Sand in Our Souls

Sand in Our Souls

THE BEACH IN AUSTRALIAN HISTORY

Leone Huntsman

To Lisa

With best wishes

Leone Huntsman

MELBOURNE UNIVERSITY PRESS

MELBOURNE UNIVERSITY PRESS
PO Box 278, Carlton South, Victoria 3053, Australia
mup-info@unimelb.edu.au
www.mup.com.au

First published 2001
Text © Leone Huntsman 2001

Design and typography © Melbourne University Press 2001

Designed by Lauren Statham, Alice Graphics
Printed in Australia by McPherson's Printing Group

National Library of Australia Cataloguing-in-Publication entry

Huntsman, Leone.
    Sand in our souls: the beach in Australian history.
    Bibliography.
    Includes index.
    ISBN 0 522 84945 8.
    1. Beaches—Australia—History. 2. Beaches—New South
    Wales—Sydney—History. 3. Recreation—Australia—
    History. 4. Australia—Social life and customs. I. Title.
333.780994

Contents

Illustrations

Acknowledgements

When *Sand in Our Souls* began its life as a thesis exploring perceptions of the beach in Australian literature, I could not have anticipated the way it grew in scope and purpose, especially in relation to the history of the beach in Australian life. Transforming the thesis into a book was a totally new challenge and a largely solitary project. However, I am grateful to those who contributed in various ways to its realisation:

Adrian Mitchell for his invaluable guidance in the early stages; Andrew Taylor and Peter Kirkpatrick for their constructive criticisms and their encouragement; Donald Denoon, for his encouragement and assistance; Pat Adamson, of the Cottesloe Society, Western Australia, for generously supplying information about Cottesloe Beach; Edwin Jaggard for his paper, 'The Australian Surf Lifesaver as a National Symbol 1920–1960'; Elida Meadows, Margaret Roberts and Tina Graham, Local Studies Librarians at Waverley and Warringah Council Libraries, for their ready assistance and interest; the Librarians of the Mitchell Library and State Library of New South Wales for their authoritative guidance and help; and the editors at Melbourne University Press for all they have done to bring this work to completion.

I also wish to thank the following for permission to reproduce copyright material (as well as those acknowledged in the text):

The Bundanon Trust, for Arthur Boyd, *The Beach*.

ETT Imprint for an extract from Mary Gilmore, 'Old Botany Bay', *Selected Verses*.

HarperCollins Publishers for an extract from 'Beach Burial' by Kenneth Slessor.

Margaret Connolly and Associates Pty Ltd for extracts from 'Noonday Axeman' and 'On Home Beaches' by Les Murray.

Mudrooroo Nyoongah for 'Beached Party'.

Toni Robertson for her screenprints *Canberra Beaches 1, 2* and *3*.

John Spooner for 'The problem raising a pogrom'.

University of Queensland Press for extracts from poems by John Blight, Bruce Beaver and Andrew Taylor.

Les Wicks and Sidewalk Poets for 'The Summer Sumos'. This poem also appeared in the *Tasmanian Poetry Festival Programme*, in *Written on Sand* (with Waverley Council), and the poet's latest anthology, *The Ways of Waves*.

Waverley Library Local Studies Department for images from the collection, and from George B. Philip's *Sixty Years' Recollections of Swimming and Surfing in the Eastern Suburbs and Kindred Subjects*.

Strenuous efforts have been made to obtain permission to use copyright material reproduced in this book. I would be pleased to hear, through the publisher, from copyright holders whom I have not been able to contact.

Finally, I thank my husband Bob for his support and patience with my preoccupation during this long period. And I dedicate this work to Australia's beaches, where many of the ideas explored herein suggested themselves to me.

Leone Huntsman
Sydney 2001

Introduction

THE BEACH LOOMS LARGE in my memories of growing up. My mother lived with her family in Bondi before she married, and several aunts, an uncle and their families still lived there when we were children. Two of my uncles, my childhood heroes, were Bondi lifesavers. We visited often, always going to the beach, joining the swarms that settled on the sand every fine weekend in summer.

Growing up an eager and omnivorous reader, I came to know the Australian books in print at that time: *Dot and the Kangaroo, The Magic Pudding, Seven Little Australians*. Later I graduated to the grimness of *For the Term of His Natural Life*; Henry Lawson's short stories with their brief spurts of bleak, ironic or insane humour leavening their portrayal of the hopelessness of rural poverty; the poetry of 'Banjo' Paterson: 'The Man from Snowy River' and 'Clancy of the Overflow'. Although I enjoyed bushwalking and loved the beauty of the bush, the world described in these stories and poems was not the one I and most of the people I knew inhabited.

While Australians are supposed to love the bush, more and more they prefer to live on the coast. The author of *The Coast Dwellers*, Phillip Drew, illustrates a common coastwards migration in the lives of his parents. They moved from Glen Innes, on the New England tablelands, to Coffs Harbour, on the New South Wales north coast, in

1947. The population of Coffs Harbour then was 4787; of Glen
Innes, 5453. By 1991, 50 190 people lived in Coffs Harbour, while
Glen Innes virtually stagnated at 6130. As Robert Drewe has written,
'Australians make or break romances at the beach, they marry and
take honeymoons at the beach, they go on holidays with their children
to the beach, and in vast numbers retire by the sea'.[1]

While most of us could recite a verse or two of 'My Country' by
Dorothea Mackellar, and sing along, if with some embarrassment, to
the tune of 'Waltzing Matilda', it seems that we have lacked the *words*
with which to express our attachment to the beach. *Images* of the
beach are all around us—in advertising, in the newspapers, in news-
reels and magazines. When a 'Turn Back the Tide' concert was held
on Bondi beach on Good Friday in 1989 to protest against the pollution of Sydney's beaches, it was reported that a quarter of a million
people attended—far more than the 50 000 the organisers had hoped
for. Given this evidence of the love affair with the beach, it has been
difficult to find anyone attempting to *process* the experience of the
beach intellectually. In 'Nation and Identity: Bondi' Anne Game commented that 'There has been surprisingly little written by academics
on Bondi, and I suspect that it is regarded as a not quite proper object
of analysis'.[2] Have Australian intellectuals decided that the beach is
too trivial a subject to warrant serious consideration?

One reason for the apparent absence of the beach from what might
be called 'high culture' in Australia could lie in collective ignorance of
its history. The bush, the landscape, *was* Australia as it presented
itself to the first explorers and settlers; but when did the beach become
significant? I had a vague memory of a man named Gocher breaking
the law by going swimming at Manly in Sydney early this century,
with everyone going to the beach after that. But a more determined
search for a definitive history of the beach in Australia was fruitless.
Documentary evidence relevant to this development—how and why
the beach became a prominent part of 'the Australian way of life'—
proved to be fragmentary and elusive.

The absence of the original inhabitants' experience of the beach
from the historical record, however regrettable, is understandable. The
coastal Aboriginal people of south-eastern Australia were the first to
be reduced by disease, violence, dispossession and demoralisation in
the face of European contact, their way of life destroyed, their stories

apparently lost. What is less explicable is the silence of historians with respect to the place of the beach in Australian life since 1788. Among a recent proliferation of works on Australia's social and cultural history, I expected that some writers would have found it interesting and worthwhile to investigate the development of the relationship between Australian people and their beaches since 1788; for such a study could show us how customs, attitudes and values change in the process of accommodation to a new environment. This might lead us to a deeper understanding of the process of enculturation itself.

Despite its potential significance, one will look in vain for a history of the beach in Australia. Geoffrey Dutton's *Sun, Sea, Surf and Sand: The Myth of the Beach* is an entertaining survey of references to the beach in painting, photography and literature, but in no way is it a systematic history. There are, of course, local histories telling of events and people involving the beach in particular localities, histories of various lifesaving clubs, and collections of facts and anecdotes about the beach, such as Lana Wells's *Sunny Memories: Australians at the Seaside*; but there are no scholarly treatments, generalisations based on a painstaking study of primary source material, or interpretations that seek to link the beach to other important aspects of Australian life. A British historian, John Walton, makes a comment regarding the history of English seaside resorts that could be applied *a fortiori* to the attention paid to the beach by Australian historians: 'The rise of the seaside holiday industry sometimes receives a passing mention in textbooks on British History in the nineteenth and twentieth centuries. Often these references are wildly inaccurate, and invariably they fail to do justice to the importance of the subject'. Walton writes at the conclusion of his detailed investigation of the English seaside resort that 'Further research . . . is obviously needed, but the situation also demands some ambitious works of well-informed synthesis, even though many of their conclusions will be tentative and interim in nature'.[3]

It has been necessary, then, for me to undertake my own historical study, which, while 'tentative and interim in nature' seeks to achieve a 'well-informed synthesis', linking the changing significance of the beach to other developments and forces in Australian history.

Given that there were significant differences in the history of the beach in different parts of Australia, relating to differences in climate, social factors and the accessibility of ocean beaches to major population centres, the history of the beach in Sydney is the main point of reference, for several reasons. Sydney was the first European settlement, the place from which British law and custom spread to the other colonies, and with it regulations and attitudes relating to bathing. Laws similar to those in New South Wales were passed in South Australia, Western Australia, Victoria and Tasmania;[4] in Queensland also, as a history of its lifesaving movement acknowledges, the early rules governing surf bathing were modelled on those in New South Wales: 'New South Wales must be regarded as the home of surf bathing in Australia . . . it was natural that [public safety measures on the beaches] should emanate from the source of origin of this popular pastime—Sydney'.[5]

Sydney's ocean beaches provided the setting in which aspects of a distinctive beach culture were first recognised and celebrated; the example of Sydney influenced the idea of the beach among Australians in other parts of the continent; and the Surf Life Saving Association, to which the hundreds of surf lifesaving clubs were affiliated, had its headquarters in Sydney, assisted in the development of clubs in other states, and set in place the model adopted by clubs Australia-wide. In Western Australia, for example, the first surf lifesaving club at Cottesloe beach was established in 1909 independently of those on the eastern seaboard; but it sought the advice and adopted the techniques of New South Wales clubs and affiliated with the New South Wales Surf Life Saving Association in the early 1920s.[6] Hence my generalisations are mostly based on primary sources relating to beaches in Sydney; but I have also noted examples, exceptions and differences in other parts of the country.

I have also explored the ways in which writers and artists have interpreted the beach over the period of European settlement; for, just as the facts of the history of the beach show one aspect of a population's adaptation to a new environment, so what David Malouf in his 1998 Boyer lectures called 'that great process of culture', whereby the phenomena of our lived world are translated into symbolism, into consciousness, is an index of adaptation at a deeper level—in the hearts and minds of the people who have become Australian. I have therefore looked at the ways in which the idea of the beach has been treated and imaginatively transformed, and the light this casts on the incorporation of the beach within Australian culture.

Reflecting on the history of the beach and its place in Australian life today, I was engaged by a more general question: how has the beach influenced the development of Australian culture and the sense of our national identity so often a subject for debate? Traits and qualities of character associated with the experience of bush life were used for many years to define what was typically Australian. Could one argue today with equal or greater justification that the experience of living with the beach has shaped Australian culture in hitherto unrecognised or unrecorded ways? My answers to these questions are necessarily speculative; I advance them tentatively in the knowledge that they will provoke disagreement and debate.

It is time that somebody asked them. It seems to me that the place of the beach in Australian life is too prominent, our attachment to it too deep, for its history to remain unrecorded and its deeper significance to be ignored and unexamined.

My use of the term 'the beach' incorporates the constellation of meanings associated with the experience of the beach in Australia. The following section sets the beach in its geographical and physical context, while the final section of this Introduction explores the emotional context in which the beach experience is located.

I hope that what I have written resonates with Australian readers and illuminates the significance of experiences we are prone to take for granted. I also hope that it helps readers from different cultural backgrounds to understand us better. For me at least, the search for answers has been an exhilarating and enlightening journey.

Australia's beaches

AUSTRALIA IS AN ISLAND CONTINENT bounded by a coastline about 36 700 km in length, or more than 120 000 km if estuaries and the 1800 islands are included. In a sense, it can be said that Australia is a nation contained within a beach.[7]

The great oceans—Pacific, Indian and Southern—that roll onto the edge of the continent meet a shoreline consisting of three main types of feature: rocks and cliffs; beaches and dunes; and mudflats and tidal plains. The distribution of these features is shown on page 6.[8]

While the headlands enfolding the beaches are composed of rocks millions of years old, the beaches themselves are only about 6500

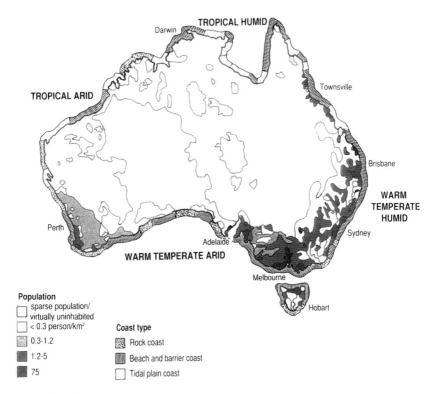

Australia's beaches.

Source: P. Dale, *Managing Australian Coastlands* (after Thom, 1984); with permission, Pearson Education Australia, publishers.

years old. The coastline at the height of the previous Ice Age about 10 000 years ago was 20 to 60 km offshore, to be gradually submerged as the icecaps melted and the sea rose to its present level.

What is a beach? It is a wave-deposited accumulation of sediment, usually quartz sand grains, together with other minerals and rock, shell and algal fragments, and sometimes cobbles and boulders. Australia is fortunate in that many of its beaches consist of soft sand, often white or pale gold in colour. While the composition of the sand varies from beach to beach, Thomas Keneally's description of the sand on one of Sydney's northern beaches in *Woman of the Inner Sea* could be applied to that on hundreds, perhaps thousands, of other beaches around the Australian coast: 'Sydney sand, that ideal childhood sand— not powdery and bleached, not black and volcanic, not shingly and hostile to bare feet . . . Soft enough for a child to launch himself onto, shoulder or stomach first, without pain; compact enough for the construction of fantasy'.[9]

The sand of the beach rests on bedrock geology, and the beach itself extends from the upper limit of wave swash (the broken wave spending itself as it spreads over and sinks into the sand, reaching furthest at high tide or in stormy weather) out across the zone of surf to where the waves begin to move the sediment towards the shore.

Although every beach is unique, beaches along one part of the coast may differ in a general way from those in another region. The map divides the continent and its surrounding oceans into climatic regions—temperate/tropical; arid/humid; however, because politically Australia is a single nation, it is often easier to refer to the characteristics of beaches belonging to the various states and the Northern Territory.

Beaches occur along most of the coastline in the states of New South Wales, Victoria and South Australia. This is also the part of the continent first settled by Europeans, and has the highest population density. About 60 per cent of the New South Wales coast consists of 721 sandy beaches, ranging from long sweeping beaches up to 26 km long to small, deeply embayed beaches only a few metres in length. The waves of the Pacific Ocean roll virtually unimpeded as surf onto the ocean beaches all the way up the coast to Queensland's southern beaches. The Tasmanian coast, too, mostly consists of beaches, except in the south.

In the tropical waters of North Queensland, the Northern Territory and Western Australia, coral reefs form a barrier protecting the coastal beaches from the full force of the ocean waves, so they have no surf to speak of, except in cyclonic weather. Saltwater crocodiles may inhabit these tropical beaches; and at the hottest times of the year large numbers of deadly poisonous box jellyfish are carried towards the beaches, rendering them distinctly uninviting to humans.

Along the south-eastern coast and on the coast of Tasmania the beaches are often short—their average length in New South Wales is just over a kilometre—and contained between rocky outcrops, steep cliffs or headlands. In other places—the Gold Coast of southern Queensland, the Eighty-Mile Beach of north Western Australia, the Ninety-Mile Beach in Victoria, and the Younghusband Peninsula–Lacepede beach in South Australia—they present a long, barely curved line of sandy dunes to the oceans. Because most of Australia's continental shelf is steep and narrow by world standards, its ocean beaches (where unprotected by reefs) are typically pounded by waves more active and vigorous than those found on many other coastlines—particularly those of Europe.

For historical reasons that are explored in this book, the quintessential Australian beach is a surfing beach—that is, one that faces the open ocean, and where waves build in height before crashing as breakers onto the sand. Sandy beaches without surf are located in sheltered bays and inlets such as Sydney Harbour; sandy stretches of riverbank are also sometimes also thought of as beaches. These places possess attributes of *beachness* to a greater or lesser extent, depending on how closely they approach the qualities of the ocean surf beach.

The appeal of the beach

YOU LIVE ONCE BUT YOU SURF FOREVER!
—message chalked on the path leading to North Narrabeen beach, 1996

When we go to the beach and cross the threshold from the sand to the sea through the fringing waves, we gain 'access, incomparably literal sensuous access, to that vital level of the self which is continuous with infancy'.[10] As we move into deeper water we relive the experience of immersion, of merging into oneness with the vast undifferentiated matrix. We discover again the joy of play: of dancing through the froth, gliding up the wave face or diving through it (or, at a higher level of grace and skill, riding the wave front as bodysurfer, boardrider or windsurfer). We are enveloped in total sensory stimulation as the cool silky water slides around our bodies, the foam fizzes over the surface of our skin, the roar of the waves fills our ears, the taste of salt in our mouths, as the body of the infant responds with ecstasy to stroking, touching, murmuring, feeding.

And after we live this experience we return to the land, to the sand, where we may lie in drowsy bliss, just as the sated infant sleeps, all tension spent. Or we may engage in different kinds of play: the child's busy engrossment in the building of castles and elaborate sandworks; the adult's walking along the beach and back again, to nowhere, to no purpose, in contented solitude or easy conversation with a companion; the fisherman's dreaming into the gathering sunrise or the fading dusk. Or we may sit or stand higher up the beach to watch the waves where their rhythmic, repetitive beat, their perpetual advance and retreat, bring a kind of calming reassurance: the sea, always there, though others might vanish, hurt us, abandon us, be unavailable.

The fundamental attraction of the beach lies, then, in its being one of the opportunities that life now and then offers for direct recapturing of

> the joy of a creature who knows time and senses its own separateness, who has become familiar with striving and with the ebb and flow, the melting together and drawing apart, that form the living tie between its fragile individual existence and the hurtful, entrancing surround; it is the joy of a creature who remembers and anticipates less primitive ways of feeling and, suspending what it knows, what it remembers and anticipates, surrenders itself to the melting, flowing moment. So while this joy is not the lost pure euphoria of infancy, it does echo that euphoria clearly enough to offer us episodic, momentary recapture of its flavour ...[11]

When I read this description by Dorothy Dinnerstein in *The Mermaid and the Minotaur*, it seemed to me to come close to capturing the emotional and sensory responses associated with enjoyment of the beach. She cited art, religion, and pleasure in nature as examples of forces that might evoke responses of this kind. But in Australia the physical envelopment by moving water and near-total immersion in the 'entrancing surround' experienced at the beach provides a particularly pure example of 'surrender to the melting, flowing moment'. Being-in-the-surf is also qualitatively different from swimming or floating in lake, pool or river because the ever-changing, ever-moving waves, foam, spray and sand accentuate the playful, interactive quality of the experience. In the surf the energy of the body at play synergises with that released by the wave:

> all the energy so carefully gleaned from the winds of the distant storm and hoarded for a thousand miles of ocean crossing is gone, expended in a few wild moments [as the wave breaks]. Because the energy is released so rapidly, the energy density in the surf is actually much higher than in the storm which originally created the waves.[12]

This brings to mind the words of the poet William Blake: 'Energy is the only Life, and is from the Body . . . Energy is Eternal Delight'.[13] It is during these playful moments that we are most true to ourselves, according to Freud: 'Man is only completely a man when he plays'.[14] And Freud is not alone in identifying play as an essential human activity, the potential of which is often perverted or destroyed by civilisation. The Christian theologian, Jacob Boehme, wrote that

> As God plays with the time of this outward world, so also should the inward divine man play with the outward in the revealed wonders of God in this world, and open the Divine Wisdom in all creatures, each according to its property. Adam fell when this play became serious business.[15]

The intrinsic eroticism of beach activity is manifest in its playfulness. Yet the beach is not pure, unalloyed joy: that allusion to the '*hurtful*, entrancing surround' acknowledges the ambivalence that is inescapably part of human experience. At the beach we know our helplessness when waves dump us or the rip drags us this way or that. We feel our own weakness in the grip of that overpowering strength; mingled with our joy is a fear of the perils that lurk in the opaque depths—the sharks, the biting and stinging creatures, the unimaginable. Thus awareness of the potential for danger as well as delight is always with us; but as long as it remains 'an undercurrent', the intensification of sensory arousal associated with this awareness may actually increase our pleasure.

Testimony to this pleasure is not hard to find:

> That crowded beach [Bondi] had a sound, a roar of excitement. You could say it was joy . . .[16]

> I can remember one crystalline morning when nothing seemed more beautiful than the look, the sound and the smell of the green and white Pacific. I launched my board onto that swaying transparency, paddled it over the rainbow spray and the bucking waves singing 'shenandoah' at the top of my voice and certain that nothing anywhere in the world could match this joy.[17]

and

> There is nowhere else I'd rather be, nothing else I would prefer to be doing. I am at the beach looking west with the continent behind me as the sun tracks down to the sea. I have my bearings.[18]

Some would disparage the delight so intensely felt by these beachgoers as a pleasant but essentially trivial diversion from the serious business of life; but Dinnerstein is emphatic that such joy is of vital importance. It supplements the other compensations that life offers and that help to assuage our basic, universal and inconsolable grief—a grief which arises, first, from separation from the mother and consequent loss of the infant illusion of being all-powerful; and later, from the realisation that we must die. These other compensations are *history-making*—the world's pool of 'memorable event, communicable insight, teachable technique, durable achievement'; and *work*, 'the quest for mastery, competence, enterprise, in place of the old joy of passive, effortless wish-fulfilment'.[19]

To the extent we strive to shut out from our minds and hearts the certain prospect of death, trying to act as if we were immortal, we are unable to live in the present and to surrender ourselves to whatever pleasure life can offer us. It is crucial for our psychological health and wholeness to for us to embrace opportunities for enjoyment of the moment—opportunities of which the beach provides, in Australia, a readily accessible example.

The beach therefore holds potent meaning for human beings irrespective of culture, since it invites us to relive the 'early carnal joy' experienced in infancy. This helps to explain why the appeal of the beach is so fundamental. In many countries practical considerations of climate, geography, history, accessibility of the ocean and cultural inhibitions limit, discourage or prevent the expression of this attraction; but in Australia a combination of favourable climate, geography, accessibility, and—eventually—history and culture, have combined to enhance the ability and the inclination of Australians to respond to the lure of the beach.

Today the beaches are freely available for our enjoyment. While this freedom is now taken for granted, it has not always been the case. The reasons stretch back to the beginnings of settlement and were strongly influenced by our European inheritance, which affected perceptions of the beach even before British settlement.

PART 1

The Evolution of the Australian Beach

1

First Impressions

Brief encounters: the beach and culture contact before first settlement

IN EXPLORING THE HISTORY of crosscultural conflict between Europeans and the inhabitants of the Marquesas Islands in the Pacific, Greg Dening uses an overarching metaphor—introduced in the title of his book, *Islands and Beaches*—to understand and to explain the process of culture contact itself. An 'island' is the culture constructed by a people; a 'beach' is the boundary between cultures. As newcomers cross that boundary, bringing with them all the cultural meanings and phenomena from their own 'island', they change the culture of the newly entered 'island' forever.[1]

The ships of European explorers can hardly be said to have penetrated the 'island' of the Australian continent before 1788. They skittered along the coastlines, the explorers and their crews viewing the native inhabitants on the beach and never penetrating far beyond it. But to their perceptions of the new land they brought the values of *their* 'island'—of cultural and moral superiority, imperial rights to exploration and acquisition, appraisal of opportunities for exploitation and profit, and the Enlightenment ideal of the advancement of knowledge through the observation and recording of new phenomena.

Thus first impressions were filtered through existing preconceptions, starkly revealed in Sir Joseph Banks's description of the people seen from Captain James Cook's *Endeavour* when it first touched on the Australian continent in 1770:

> In the morn we . . . [discerned] 5 people who appeared through our glasses to be enormously black: so far did the prejudices which we had built on Dampier's account influence us that we fancied we could see their Colour when we could scarce distinguish whether or not they were men.[2]

Here Banks refers to William Dampier's unfavourable accounts of West Australian Aboriginal people in published accounts of his landings in 1688 and 1699, and reveals his own awareness of the extent to which perception was influenced by expectation.

We have no corresponding account of the Aboriginals' interpretation of the ships and strangers they saw from the beach. While Banks and his scientific colleagues meticulously catalogued 'facts' about Aboriginal people in the same way as they named and classified new plants and animals, the *meaning* of the Aboriginals' behaviour on the beach eluded them. They observed three main kinds of response to their presence: attempts to repel them by threatening gestures and displays of weapons; apparent indifference as the people went about their daily tasks of carrying wood or spearing and cooking fish; and ignoring them, running away or melting into vegetation beyond the beach.

Was this behaviour cowardice, as Banks chose to label it—or a prudent withdrawal from contact until more understanding of the newcomers' motives could be gleaned or these unsettling apparitions disappeared for ever? Whatever the reason, no relationship between newcomers and inhabitants could be established during these fleeting encounters. The Europeans were baffled by the Aboriginal people's indifference to the goods they brought with them. They threw beads, ribbons and cloths as presents into a 'house' near the beach, only to find the next day that every individual thing they had thrown there was left behind, untouched. There was an apparent refusal on the part of the Aboriginal people to accept any offerings that would have established a relationship of reciprocity between the two peoples. On the other hand, the Europeans had no qualms in taking with them all the 'lances' (spears) that they found in one of the houses, an early indication of their assumed right to appropriate whatever was of interest or profit to them.

The early and sometimes unfavourable judgements of the Aboriginal people expressed by early explorers co-existed with a rather wistful envy of their carefree way of life as contrasted with that of effete Europeans—a sentiment influenced by another cultural belief in the virtues of the Noble Savage. Thus Captain James Cook wrote:

> From what I have said of the Natives of New-Holland they may appear to be some of the most wretched people upon Earth, but in reality they are far more happier than we Europeans; being wholly unacquainted not only with the superfluous but the necessary Conveniences so much sought after in Europe, they are happy in not knowing the use of them. They live in a Tranquillity which is not disturb'd by the Inequality of Condition: the Earth and the sea of their own accord furnishes them with all things necessary for life, they covet not Magnificent Houses ... they seem'd to set no Value upon any thing we gave them ... this in my opinion argues that they think themselves provided with all the necessarys of Life and that they have no superfluities.[3]

Before the first settlement was established in Port Jackson, Governor Phillip noted on 22 January 1788 that he had named one of the harbour's inlets Manly Cove because of the confidence and manly behaviour shown by the natives there—thereby naming the place that later became part of one of Sydney's premier beach resorts.

The brief encounters on the beach only dramatised the difference between the two peoples. Each remained an enigma to the other. Dening's 'beach' was more of a chasm than a boundary, a seemingly unbridgeable gap in understanding between the two cultures that was to have tragic consequences in the years to come.

The early years: 1788 to the 1830s

AFTER THE FIRST FLEET had landed on 'the fatal shore',[4] the earliest interactions between the new settlers and Aboriginal people took place around the beaches of Port Jackson, Botany Bay, Pittwater and Broken Bay. The newcomers observed that the natives subsisted mainly on the fish and shellfish that they drew from the waters surrounding the settlement. The early diarists described in some detail the different functions of men and women with respect to fishing: the way they broiled the fish they had caught over little fires in their canoes; the fashioning of fishhooks and the construction of canoes. Joseph Lycett's painting *Aborigines Spearing Fish, Others Diving for Crayfish, a Party Seated Beside a Fire Cooking Fish* shows a division of labour between the sexes, with women catching fish from the canoes, swimming or diving, the men spearing fish from the rocks. Cook had also observed this separation between the roles of men and women in the 'primitive' societies encountered during the voyage—in Tierra del Fuego, Tahiti, New Zealand, and now, it was evident, in New South Wales. In this one respect at least, the settlers must have been reassured that the natives, in other ways so alien, were like them.

The Eora people living around Port Jackson were proficient swimmers. In 1791 Bennelong and several others swam out to rescue

Joseph Lycett (c. 1775–1828), *Aborigines Spearing Fish, Others Diving for Crayfish, a Party Seated Beside a Fire Cooking Fish*, c. 1817.
Watercolour, 17.7 × 28 cm

Source: 'Drawings of the natives & scenery of Van Diemans [*sic*] Land', National Library of Australia, R5686. By permission of the National Library of Australia a group of settlers whose boat had overturned in Farm Cove; they returned those rescued to shore and dried out their clothes over a fire. The name 'bogie hole', derived from an Aboriginal word meaning to bathe or swim, was often used until quite recent times for a swimming-place. When I was a child we called the smaller rock pool at the northern end of Bondi beach the bogie hole, and in his *Oxford Dictionary of Australian Colloquialisms* G. A. Wilkes notes the first recording of the word in an utterance by Colbee, one of the Aboriginal people captured by Governor Arthur Phillip.[5]

Early bathing and swimming

There is considerable evidence, scattered and fragmentary though it is, that the settlers greatly enjoyed bathing in the waters of the harbour. Early records suggest that convicts, soldiers and early colonists needed no urging to follow the example of the Aboriginal people and to enter the water—in fact, they persisted in doing so, despite officialdom's efforts to discourage them.

Lack of familiarity with the water meant that few of those who lived in Britain or Ireland could swim, so one might assume that this applied also to the colonists. The evidence, however, suggests that the ability to swim was widespread. It is likely that some learnt the skill (and the pleasure to be derived from swimming) by watching the original inhabitants enjoying themselves in the water. The historian Michael Cannon conjectures that 'no doubt the hotter climate, combined with easy access to beaches and rivers [and bay and harbour shores] encouraged a good deal of bathing simply for the sake of coolness in summer'.[6] Most of the First Fleet diarists allude to the heat of that first summer, Watkin Tench noting that it 'felt like the blast of a heated oven . . . it was allowed by every person, to surpass all that they had before felt, either there or in any other part of the world'.[7]

By 1803 bathing was so common that Governor King apparently felt it necessary to restore some decorum, possibly using the dangerous creatures lurking in the water as an excuse for what may have been an attempt to uphold propriety when he issued a government dispatch published in the *Sydney Gazette* on 20 October of that year:

> This Bay and Harbour in general,—being unfortunately full of Voracious Sharks and Stingrays only, it is recommended to the Convicts not to go into the water without the utmost precaution

and they are positively prohibited from bathing in front of the Encampment.

Whether or not the convicts heeded this injunction, the Fig Tree, overlooking Woolloomooloo Bay, remained a very popular bathing spot, providing trees and rocks for shade, for diving, and for conceal-ment while changing. (This was the site of what was to become the Domain Baths, first enclosed in 1860, opened as the Domain Baths in 1908, renamed the Andrew 'Boy' Charlton pool in 1968, and still in use today.) The *Ben Bolt*, an abandoned hulk, was sunk near the shore, and wooden fences built out to it to form the sides of an enclo-sure, supposedly as some protection against sharks (but since one could dive and swim underwater around the submerged sides of the hulk out into the harbour, the protection was more psychological than real). Later this swimming 'enclosure' was enlarged with the addition of another hulk, the *Cornwallis*.[8]

In the 1820s Surgeon Peter Cunningham's assessment of the characteristics of the new generation of Sydney's inhabitants, the currency lads and lasses, included the observation that 'They [the girls] are very fond of frolicking in the water, and those living near the sea can usually swim and dive like water-hens'.[9] By 1834 the *Sydney Gazette* of 18 February pronounced that 'bathing is now the favoured recreation in Sydney'; a visitor observed that 'Swimming matches . . . take place occasionally and are well contested . . . It is an amusement to which the youth of New South Wales are very partial, scarcely anyone over the age of three or four being ignorant of the art'.[10] In 1847 a writer in *Heads of the People* referred to a bathing place 'commonly called the Fig-Tree' near Mrs Macquarie's Chair (in the Botanic Gardens) and

> which is often . . . the place of concealment of those outlaws . . . [who] play truant and learn to swim instead of learning to write. Then comes Robinson's bathing houses, beyond which is another bathing place called the 'steps'. This is the favourite resort of the younger boys, who not having yet learnt the art of swimming, are content to splash and paddle about like a brood of young ducks in a horse-pond.[11]

Bathing seems to have gained early popularity as an enjoyable activity in its own right, not just as a way of cooling off in hot weather. The *Sydney Gazette* of 13 June 1829 noted that 'a number of bathers are still to be seen every morning, notwithstanding the sharpness of the air in the early part of the day'.

Other visitors observed that 'So much . . . was bathing the fashion that it was impossible to walk out any time of the day, by the waterside about Sydney, without being annoyed by bathers in all directions'[12] and 'Where there is so much bathing it may naturally be supposed there are good swimmers, and Sydney is celebrated for them'.[13]

Writing about leisure pursuits in early colonial times, J. W. C. Cumes cites records of people bathing in other colonies, and speculates that many colonists must have enjoyed themselves by swimming from the earliest days of settlement. He concludes that swimming must have been a more general recreation than written records disclose, and sees this as evidence that an indigenous style of recreation and amusement was developing.

Sydney, the seaport town

Until the late 1830s a maritime culture dominated the town of Sydney, and this was true of the other colonies in their early days of settlement. Commerce and travel between one settlement and another was by sea. As Ross Gibson points out, Sydney was a 'highly sea-conscious town':

> Sydney Town surged with ocean-workers. The whaling industry was the staple of the colonial economy for decades . . . there were seal-hunters, timber-getters and opportunistic traders . . . The shoreline around the Tank Stream surged with opinions, desires and worldviews brought in from the ocean.[14]

It is intriguing that so little trace remains in our collective memory of this early maritime experience. Alan Frost ponders the question: 'Why did our progenitors on the Cumberland Plain not find their life on the edge of the great ocean distinctive enough to offer a separate identity? Why did we develop no legend of Pacific identity?'[15]

It may simply be the case that a general amnesia about this early period prevailed because of the overriding truth about it: that Sydney and the other early colonies were then predominantly settlements of convicts. Certainly most of the paintings of this early period omit their presence; and having a convict ancestor was a shameful secret until recently, when it has become a more positive discovery, a link with the beginnings of settlement. But a more specific reason might be that, despite maritime comings and goings, the settlements themselves

were founded in estuaries, rivers and bays away from the ocean shores.
A primary requirement for settlement was safe harbourage for the
ships on which each colony depended for its lifelines to other colonies
and the imperial power; but this choice of site suited the personal,
psychological needs of its residents as well.

To understand their attitudes it is necessary to hark back to the
beginnings of European settlement, to put oneself in the place of those
who made the long voyage out from Europe, whether involuntarily
(convicts), in the line of duty (military, navy and government person-
nel) or in the hope of a better life (free settlers). Arrival in the new
land meant the end of months at sea, a time of tedium and discomfort
at best, more often a time to be endured with as much fortitude as
could be mustered, marked by storms, seasickness, awful food, illness
and death, especially of infants and small children.[16] In early memoirs
and records, writers seemed to play down the human and practical
problems of life at sea.[17] It was as if those months on board were a
nightmare, to be forgotten as quickly as possible.

Even setting aside the aftermath of this universal experience, there
were other intensely ambivalent ideas and emotions associated with
the ocean and its fringing shoreline. For the convicts the beaches
constituted a sea-fence, one wall of the prison constraining and
confining them, as well as a hint of the possibility of escape. For all the
settlers, the sight of the sea with its limitless horizon was a piercing
reminder of their distance from the civilised world, from families and
loved ones. Even today, we refer to the other countries of the world
collectively as 'overseas'—a way of proclaiming their distance from us.

These feelings came to the fore in these early days in the major
form of self-consciously 'literary' writing: poetry—although, as
Elizabeth Webby notes, 'that is too grand a title for most of the . . .
"poetic effusions" offered to the public'.[18] Many 'poems' appeared in
the newspapers, gazettes and magazines published in those early days,
mostly four- or eight-line stanzas, formal and elevated in their tone in
accordance with the conventions of eighteenth-century poetry.

'Gloom and doom' could be chosen as the key phrase summing up
the subject-matter of early Australian 'sea' poetry/verse. Shipwrecks
were the most evocative form of catastrophe (after earthquakes) and
the most common form of accident in late eighteenth-century Europe;[19]
and storms and shipwrecks are by far the most common subject of
these verses. Titles such as 'Sonnet: written on a storm at sea', 'The

Storm: a Fragment', 'The Missing Steamer', 'The Wreck' are sprinkled throughout the pages of early newspapers. Those not about storms and shipwrecks are mostly verses about drownings, burials at sea, feelings of homesickness and exile, and pious thoughts about God and man's place in the scheme of things.

Even when the place where meditation was inspired by the sight of the sea was explicitly Australian, it was scarcely recognisable in the conventionally English form in which it was described. Henry Halloran, one of the more celebrated and prolific early versifiers, wrote 'Australian Scenery, Bondi Bay'—perhaps the first literary treatment of this favourite beach; but as Webby comments, it is neither particularly Australian nor scenic. There is an interesting editorial note at the end of the poem: 'The word *Bondi*, in the language of the Aboriginal people, signifies *falling*, and is peculiarly apposite to the continual falling of waters at this spot'.

Henry Halloran refers to topographical features of the beach—the 'South-East point', the 'sweeping bay', the 'frowning headland' at the North-East end; but generally the beach he describes would not be recognisable to an observer of the blue-and-gold playground that is Bondi today:

> Thro' a long vista of embow'ring trees,
> Which give their sear leaves to the rustling breeze,
> The wide expanse of Ocean meets the eye—
> The awful emblem of Eternity!
>
> From North to South a sweeping bay extends—
> The South-East point in rocky masses ends—
> While here or there, upon th'untrodden shore,
> Are strewed the 'thwart, the helm, the broken oar,
> The fragments of a sail, the splinter'd mast—
> The fisher's toy! The victim of the blast!
> But where's the fisher? Did the laughing gale
> Close round his head? Did ev'ry effort fail?
> No tongue can tell; perchance he found a grave
> Beneath the azure mantle of the wave . . .
>
> To the North-East a frowning headland rears
> His giant form: on his rough brow appears
> The scar of time: magnificently rude.
> He towers above the deep; . . .
>
> The white-haired waves, from Ocean's bosom thrown,
> Roll to the shore with melancholy moan . . .[20]

The beach was a stage from which Halloran could observe and meditate upon the power and immensity of the ocean and man's insignificance. A barque disappearing over the horizon is a symbol of the brevity of life: the beach an excuse for moral homily, not a place to observe, experience and enjoy in its own right.

Another of Halloran's poems refers to a popular Sydney beach: 'Pages from My Scrapbook of 10 Years Ago: Coogee, On the Sea-Coast'.[21] He refers to a sunset, the birds returning to their young on 'this fragrant and untrampled sod'; but the burden of the poem is another religious/philosophical meditation, and Coogee, the place itself, is insignificant.

There is an intriguing exception to the general failure by the versifiers to observe and to record what actually lay before them. 'Lines Written by the Sea-Side', published in the *Monitor* of 1 November 1827, begins with a reference to a sunset. But instead of the usual conventional pieties, suddenly the anonymous writer describes an experience:

> I was not lonely—dwellings fair
> Were scatter'd round and shining there—
>   Gay groups were on the green,
> Of children, wild with reckless glee,
> And parents that could childlike be
>   With them, and in that scene ...
>
> The breezy murmur from the shore,
> Joy's laugh re-echoed o'er and o'er
>   Alike by sire and child—
> The whistle shrill—the broken song—
> The far-off flute-notes, lingering long—
>   The lark's strain rich and wild ...

The writer conforms to fashion in the final stanza, rounding off with worthy sentiments; the 'sea-side' itself is not described; but he or she has defied convention by peopling the shore, and with happy people enjoying themselves—not shipwrecked sailors or drowned lovers.

Generally, however, the days of swimming and splashing about in the waters of the harbour (and in the rivers and bays around other early settlements) seem to have gone largely unremarked and unrecorded. As far as prose is concerned, in his history of Australian literature H. M. Green writes of the small body of fictional writing in what he categorises as the First Period of Australian literature, from 1789 to 1850, that it

> throws some light on the life of the large and small settler; of the station-owner, so far as farm and station owner were distinguishable; of the country gentleman, an English type ... of convict servants, and of bushrangers. Then, and for a long time afterwards, the countryside was to remain the centre to which writers and readers naturally turned; indeed ... it occupies the background, as well as often enough the foreground of Australian fiction still.[22]

It appears that the ascendancy of the bush in the minds and hearts of writers was established early, and that their imaginations were not engaged by our maritime history or the attractions of the coast.

The desire to record and document the growth of the colony resulted in many sketches and paintings of panoramic views from various vantage points around the harbour. Proof of the new civilisation's triumph over nature, the inevitable victory of building and cultivation over wilderness, was an underlying theme in early paintings by artists such as John Lewins, John Glover and Conrad Martens. Tranquil scenes of substantial homes amid well-tended gardens or pastoral surroundings also often included forests of eucalypts framing the edges of the picture or in the background—'wilderness' in retreat. Similarly, the inclusion of small groups of Aboriginal people near the margins of paintings presented them as receding from the new society-in-the-making.

The reliance of the settlements on their sea-links is hinted at in the profusion of ships anchored in river or port, or tidily moored at wharves. Paintings of the coastline, like the early depictions of Sydney Town, combined a desire to represent the picturesque with a kind of pictorial mapping—showing the topographical features of land seen across bodies of water (as in John Skinner Prout's *Maria Island from Little Swanport, Van Diemen's Land*, c. 1846). There were also paintings of ships foundering during storms at sea or being wrecked on rocks near the coast, as well as lively scenes of whale chases.

Just as convicts are largely absent from the formal paintings and drawings surviving from this early period, so are the frolicsome settlers, soldiers and convicts in the waters around Port Jackson. The only people shown relaxing and enjoying themselves on the sheltered beaches are Aboriginal. Of course the beaches were places of serious business for the coastal Aboriginal people, who derived much of their food from the sea. The titles of Joseph Lycett's lively and interesting paintings of Aboriginal life describe the activities depicted: *Aborigines Feeding from Beached Whales*; *Fishing by Torchlight, Other Aborigines beside Camp Fires Cooking Fish*; *Two Aborigines Spearing Eels* (and *Aborigines Spearing Fish . . .*, see page 18).[23] Around Tasmania the women did all the diving for shellfish, their skill described by James Backhouse:

> These women seem quite at home in the water, and frequently immerse their faces to enable them to see objects at the bottom. When they discover the object of their search, they dive, often using the long stems of the kelp to enable them to reach the bottom; these they handle as dextrously as a sailor would a rope in descending.[24]

This is an evocative image for anyone who has watched the tan-brown forests of giant kelp writhing in the waters around Tasmania; in those cold waters, it can hardly have been fun for the women. But it was an image of idyllic idleness that was portrayed in paintings such as the convict Thomas Watling's *A Group on the North Shore of Port Jackson, New South Wales*, painted in the 1790s, and George Angus's *Rapid Bay with an Encampment of Yankalillah Blacks* (1847). As Geoffrey Dutton observes of Watling's work, this is 'a classic Australian scene, a barbecue on the beach . . . it is certainly typical that a man, not a woman, is in charge of the grilling.'[25]

The way of life presented in these paintings of carefree natives was potentially subversive. Tench had written matter-of-factly in his journal that 'All savages hate toil, and place happiness in inaction: and neither the arts of civilized life can be practised, or the advantages of it felt, without application and labour'.[26] Here he sums up the threat their perceived indolence would pose to the established order if the new settlers were to emulate their behaviour, according pleasure a higher value than industry. For work had a redemptive function in a colony where hard-working convicts were rewarded by being given tickets-of-leave and allowed to set up their own enterprises, and others were assigned to work with free settlers, or in labour gangs in the prisons.

At the dreadful penal settlement of Norfolk Island, scenes not unlike that portrayed in *A Group on the Shores of Port Jackson* occurred on an extraordinary day, described by Robert Hughes in

The Fatal Shore, when the reformist superintendent, Alexander Maconochie, opened the gates of the prison and released the prisoners to celebrate the Queen's Birthday.[27] They were able to wander as they pleased on the island, swim in the sea, stretch and frolic on the sand. They barbecued their food, performed plays, music and poetry, and all returned obediently to their cells before the hour of curfew. This excursion caused a furore when the citizens of Sydney heard about it, and Maconochie was soon moved to another post. The possibility of redemption through play rather than work was unthinkable; for if work was seen as morally good in itself, so idleness must be immoral. Where would the new colony have been if the new settlers had followed the example of the Aboriginal people, according pleasure a higher value than industry and adopting instead an attitude to work summed up in verse in the *Bulletin* in 1907:

> I'm a vagrant free from labour,
> Work was never meant for me . . .
> And I'm quite content to idle,
> Doing nothing by the sea.
>
> All the city work and clamour
> And the clang of wheel and hammer
> Never did my soul enamour,
> Now I laze by shadowed lee,
> Where the sleepy wave is creaming,
> Yellow sand, and free from scheming,
> Emulate the lizard, dreaming,
> Doing nothing by the sea.[28]

Wariness of the temptation to indolence and distaste for the 'indecency' of the unclothed swimmers seemingly emulating the original inhabitants simmered among official and respectable inhabitants, but was not yet overt or coercive. For a brief time it seemed that the new settlers might continue to follow the Aboriginal example in freely enjoying the opportunities for refreshment and pleasure that bathing and swimming in pristine waters and a warm climate afforded them. As they sought to construct a congenial way of life in their new environment, however, an idea of the beach that they brought with them from England—the beach as seaside holiday resort—soon became more salient.

2

The Triumph of Respectability

OFFICIAL CONCERN ABOUT the naked bathers in the harbour as early as 1810 had led to the publication of an order by the Governor's Secretary in the *Sydney Gazette* of 6 October of that year:

> A very indecent and improper Custom having lately prevailed, of Soldiers, Sailors and Inhabitants of the Town bathing themselves at all hours of the Day at the Government Wharf, and also in the Dock-yard . . . no person shall Bathe at either of these places in future, at any Hour of the Day; . . . the Sentinels . . . to apprehend and confine any Person transgressing this Order.

Disapproval grew until in 1833 bathing in the waters of Sydney Cove and Darling Harbour between the hours of 6 a.m. and 8 p.m. was banned, with these restrictions being extended to all beaches within view of a public place or resort in 1838, and applied gradually to new townships and municipalities as they were proclaimed.[1] Not everyone complied with these bans, as a scandalised correspondent pointed out in the *Sydney Gazette* of 28 January 1841:

> Hint to the Police—I wish you would call attention in the Gazette to the fact, that *boys* and *girls* (the latter big enough to wear stays) were bathing publicly together at the end of the street leading to the Commercial Wharf, and close to the place, and at the very time, when people assemble for the steamers, on Monday last at 4 o'clock. One young girl standing in the water told a bigger

standing out, both naked, 'not to be a b—y fool'. There were sundry little girls and big boys looking on. One of the naked girls deliberately came out, put on her shift, stays, frock, &c., in the presence of the boys, who were all looking on.—Co-respondent.

There were other sporadic reports of people defying these orders, and soldiers continued to bathe nude along the shores of Darling Harbour. However, the same W. R. Govett who complained about 'being annoyed by bathers in all directions' wrote of the prohibition on bathing that it 'was duly observed by the inhabitants'.[2] One incentive to comply with laws regarding bathing was the imposition of fines. People could be fined up to a pound if caught—a considerable sum for a working man. Bathing and swimming in daylight, in the open, disappeared from the public gaze.

Unease among government officials about disorderly conduct was not the only reason why these bathing bans were imposed and obeyed. From the 1830s onwards the population of the new colonies became more complex and diverse. Up until 1830 there had been only 15 700 free immigrants and nearly 61 000 convicts, but by 1850 more than 191 000 free immigrants had arrived, outnumbering the convict population of 144 615.[3] Colonial society was growing larger and more complex, with a significant section of the population concerned about status and respectability, and prosperous enough to reproduce in the new land the practices, fashions and customs of the homeland most of them had left behind. These free settlers brought with them the English idea of a seaside resort—a form of leisure more in tune with aspirations to social standing and propriety than the anarchic bathing practices hitherto enjoyed by the less respectable classes.

The English seaside resort[4]

FROM ABOUT 1660 ONWARDS England had seen the rise of the spa town as a focus for the social life of the aristocracy and the landed gentry. The drinking of spa water was considered to have therapeutic benefits, and this became the ostensible reason for visiting spa towns in the fashionable season and engaging in the hectic round of balls and social amenities they provided. A hierarchy prevailed among the spa towns reflecting the social position of their clientele.

By the mid-eighteenth century the seaside resort was developing as an adjunct to the spa season. As spa water was considered to be healthful, so also the drinking of seawater was successfully promoted as a remedy for such afflictions as scurvy, jaundice, gonorrhoea and gout. Those who had patronised the spas now also visited the seaside resorts, often drinking copious quantities of seawater and bathing from beaches or bathing machines. Hard as it is for us to imagine today, the drinking of seawater in quite copious amounts was a medically approved fad in the late eighteenth century. A visitor to Lyme Regis in 1792 noted that 'Decent looking men used to go down to the beach three or four times in as many hours, and drink a pint of sea-water each time'.[5]

The invention of the beach in modern Western culture dates from the discovery of the virtues of seawater during this period.[6] Dr Russell, a leading protagonist of its healthful benefits, specified the features of 'the salubrious beach' in some detail. It should be 'neat and tidy'; away from any river mouth, so as to ensure that the waves would be high and the water sufficiently saline. It should be sandy and flat, making it easier to cross in a bath chair. The shore should be bordered by cliffs and dunes suitable for walking and horseback riding.

The Prince of Wales set the seal of royal approval on the then-small resort of Brighton by visiting it in 1783 and building his Royal Pavilion there. As with the spa towns, a hierarchy of prestige developed among the seaside resorts, which by late in the century had superseded the spas as 'the place to stay' for those who wished to be in the forefront of fashion.

The provision of stagecoach services to the resorts broadened the social composition of the visiting population as the middle classes, ever anxious to emulate their betters, began to spend two or three weeks at the seaside in summer. With the coming of the railways from the 1840s onwards, the numbers of holidaymakers increased exponentially. By late in the century even members of the working class took advantage of cheap excursion fares both for day trips to resorts and for holidays, as the custom of taking a holiday became a possibility for them as well. Hotels of varying levels of style and luxury were built, with visitors of more modest means occupying lodging-houses or renting cheaper, more primitive forms of accommodation. Collectively the resorts provided escape from the crowded towns and cities, and from the formalities of everyday life.

At first, when the resort population was more socially exclusive, their attraction was supposedly the opportunity for therapy and improvement rather than pleasure. Bathing was a grim and hasty ritual, undertaken in the chill of early morning, most often from a bathing machine, a kind of caravan-cum-dressing room on wheels pulled by a horse down to the water's edge, wherein the bather could undress and enter the water (usually naked, with privacy provided by immersion in the water). Immersion was normally brief, half an hour at most, in some places assisted by formidable women called 'dippers', who would grasp a hesitant would-be bather and plunge him or her into the water. The victim was usually a child or its mother—the bathing-machine was less popular with men, who ran into the sea naked until restrictions on this freedom forced many of them to retreat to the bathing-machine as well.

The shock to the body of the cold water was considered to be beneficial, and was sometimes followed by a massage with seaweed, and a rest. Feeling virtuous at having endured this ordeal, the holiday-maker could proceed to enjoy the other amenities provided at the resort. The assembly room and circulating library, with coffee- or tea-rooms attached, became the focus for social gatherings. Those of a less frivolous bent might engage in the popular passion for collecting pebbles, shells, seaweed and assorted marine life, a craze that was at its height in the 1850s and 1860s but had largely died out by the end of the century, mainly because it had resulted in the destruction of most easily accessible marine specimens.

The pursuit of pleasure as the real aim (apart from keeping up with the fashion) of the seaside holiday came to be implicitly acknowledged and accepted. Many forms of entertainment were provided for resort visitors, sometimes by vigorous private entrepreneurs, more often, and particularly in the case of successful resorts like Blackpool and Bournemouth, by local government, which generally assumed control over the regulation of seaside resorts throughout Britain.

Piers were first built for the landing of people and supplies arriving at resorts by steamers. Soon they were being used as places for promenading over the sea, for fishing, for viewing back towards the resort and the coastline, and sites where entertainment could be provided. Promenades were also built along the seaside, gardens were landscaped, and the 1870s saw a vogue for aquariums. Characteristic seaside entertainments were band recitals, black-and-white minstrel shows, Punch and Judy shows, and donkey rides and stalls on the beach. So many vendors set up their wares on the sand that the Blackpool Town Clerk in 1895 listed 316 'standings of the foreshore' and there were thirty-five phrenologists on the beach on one long weekend holiday.

In the early days of the English seaside resort in the mid eighteenth century, mixed nude bathing was normal. This was the period when resorts were the preserve of the upper classes, with their relaxed attitudes to morality. As resorts became more popular, however, the middle classes, with their concern for respectability and propriety, set the moral tone at the resorts. Since 'Leering through lorgnettes . . . was the favourite male pastime on the beaches of the day',[7] women began to wear a kind of flannel cloak to cover themselves during their ritual bathe, and mixed bathing was no longer practised—in Blackpool in 1788, for example, a bell was rung when it became the hour appointed for ladies to swim, and men were supposed to make themselves scarce. Regulation of bathing in England was often unwelcome, and controversy raged over restrictions on mixed and nude bathing. Rules were local, and their severity, and the rigour with which they were enforced, varied from place to place and from time to time.

Hence, at the time Australia was settled, permissiveness regarding 'public decency' while bathing was gradually giving way in England to a moralistic disapproval of the mixing of the sexes and the sight of the naked human body, and a distaste among women for being ogled by men.

The craze for the seaside spread to Europe, with a delay of some thirty years as it made its way along the coasts. Patterns of social life evolved in the continental beach resorts, based on the English model. But English inventiveness was fundamental in the development of seaside holiday-making in Europe, with the aristocracy playing the pioneering role there, as in England.

Resorts in the Australian colonies

FROM THE 1830S ONWARDS the forms of relaxation fashionable in the colonies were modelled on those of the English gentry. The spa tradition was copied, and about 200 spas were established in Australia where springs containing suitable minerals had been found.[8] Bath houses on the English model were built for users of a special class, such as the Military Bath House in Erskine Street fronting onto Darling Harbour in 1822, and the Governor's Bath House in the Domain in 1828.[9]

Baths and bathing machines

To enable law-abiding citizens to continue to enjoy bathing, baths were built—'a hasty repressive reaction to screen the nudity of the colonists who insisted on bathing in the sea.'[10] They were well-screened from public view, with high wooden fences on the shore side, often completely enclosed by timber, and with individual dressing-sheds along the walkways.

The first public baths in Sydney harbour were completed in about 1826; Adelaide Marine Baths were established in 1839 for 'a respectable married female [clientele] previously accustomed to Baths in

Fig-Tree Baths, Domain: Sydney's first swimming spot on Woolloomooloo Bay, later to become the Domain Baths, then the 'Boy' Charlton pool. (*Illustrated Sydney News*, 28 September 1872, p. 1)

Source: Mitchell Library, State Library of New South Wales

This photograph of the Domain Baths, taken late in the nineteenth century, shows the walkways and wooden fences enclosing the baths. These structures were insufficient, however, to hide from scandalised onlookers the figures of nude boys, who wave cheekily at the cameraman.
Source: Government Printing Office Collection, State Library of New South Wales

England'.[11] By 1853 there were four Sydney Harbour baths for use by the public; and by 1882 there were at least five more. Some harbourside residences had their own private baths. Baths were also built in resorts in other colonies, a splendid establishment at Melbourne's St Kilda being completed in 1860. Baths also formed part of the attractions at popular resorts like Clifton Gardens and Manly in New South Wales, and Glenelg in South Australia. There were separate men's and women's bathing arrangements, with a few hours a week being set aside for women's swimming, the baths being the preserve of men at other times. (Had the allocation of times been proportionate to the demand for swimming, much more time would have been allowed for women to swim.)[12]

A correspondent to the *Newcastle Herald* of 13 July 1883 proposed a design for a swimming pool that took to extremes the desire to screen swimmers from the eyes of the general public. He suggested that the bogie hole there could be excavated to three times its present size, with a sea-wall on the east side, a roof over it to join with the cliffs, the two ends framed with hardwood, and the whole covered with corrugated iron. 'I would then place to the southward a tube of iron with a valve on the top—the tube to be tapered outwards to the sea, and terminating with a funnel-shaped mouth'. Claustrophobic swimmers would have been well advised to avoid the Newcastle Bogie Hole Baths had they ever been built to this design!

The bathing machines that were such a feature of English seaside resorts also began to appear in Australia as another means of preserving the modesty of those who wished to bathe. It seems that they were used by well-off women as a way of gaining the privacy they deemed necessary. As early as 1827 a bathing machine built in Hobart became one of that town's most fashionable amusements for women, and there was one bathing machine at Glenelg in 1845. Wheeled bathing boxes appeared at Manly (South Steyne) in 1860, and at Coogee and Clifton Gardens, with an Australian modification of the English model—a kind of sharkproof cage in front.

Coogee Bay in the 1870s, showing wheeled bathing machines with their sharkproof cages in front. (E. A. Holloway)

Source: G. B. Philip, *Sixty Years' Recollections of Swimming and Surfing in the Eastern Suburbs and Kindred Subjects* (1940)

When a *Sydney Morning Herald* article of 23 January 1907 advocated the reintroduction of bathing machines it conceded that 'Many years ago a few bathing machines were placed at Coogee, but they were not generally used'. The Commission on Surf-bathing in 1911 recommended against their reintroduction, stating that they were not suitable for the beaches here, as the wheels sank too easily into the soft sand. Yet their use was apparently widespread enough for them to be blamed for a general lack of swimming proficiency among women, the Ladies' Own Column in the *Illustrated Sydney News* of 3 March 1876 complaining that 'Bathing machines where they are used, generally stand in such shallow water that to dive from them (let alone swim) is impossible, as the head would strike against the bottom'. The writer went on to instruct readers, in tedious detail, on the art of floating in the water—a capacity that had been embraced so unselfconsciously by Sydneysiders in the earlier years of the century:

> If you are afraid to throw yourself in backwards from the lower step at first, walk out into the water till it is about as deep as the length of the arm, stoop and wet the head thoroughly to prevent headache, then *sit down*. Now place both hands, palms downward, on the ground, then stretching out the right leg bring it to the surface, and next the left one, bringing them both together. The weight of the body is thus thrown on the arms which may bend a little, but don't mind that. Now raise one hand, bring it slowly to the surface, stretch it out at right angles from the body, then do the same with the other; the centre of the body sinks a little deeper than the extremities, but the entire person is now on top of the water; and if all this have been slowly and methodically done half the battle is over, for you *will actually be floating*, and you may stay in this position just exactly as long as you please . . .

Drowning (usually in inland rivers) was a major cause of death in the nineteenth century, and this had led to a realisation that it was a good thing for people to be able to swim. Yet concern for modesty and for hiding bathers and swimmers from public view had clearly overridden the primary reason for engagement in such activities— freedom of movement in the water and the exercise of life-saving and pleasurable skill. The original English rationale for bathing—as health-giving ritual rather than enjoyable recreation—again held sway for those who submitted themselves to the constraints of the bathing machines.

Seaside resorts

'Seaside resorts' had begun to be established around Sydney, promoted for their therapeutic value and bracing clean air. In the 1840s Botany Bay first became established as a celebrated resort, with two good hotels; Clontarf, Watson's Bay, Mosman's Bay and Chowder Bay were popular resorts reached by ferry. Cremorne Gardens, opening in March 1856, was proclaimed by the *Sydney Morning Herald* as 'among the best of those places of a holiday resort of a superior order in Sydney'. Bondi became popular as a privately owned picnic ground and amusement resort between 1855 and 1877. By the 1870s Balmoral, The Spit, Cremorne Gardens, Athol Gardens and Clifton Gardens were all popular Sydney harbour resorts.[13]

Such developments were also occurring in the other colonies. In 1840 Port Melbourne (then called Sandridge) was promoted as a health resort, and in 1845 Brighton became popular after a particularly severe winter and a whooping cough epidemic in Melbourne. St Kilda was connected to Melbourne by steam rail in 1857.[14] In the 1850s Swansea in Tasmania was promoted for its sea-bathing. Cleveland and Sandgate were favourite Queensland seaside resorts in the 1860s, while Glenelg and Robe in South Australia acquired the status of resort at about the same time (Robe becoming fashionable because of the patronage of the Governor, Sir James Fergusson; Sandgate because Governor Bowen adopted it as his resort). A leader article in the *Newcastle Chronicle* of 17 November 1866 noted that

> Victorians, not content with their charming retreats at Brighton and St Kilda, flock in scores across to Launceston and Hobart Town, and there while away weeks, and even months, just as the weary and smoke-begrimed Londoner quits the glowing pave of the 'little village' for the wooing air or salt-fresh gales of Scarborough and Dover.

The editorial went on to manifest a bad case of colonial cringe: 'We are well aware that it will be years (perhaps centuries) before any approach to the English standard of perfection can be made in these remote offshoots to the British crown . . .'

The most ambitious attempt to create a popular seaside resort was probably the plan of Henry Gilbert Smith to build 'the Brighton of Sydney' at Manly. An English businessman and entrepreneur, Smith recognised Manly's potential, and his application for subdivision included a note to the effect that

> the object has been to give such a character to these Marine Retreats that they may become favourite Resorts of the Colonists. The promenades and squares indicated on the plan will be the means of ensuring health and amusement to residents and visitors.[15]

In 1853 Smith bought or leased much land at Manly, and proceeded to develop the area. Hotels and guest houses began to proliferate, and Manly was promoted as a holiday destination for country people needing an annual dose of sea air. Smith named a broad street linking the harbour side of Manly to the ocean beach the Corso, after the Corso in Rome. The walkways along the ocean beach were named South and North Steyne, after the thoroughfare at Brighton. A company was set up to provide ferry services from Circular Quay to Manly, and families travelled there in their best clothes to 'take the air'. Fairy Bower, a small ocean beach to the south of the main ocean beach, became a popular spot for picnics and church outings. The area was laid out with ornamental seats, winding paths and steps, and a tea-room on the English model.

Smith also made it his business to 'improve' the look of Manly by planting Norfolk Island pine trees everywhere. It's hard to agree that the Norfolk pines were an improvement when one reads a description of Manly in the 1880s:

> Flowers fill all the bush about Manly in the spring. Heath-like epacrids of many varieties carpet the table-lands; wattles of various shades of yellow bloom in the scrub on the flats; waratahs or native tulips shine like crimson cones in the gullies; the aromatic native roses and other boroneas grow in profusion; the gold and silver stars of Bethlehem lie thickly tufted on the ground, and on many rocky faces of the coast ravines are beautiful orchids called rock-lilies.[16]

Many of these species can still be seen in the former army and St Patrick's Seminary areas around North Head, but they have disappeared from the Manly beachside.

In his thesis on the history of Manly Peter Triglone states that he has been unable to discover Smith's reasons for the choice of Norfolk pines, speculating that the verticality of the pines provided a contrast to the low native heath; they might have been thought to help prevent sand movement. It might also have been the case that the characteristic pine shape and colouring of the Norfolk pines gave a more European look to the beach than the cabbage-tree palms and wildflowers indigenous to the area, and that they provided a 'frame' through which the ocean could be viewed. Whatever the reason, the planting of Norfolk pines established a fashion that was copied on many other Australian beaches, extending up to some of the Gold Coast beaches in Queensland, down to Tasmania, and across to Cottesloe and Scarborough in Western Australia.

The English nineteenth-century mania for collecting plant, animal and marine specimens was also promoted here. *Cassell's Household Guide* recommended these pursuits as a learning device for the young, while in 1859 the Australian *Building Times* commended seaweed and seashell collecting as a 'field of interesting occupation for the leisure of the gentle sex'. Seaweeds were pressed and dried, mounted or arranged to form a picture. Shell collecting was described by *Cassell's* as a 'never-ending occupation, of the most useful and instructive kind'.[17]

One of the earliest Australian beach paintings, *Brighton Beach* by Henry Burn (1862), features a rather muddy-coloured beach, reflecting a sky filled with a dust-storm or industrial haze. It is viewed from a vantage point above and at a distance from the beach, with a fluttering tricolour flag, buildings and elaborately costumed figures along the top of the bank competing for the viewer's attention. Its affinity is more with English illustrations of 'the seaside' than with later beach paintings.

Brighton Beach also shows a pier at one end of the beach. As at English seaside resorts, piers and jetties began to be built around the Australian coastline. The jetty at Glenelg was one of the earliest to be built, being constructed within four years of Glenelg's becoming a municipality; it was opened by the Governor in April 1859. A kiosk and an aquarium were later built on the jetty. A token cargo of imported produce was unloaded at the opening ceremony, but it was not until 1865 that a 'genuine' cargo (of coal) was unloaded at the jetty. Interest in attracting shipping to Glenelg lapsed, however, and the jetty was only used by anglers and holidaymakers.[18]

Some piers were used for landing passengers and supplies by sailing boat or steamer. But the jetty at Cottesloe, built in 1906, was always intended 'to be used for promenade and pleasure only'. Built by the Cottesloe Roads Board, the precursor to the Cottesloe Municipal Council, the pier had a bandstand, was 382 feet in length, was very popular and attracted huge crowds.[19]

In Sydney's eastern suburbs Coogee had the Palace Aquarium, opened in 1887, with associated swimming baths and amusement grounds with manicured lawns, grottoes of luxuriant tropical plants and large refreshment rooms. Bondi's Aquarium with its landscaped grounds, also opened in 1887 at Fletcher's Glen, Tamarama. It was replaced in 1906 by Wonderland City, an amusement complex containing sideshows, a switch-back scenic railway, slippery dips and underground rivers.[20]

At the picnic grounds and pleasure resorts those who belonged to what respectable members of society darkly referred to as the 'rough' or 'larrikin' element often enjoyed themselves in rowdy and boisterous fashion. In early 1881 the *Bulletin* published a scathing account of 'the orgy' into which the 1880 Boxing Day picnic at Clontarf

The Aquarium, Fletcher's Glen (Bondi): one of the many amusements available to visitors to 'the seaside' in the late nineteenth century. (E. A. Holloway)

Source: G. B. Philip, *Sixty Years' Recollections of Swimming and Surfing in the Eastern Suburbs and Kindred Subjects* (1940)

Picnicking at Bondi beach in the 1890s, looking north. The isolated cottage of 'Nosy Bob', the colony's official hangman, can be seen in the distance among the sandhills. (Photographer: Henry King)
Source: Waverley Library Local Studies Collection

descended: 'As their blood warmed by dancing, and their passions became inflamed by liquor, the scene became indescribable'. The proprietors of the Clontarf hotel sued the *Bulletin* for libel, and the case became a *cause célèbre*, with the guardians of respectability supporting the *Bulletin* by raising funds to assist its proprietors, Haynes and Archibald, to have the Court finding against them reversed.[21]

For the 'pushes' (gangs identified with particular localities), fighting rival 'pushes' or the police rounded off a good day out. On Boxing Day 1884 a 'riot' occurred at Bondi, culminating in three men being sentenced to eight years' gaol and two years' hard labour for maliciously wounding a constable.

In his reminiscences of Manly at the end of the nineteenth century Arthur Lowe recalled the way the working girls from the city— barmaids, shop- and factory-girls—would throng to Manly on their

Manly beach on a public holiday. (*Illustrated Sydney News*, 16 December 1865)
Source: Mitchell Library, State Library of New South Wales

The beach and pier at Coogee, 1920–30.
Source: Bicentennial Copying Project, State Library of New South Wales.

Sundays off: 'There was seldom a man to be seen amongst the large number that came to Manly in those days. Probably they'd had enough of the mad male for the week past, and were entitled to a day without him'. Footballers and surfers would gather at the wharf to watch the spectacle as the girls raced to catch the last ferry back to Sydney on Sunday night.[22]

Meals or refreshments could be obtained at restaurants, hotels, or shops and stalls selling all kinds of food. Picnics, another English pastime transplanted to the colonies, were very popular among daytrippers. People dressed up in their best clothes, food was packed and transported in hampers, and at popular picnic spots there was often a kiosk where hot water could be obtained for making tea.

Thus the idea of the English seaside resort was copied in the colonial setting. Colonial society sought to reproduce in Australia the structures, features, fads and social complexities characteristic of English seaside resorts. As in so many other aspects of colonial culture, the ways things were done in the Home country were adopted, irrespective of their suitability for the new environment. And the ascendancy of this imported model was aided and abetted by the strong and sustained official opposition to unregulated bathing and swimming.

3

Writers and Artists, the Bush and the Beach

THE POPULARITY OF RESORTS and picnic grounds does not seem to have stimulated the imaginations of writers in the latter part of the nineteenth century. There are a few references to members of the colonial upper class picnicking or swimming at harbourside or bay beaches: Blanche Mitchell, the fifteen-year-old daughter of the explorer Sir Thomas Mitchell, wrote in her diary of her flirtations with officers at a picnic at Coogee.[1] Eliza Chomley recalled 'scurrying into our bathing gowns and into the water . . . [from her home on Melbourne's bayside] Of course there were no bathing boxes or restrictions of any kind'. In the mid-nineteenth century (Mrs) Thomas Anna Cole scorned to be kept out of the water by cold or by the threat of sharks but frequently refrained, regretfully, from bathing if there were men swimming on her part of the beach, or if the gardener was working within sight.[2]

While most children's books were preoccupied with bush themes or were imported from England, there is a brief reference to the coast in Ethel M. Turner's *Seven Little Australians*, where Judy's banishment to boarding school follows her impulsive excursion with the younger children to the Bondi Aquarium. Other works set in this period containing allusions to the beach were written at a later time—for example, a picnic episode in Patrick White's *Voss*, and the family's holiday beach house at Flinders in Martin Boyd's *Lucinda Brayford*.

In magazines such as the *Bulletin* and the *Australian Town and Country Journal* the dominant motifs were imitation of English models and conventions, combined with an inability or refusal to observe and draw upon the distinctive characteristics of the local beach or seascape. Thus, one story describes a girl coming to the shelter of a hut from the storm-racked beach, seeking forgiveness despite her moral ruin; her hardhearted religious mother spurns her, even as her kind, irreligious stepfather urges clemency.[3] The dark forces of Nature mirror those in the hearts of human beings. It is reminiscent of a similar scene with Pegotty's daughter ruined and abandoned by Steerforth in *David Copperfield* at Yarmouth rather than a sunny Australian beach.

Verses by such popular late nineteenth-century poets as George Essex Evans, Victor Daley and Roderic Quinn were generally similar in tone and subject to those written earlier in the century, reflecting a mood of quiet contemplation as the ocean, observed from the beach, provokes meditation on the brevity of human life and achievement, or remembrance of love past. Christopher Brennan summed up the prevailing tone of Australian 'sea' poems of this period in these words:

> the irresistible melancholy of the sun,
> the irresistible sadness of the sea.[4]

Whenever a poem of this period is set on a beach, its imagery has a static quality: the perspective is that of a viewer describing a painting, rather than the viewpoint of one who is 'in the frame'.

There is only one notable nineteenth-century Australian poem to express the emotions evoked by the experience of swimming, of envelopment by the ocean—Adam Lindsay Gordon's 'The Swimmer':

> I would that with sleepy, soft embraces
> The sea would fold me—would find me rest
> In luminous shades of her secret places,
> In depths where her marvels are manifest;
> So the earth beneath her should not discover
> My hidden couch—nor the heaven above her—
> As a strong love shielding a weary lover,
> I would have her shield me with shining breast . . .
>
> I would ride as never a man has ridden,
> In your sleepy, swirling surges hidden,
> To gulfs foreshadow'd through straits forbidden,
> Where no light wearies and no love wanes.[5]

Gordon wrote from his own direct experience. He lived in the small South Australian seaside town of Robe for almost nine years while he worked as a horsebreaker. His employer noted (as recorded at the Robe History Interpretative Centre) that 'Gordon was … a regular all-weathers early bather … I have seen him swim out until you lost sight of him among the waves'. Gordon wrote that he was never happier than during this time, and when he committed suicide a few years later he chose to do so by shooting himself after riding his horse into the waves at Brighton Beach in Melbourne. But though his poem 'The Sick Stockrider' was simple and sentimental in comparison with 'The Swimmer', it was infinitely more popular. This reflected the significance of the bush in the minds and hearts of writers in the latter part of the nineteenth century, and the relative indifference to the coast and the beach summed up in A. B. (Banjo) Paterson's poem 'To the Future':

> We cannot love the restless sea,
> That rolls and tosses to and fro
> Like some fierce creature in its glee,
> For human weal or human woe
> It has no touch of sympathy.
>
> For us the bush is never sad:
> Its myriad voices whisper low,
> In tones the bushmen only know,
> Its sympathy and welcome glad.[6]

The pervasive presence of the bush in Australian art and literature contributed significantly to the establishment of an Australian sense of national identity. Why did the beach make no comparable contribution?

The terms 'Australia' and 'Australians' had come into general use as terms for the continent and its inhabitants early in the nineteenth century; Matthew Flinders had suggested its use, and it was promoted by Macquarie.[7] Ideas about what it meant to be Australian were developing throughout the nineteenth century; the real impetus, however, came in the 1880s and 90s, and was driven by a number of forces. Broadly, it was related to the rise of nationalism in nineteenth-century Europe; but here, local conditions made the definition of 'Australianness' a prominent and engrossing issue. Debates that would lead to the Federation of the colonies were under way; the native-born now outnumbered those born overseas; and writers had become sufficiently numerous, widely published and widely read, to form a new and influential intelligentsia.

The ways in which writers and artists defined a newly emerging nation's sense of itself have been well documented and analysed by literary historians and cultural critics.[8] The idea of 'the bushman' as a representative national type was especially influential. Qualities were ascribed to the bushman, the casually or precariously employed itinerant bush worker, which were later and famously summed up as 'typically Australian' by Russel Ward:

> [he] is a practical man, rough and ready in his manners and quick to decry any appearance of affectation in others. He is a great improviser, ever willing 'to have a go' at anything, but willing too to be content with a task done in a way that is 'near enough' . . . He is a fiercely independent person who hates officiousness and authority . . . Yet he is very hospitable and above all, will stick to his mates through thick and thin . . .[9]

As early as 1897 Francis Adams in *The Australians* had written that the bushman was 'the one powerful and unique national type yet produced in Australia'; and the works of immensely popular writers like Lawson, Paterson, Furphy, and Adam Lindsay Gordon reinforced a belief that the traits attributed to the bushmen epitomised the 'Australianness' that was now so valued.[10]

Another legend associated with the bush, not as closely tied to the idea of national identity but profoundly influential, was pioneering—a legend which, like that of the bushman, was promoted through literature and art. 'Pioneers' originally meant immigrants who had come to the colonies in their early years; but by the 1890s it had come to mean those who first settled and worked the land. The large claim advanced for the rural pioneers was that they 'made the land' through their labour, as in Henry Lawson's 'How the Land Was Won':

> They toiled and they fought through the shame of it—
> Through wilderness, flood, and drought;
> They worked, in the struggles of early days,
> Their sons' salvation out.
> The white girl-wife in the hut alone,
> The man on the boundless run,
> The miseries suffered, unvoiced, unknown—
> And that's how the land was won.[11]

And, more recently, Les Murray celebrates those who worked the land in 'Noonday Axeman':

> A hundred years of clearing, splitting, sawing,
> a hundred years of timbermen, ringbarkers, fencers
> and women in kitchens, stoking loud iron stoves
> year in, year out, and singing old songs to their children
>
> have made this silence human and familiar . . .[12]

All of those who worked the land could be included in the category of pioneer: squatters, selectors, small farmers. Even the convicts were rehabilitated as pioneers, in Mary Gilmore's succinct words in 'Old Botany Bay':

> I split the rock;
>   I felled the tree:
> The nation was—
>   Because of me.[13]

The pervasive presence of the bush has led to a view of our literary heritage that is neatly summed up in Nigel Krauth's memories of what he learned at school:

> I had the constant impression in childhood and adolescence that Australia lay somewhere to the west—out there—where I hadn't been. And was another country . . . the great classics of Australian literature had nothing to do with me or the country that I was familiar with [he grew up near Manly]. The Western Plains, the Vision Splendid, the Overflow (where the hell was the Overflow?) the Bush, the Outback—where *were* these places?[14]

From the earliest days of settlement the bush has embodied the spirit and the challenge of the new land—as alien and unwelcoming wilderness, to be subdued and tamed; potential wealth, to be owned, cultivated, grazed, built on, or mined; nourishment for the soul in its vast spaces, its wild beauty and tranquillity; a place of escape, of meditation, of spiritual and emotional sustenance. Writers who came to be celebrated as definitively Australian responded to these nuances, 'singing the land', bringing a nation into being.

Artists vie with writers in the importance of their contribution to the articulation of a culture. Daniel Thomas wrote that 'works of art are a force which creates a people's way of life, of feeling and thinking. Art . . . is the principal means by which "Australia" has been invented and created'.[15] Artists were as potent an influence in linking the bush with Australianness in the late nineteenth century as writers were. Some artists earlier in the century, most notably Eugene von Guérard, had painted landscape as wilderness, Guérard's broad and sweeping vistas of mountain and coastal scenery attempting to represent the awe-inspiring and the sublime. But by the 1890s the light-filled, tranquil landscapes of the Heidelberg artists were depicting a countryside tamed for profit and pleasure. Intensity of light, sunny colours of blue and gold, bleached fields of stubble, drowsing horses and cattle, tranquil rivers, all feature in the works of Charles Conder, Tom Roberts, David Davies and Arthur Streeton. There was also celebration of bushmen and the pioneers in the paintings by Roberts, Streeton, Frederick McCubbin and many other less-famous artists.

The bush presented writers and artists with a rich lode of meaning as they helped to shape Australians' ideas about themselves. Why did the beach have so little impact on the imagination of nineteenth-century Australians?

Simon Ryan argues in *The Cartographic Eye* that our perceptions of space are socially produced, based on our expectations of what we are about to observe. When explorers and would-be squatters arrived on the coast, they were drawn inland by their expectations of what they would find. As a man entering a house notes none of the details of the entrance, his anticipatory attention drawn towards the richly furnished rooms inside, so the newcomers moved immediately inward:

> The way is won! The way is won!
> And straightway from the *barren* coast
> There came a westward marching host,
> With eager faces to the west,
> Along the pathway of the sun.[16]

Today we might argue with 'Banjo' Paterson's description of the coast as 'barren' in the light of recent estimates that Australia's marine territories could contribute between $50 and $85 billion a year to the national economy. In the nineteenth century, however, the resources to be plundered lay landwards. Land was pegged and claimed for mining; squatters occupied it and worked it, spreading their crops, flocks and herds across it. Explorers named features of the landscape, their routes inscribed on maps as graphic evidence of European society's acquisition of the land. As the first centenary of settlement was celebrated, there was confidence in the agricultural and mineral wealth of the land as guarantee of Australia's bright and prosperous future.

The beach offered no such promise. As low tide replaces high tide, as tides change with the phases of the moon and as the sea assails the beach in storms and cyclones, its shape and its extent cannot be mapped and claimed in a way consistent with legal precision. It is useless for cultivation. Nothing solid and permanent can be built on it. Nothing worthwhile will grow on it. So while the bush was useful and important in its potential for transformation into property, the beach offered no such potential, and was therefore ignored, left out of the nation-building enterprise.

As the colonies headed towards the first centenary of settlement in 1888, capital cities and inland towns were growing and prospering— or at least their well-off and successful residents were. Books like Michael Cannon's *Life in the Cities* and Shirley Fitzgerald's *Rising Damp* show that there was great poverty, disease and overcrowding in the cities; but these 'flaws in the glass' were invisible to those who did not endure them, and were overlooked in these optimistic times. Nourished by the wealth gained from the gold discoveries and from pastoral and commercial expansion, 'Marvellous Melbourne' was a city of substantial buildings, and a self-confident business and social elite.

The artists of the Heidelberg school, based in Melbourne, reflected the buoyancy and self-assurance of the period in their work—an important reason for their popularity. Even as their paintings were being completed and displayed, the depression and industrial strife of the 1890s darkened the bright picture they conveyed; and some of their paintings, notably McCubbin's, touch on the privations suffered by the rural poor—even as they romanticise them. But it is the positive mood of the paintings themselves that shapes our image of that period.

It was during the heyday of the Heidelberg painters that the beach first became an important subject in Australian art. The message that this country is now ours, we are at home in it and it is ours for profit and enjoyment—the underlying theme of their landscape paintings, and one that remained dominant in landscape painting for the next

The waves are a mere ripple on the edge of the sand. In the serene elegance of the figures on the sand and on the pier, the painting reflects a view of Nature tamed in the service of Man.

Charles Conder (b. London 1868, arr. Australia 1884, d. England 1909), *A Holiday at Mentone*, 1888. Oil on canvas, 46.2 × 60.8 cm.

Source: Art Gallery of South Australia, Adelaide. South Australian Government Grant with the assistance of Bond Corporation Holdings Ltd through the Art Gallery of South Australia Foundation to mark the Gallery's Centenary 1981, 815P14

fifty years—also applies to the beach paintings of this period. Roberts's and Conder's paintings of Coogee celebrate light, colour and pleasing scenery, just as their rural landscapes do.

However, many beach paintings of the late nineteenth century show well-dressed, obviously prosperous and middle-class people in calm occupation of the beach, strolling along the sand. *Beach Scene*, painted by J. H. Carse in 1870, showed wild waves crashing onto the sand—a reminder of the ship-wrecking ocean of earlier paintings and poems; and the people in the scene are away from the beach, at a safe distance, high on the rocks. But the waves in most of these later pictures are a bare ripple on the edge of the beach—the ocean seemingly 'knowing its place', tamed for man's enjoyment as the land had been tamed for man's profit. Only the children paddle in the water, a temporary indulgence before they too become adults, enjoying the benefits of the advanced civilisation to which they are privileged to belong.

The beach itself (and not as appropriated by artists to the generality of land and landscape), made negligible contribution to the construction of national self-consciousness and identity that was a major project of the nineteenth century and in which the bush played such a prominent part. Late in the century the beach, and all it would mean in the century to come, was yet to be discovered.

4

Beginnings: A New Century, a New Nation and the Struggle for the Beach

The ocean beaches

SINCE SETTLEMENTS had been established around sheltered harbours, rivers and bays, throughout much of the nineteenth century the areas around the beaches that lay along the open coast were undeveloped and uninhabited. Andrew Short sums up the significance of the beaches along the open coast:

> Newcomers found little use for beaches apart from running aground during storms, or loading goods and launching small boats in more sheltered locations ... The beaches were infertile and worthless, the waves a nuisance and hazard to all coastal sailors, and the dunes behind the beaches a waterless, barren wasteland.[1]

Many coastal beaches around Sydney were named and surveyed in the early days of settlement by the Surveyor James Meehan, and often the names given to them were Aboriginal, supplied by Aboriginal informants: Bondi (Bundye), Coogee, Maroubra, Cronulla, Curl Curl, and so on. The small settlement of Sydney grew to become a town, and as suburbs were built extending away from the inner city, genteel-sounding English names were bestowed upon them. But these were places that were cultivated and civilised. The ocean beaches were named and then left undeveloped for many years, their Aboriginal names reflecting their status as a useless, barbaric fringe.

In 1842 *Tegg's New South Wales Pocket Almanac* wrote of 'Great Coodgee' [Coogee] that it was a 'fine sandy bay … where all the shells and marine productions peculiar to this continent may be found', proceeding to give the scientific names of seahorses, sponges, corals, and so on, while the note on 'a very long sandy bay some 3 miles further south' [Maroubra?] states that 'the shore is strewn with large sponges, and other marine productions'.[2] It seemed that the ocean beaches were regarded more as places to visit for the collection of a variety of specimens than for any other value they might have.

Baths around the harbour and the rivers remained the only places within public view where swimming was permitted in daylight hours; but by the late nineteenth century the building of more baths was inhibited by sewage pollution, which made waters around major centres of population distinctly less enticing. An observer in 1880 commented that 'The sanitation of Sydney is a standing menace, a defiance of nature, a scandal and a reproach to our civilization'.[3] Thus the ocean beaches, with their bracing sea breezes and distance from the smelly, polluted river and harbour waters, gained in appeal as places of relief and escape from the congested town and city centres.

A general reduction in working hours in the latter part of the century meant more time for relaxation. Horsedrawn buses ran to popular beaches like Bondi, Coogee and Bronte by 1880, soon to be replaced by steam-powered, then electric trams; and Bondi's popularity grew from 1882 when private land around the beach was resumed to make the area a public recreation space. There was 'explosive' suburban development as the middle classes removed themselves from the squalor and crowding of the inner cities. Manly had long been accessible from the city by ferry, and it was a short walk from the ferry wharf to the ocean beach.

Thus people were visiting the ocean beaches in larger numbers, and some of them were living closer to them—but not yet to swim in the surf, however, or not many of them, and not during daylight hours. Natural rock pools at the ends of popular beaches like Bronte, Bondi and Coogee were popular swimming places, consolidated as baths in the 1880s; but the written record is mainly silent with respect to swimming on the ocean beaches themselves before the late nineteenth century. An exception was Newcastle, where the opportunity for the miners to rinse themselves free of coal dust and to relax by bathing at the beaches on their days off seems to have made beach bathing fairly common. This was not without its problems. There was an outraged response by the *Newcastle Chronicle* of 20 January 1866 to the arrest of persons for bathing:

> We have seen day after day clergymen, bank managers, merchants, people of all ages and conditions—even astute lawyers—supervisors of police, and police constables bathing before eight oclock in the morning, in happy ignorance that they were doing . . . wrong . . . We have the prescriptive right of at least forty years use of the beach at the back of the gaol as a public bathing place beyond the hours specified by the Act . . . thousands have been violating the law the whole of that long period.

The paper pointed out on 26 October 1872 that 'a large part of the Newcastle male population works in an occupation [mining] which makes a plunge into salt water necessary, and that to deprive them of this would expose them to the loss of health', making restrictions on bathing all the more intolerable.

The evidence suggests, however, that bathing off ocean beaches was not widespread. The ocean beach at Manly was not popular among visitors to the resort, the surf being considered too dangerous for children; and adults were still prohibited from freely entering the water in daylight. Arthur Lowe, who was born in 1879, wrote many years later of his experiences as a pioneer surfer at Manly. He claims to have been a keen surfer by the age of seven, and that there were

> No others before myself. It is not hard to explain why. People wouldn't leave their beds at 6 am to go surfing; they were not allowed by Council By-Law to go later in the day. Bathing at night was eerie. Early in the piece, people were frightened off by sharks . . . Working hours in those days were long. Transport was a problem. Many had to walk long distances to work and school, and time was therefore a very serious problem. The population was not very big anywhere, least of all around the beaches. There were quite a number of baths about populated areas, where good and comfortable, safe and very economical swims could be had. Nothing was known of such a rare sport as surf shooting at that time for it to be an inducement.

Lowe gives some persuasive evidence in support of his judgement that little use was made of the beaches for surfing:

> I knew that surfing was not in existence on any of the Sydney beaches at the time because I made it my business to find out. There were various ways. By inquiries, by travelling with my father on Court circuits, by steamboat, north and south along the coast. Also by sailing trips outside Sydney Heads . . . And many cycling excursions were undertaken on other beaches, on both the north and south side of the Harbour.
>
>   I saw a lot of the beaches in the area between South Head and Botany Bay from the seaward side. The trips with my father . . . covered a much greater area. Gosford, Newcastle, etc., on the north; Wollongong, Bega, etc., on the south. Invariably the beaches would be void of human life. Very occasionally, fishing people could be seen. I also made a trip, by a small steamer, to Newcastle . . . and carefully scanned the beaches as we slowly passed them. But very little life could be seen about them. And certainly no one surfing.[4]

At Bondi it seems to have been the local Aboriginals' enjoyment of swimming in the ocean, and lack of fear of sharks, that inspired the Europeans to follow their example:

> As far as Bondi the Beautiful is concerned, it was almost unknown to the white people until about fifty years ago (1874). Yes, it was about fifty years ago on a bright summer's day, that a party of we boys stood on Bondi Beach, watching the blacks, who were camped at Ben Buckler, enjoying the ocean waves with their wives and children . . . Said one of the boys, 'If the sharks do not touch them, what about us?' You may say that was the start of surfing at Bondi.[5]

It was as if history had turned full circle and the descendants of the first settlers were once again able to observe, learn from and copy the Aboriginal people, as their forebears had done in the early days of settlement, before the constraints of the culture they had brought with them took hold. The Bondi lads were unaware that this had happened before, of course: although George Philip wrote in his reminiscences of swimming and surfing at Sydney's eastern suburbs beaches that the children swimming at Tamarama beach were at times 'almost as naked as they came into the world, more like little aboriginals than white children',[6] there was little or no appreciation of the ironies of Aboriginal–European contact at this time. The nude bathers in Tom Roberts's painting *The Sunny South* (1887) are at ease as they approach the water from their little tree-surrounded beach. The colours of their bodies harmonise with those of the trunks and tree-limbs around them, as if they belong to a new race of Aboriginal Australians, in tune with the land; but a long time was to pass before the sense of freedom they represent became acceptable.

Restrictions on freedom to enjoy the beach

The ban on daylight bathing and swimming

As suburban development moved closer to the coastline, residents had readier access to the beaches, and discovered for themselves the pleasures of bathing in the surf. And as surf-bathing, as it was called, became more popular, so policing of the ban on daylight bathing became more assiduous. The *Police Offences Act 1901* imposed additional restrictions on beach attendance,[7] and bathers seeking to evade the law moved to the more secluded and less accessible beaches: from Bondi to Tamarama, or from Manly to Freshwater, South Curl Curl to North Curl Curl and eventually to Dee Why, with the police scaling the rocks and climbing down the gullies in hot pursuit.

Male and female daytime swimmers were caught and apprehended, and fines (increased by court costs) meant that the summonsed bathers were hard hit. Manly Council employed an Inspector of Nuisances, one of whose jobs was to remove dead animals from the streets; another, to police the daylight bathing regulations. Lowe recalled that surfers had to be out of the water at 7 a.m., as the big, portly figure of Nuisances Inspector Tom (Uncle) Skinner, with his paper-sticker and sack, pulled up: 'Out would come a huge timepiece . . . his stentorian voice would ring out, "Come on, out of that there water. It's gone 7 o'clock. I'm telling you. Or I'll book you'se names!"' The diary of a previous rather officious Inspector of Nuisances, B. J. F. Leahy, reveals that, during the sixty-seven weeks of his employment (winter included), he went looking for persons bathing after 7 a.m. on eighty mornings.[8]

Lowe suggested that one reason why the police were so zealous was that their superannuation fund was swelled by the number of convictions they achieved. Arresting those whose intention was only to enjoy their dip in the ocean must have been much easier than trying to apprehend criminals. There was also clearly class and racial

'Swimming at Bondi at Dawning Day in the 'Eighties': clearly swimsuits were not an issue for those entering the surf outside of daylight hours. (Attributed to E. A. Holloway)

Source: G. B. Philip, *Sixty Years' Recollections of Swimming and Surfing in the Eastern Suburbs and Kindred Subjects* (1940)

antagonism between the bathers (many of whom were members of the professional and business classes) and the police, their Irish brogues often mocked by the surfing pioneers who wrote about these early battles.

Resentment at police harassment increased until the laws were publicly defied, most famously in October 1902 by W. H. Gocher, a Manly newspaper proprietor who broke the law by entering the surf in daylight hours on three consecutive Sundays. Lowe was extremely scornful of Gocher's efforts: he stated that Gocher was not a surfer at all—he could not even swim, was actually frightened of the water and only went in to his knees. His was a 'grotesque and farcical [publicity] stunt', according to Lowe, and the credit for the ending of the ban on daylight bathing more properly belonged to Bondi surfers who engaged in a mass surf-in at about the same time as Gocher. (In view of the historical rivalry between Manly and Bondi surfers, for a Manly man to so ascribe credit is convincing evidence in itself!)[9]

In any case, Gocher was not prosecuted, and the *Sydney Morning Herald* of 15 November 1902 reported that the Inspector-General of Police had advised Waverley Council, which had lodged a complaint about bathers at Bondi: 'Unless . . . I receive instructions from the Government to the contrary, I do not see my way to take action beyond instructing the police that decency is to be observed'.

This policy had government backing. Lowe stated that complaints to the Chief Secretary's Department about police being too busy to protect the suburbs from crime because they were chasing surf-bathers may have contributed to the politicians' decision not to enforce the law.

But the ending of the ban on daylight bathing was far from being the end of attempts to constrain activity on the beaches. Efforts to police and control the behaviour of beachgoers persisted for many years.

Bans on mixed bathing

'Morality', in a letter published in the *Sydney Morning Herald* of 17 November 1907 opined that 'mixed bathing lowers the morals of the people and has a tendency to animalise the race'. Alderman Ogilvie of Manly thundered as late as 1917 that 'it was disgraceful to allow men and women to lie about the beaches promiscuously', and that 'separation of the sexes' should be enforced.[10]

There were practical reasons why mixed bathing became the norm, however. After several drownings it became obvious that for safety reasons it was better to have surfers together in one area of the beach where those in distress could be more easily noticed and rescued. In any case, it was impossible to enforce a rigid separation in the lively surf. Ridiculing attempts towards this end, 'HKW' in the *Sydney Morning Herald* of 30 October 1908 suggested that fences could be run out half a mile into the Pacific, no peeping allowed, 'one man allowed into a sea paddock at a time'. Councillor Scudd in Melbourne may have reminded mixed bathers that the practice was against the law in 1911, but no prosecutions ensued.[11] The Minister for Local Government thought that if surfers went out too far, a trumpet should be blown and a boat sent out to arrest them for disregarding the clarion call; but this suggestion too was ignored.[12]

Bans on sunbathing, dressing and undressing on the beach

Acquiring a suntan soon became the fashion and the aspiration of those who came to the beaches, and those unable or unwilling to follow the trend were regarded with distaste:

There is only one thing that jars the harmony of the beaches and that is the advent of a newcomer whose horrible white arms and legs seem to indicate that he is first brother to the gruesome insects found when you turn up a stone. The average healthy man or woman looks horribly unhealthy and degenerate when their white limbs appear side by side with those who have acquired the rich brown tint of the sun.[13]

But sunbathing—or sunbaking, as it was usually called in those innocent days before the causes of melanoma and other skin cancers became known—was banned. The New South Wales Government set up a Committee on Surf-bathing in 1911 to make recommendations regarding dressing-room accommodation and associated matters. The final report of the committee, containing its recommendations, was presented to the parliament on 12 February 1912. Bathers were supposed to make their way directly to and from the water by the shortest possible route; 'loitering' as they did so was forbidden. The Committee recommended the construction of enclosures wherein sunbaking could be indulged, but not all beaches were suitable; at Coogee, for example, where the beach was below the promenade, people could have looked down into any such enclosure, so it was no use building one. Sunbaking enclosures were approved for Manly, with notices prohibiting 'sun-basking' anywhere else, on pain of a £10 fine.[14] For those not taking advantage of such enclosures, an overcoat, mackintosh, or other cover-all robe had to be worn once a bather emerged from the water and mixed with 'the general public' on the beach—an ordinance referred to as the 'mackintosh rule'. Since lifesavers had to be ready at all times to undertake a rescue, an exception to this rule was made in their case. 'Lover of the Surf' complained in the *Sydney Morning Herald* on 9 January 1909 about the officiousness with which this was policed: 'Bathers may want to come out [of the water] for a minute or so, and then go back in. But during the last few weeks bathers are forced back into the water almost immediately they come out, or else told to go to the dressing sheds'.

There was argument back and forth in the newspaper 'Letters to the Editor' columns, but this regulation, too, soon fell into disuse as surf-bathing, as it was known, became more and more popular.

Dressing and undressing on the beaches was prohibited; this led to prolonged agitation for the provision of adequate accommodation.

Individual dressing sheds, or bathing boxes, had been constructed on many beaches, but they were privately owned or there was a charge for using them. With the numbers now seeking to enjoy the beaches, the provision of free dressing sheds, allowing access to the beaches for all irrespective of their income, was advocated, the surf lifesaving clubs being a powerful lobby group for the improvement of beach amenities. On the recommendation of the 1911 Committee on Surf-bathing, government money in the form of interest-free loans was made available to local councils for the building of toilets and dressing sheds.

Rules about 'suitable' swimming costumes

Argument over what constituted suitable apparel to be worn in the surf was probably the most vexed issue for the longest time. Earlier, women's costumes had been dangerously cumbersome, but by 1906 more streamlined neck-to-knee costumes were prescribed, for both women and men. The *Sydney Morning Herald* of 21 July 1906 noted that costumes should be made with dark material, and a sign on the beach at Cottesloe in Western Australia in the early 1900s told bathers, both men and women, that they were to wear 'dress of dark material—serge, flannel or flannelette extending over the shoulder to the knee'.[15]

Letter writers to newspapers generally agreed with strict dress regulations.[16] One woman, calling herself 'Australian Girl', wrote:

No true woman would exhibit herself to all who care to gaze, clad in the thinnest and lightest of gowns ... we women as a general rule are not strong enough to swim in the breakers, only going there for the pleasure of having the sweet, clean surf break over us, so our skirts are no great hindrance—we easily discard them when visiting the baths for a swim.

It was a very different matter, however, when three mayors of beachside councils proposed a regulation that was interpreted as making it compulsory for men to wear 'skirted' costumes. 'Maroubra Marauder' fulminated in the *Sydney Morning Herald* on 15 October 1907:

They go altogether too far. Why should these three Mayors seek to revolutionize civilization by enforcing a man to wear a woman's costume simply because he is bathing? ... an instance of the official mind gone mad ... Bathers are the most manly of men ... they would not for a minute tolerate the wearing of women's clothes. The manly woman may be possible, but save us from the womanly man.

The *Daily Telegraph* on 27 September 1907 published a poem, entitled 'The Skirt Scare at Manly' by 'Crow's Nest', mocking this proposed state of affairs:

> In the land of Topsy-Turvy
>   The Women are donning shirts
> And the men in the seaside places
>   Have taken to wearing skirts . . .
>
> Sing hey, for the whiskered women
>   In trailing skirts encased
> Sing ho, for the dainty fellows
>   And clasp them round the waist.

Despite the arguments of the hapless mayors that the proposed modification was not *really* a skirt, there were mass protests at Bondi and Manly on Sunday, 20 October, which took on a carnival atmosphere, especially at Bondi:

> The protest procession straggled from the northern end of Bondi Beach toward the city, following a banner upholding a dead seagull. Many men wore their sisters' petticoats, flounced, lacy, embroidered, trailing often in dust-stained yardage behind. Some strode in granny's red flannels, and many—especially those in the 200-pound and over weight bracket—wore frothy ballet frills around bulgy bellies. Others lopped chaff bags and tied these with chunks of frayed rope that even Saint Francis of Assisi would have scorned. Damask tablecloths appeared worn sarong-fashion, and more than one set of kitchen curtains finished as rags and tatters by the end of that hilarious afternoon. No more was heard of skirts for male bathers thereafter.[17]

This prompt, universal and absolute opposition tells us much about perceptions of and attitudes towards masculinity at that period in Australian history. The proposal was quickly dropped, although as late as 1927 C. D. Paterson, President of the Surf Life Saving Association, tried to induce lifesavers to vote to wear a skirted costume at interclub events—a suggestion that, though twice submitted to meetings of the Association, was decisively rejected.[18]

Many still dressed in their Sunday best to promenade on the beaches, and in the first two decades of the century surfing beach-goers were often outnumbered by crowds who were fully, respectably dressed. However, most of the regulations restricting free access to the beach quickly fell into disuse, due essentially to peaceful civil

'Surf-Bathing under mayoral conditions', *Daily Telegraph*, 16 October 1907. The cartoon ridicules the 'skirted costumes' edict, predicts the demise of the mayors responsible for it, and also has a swipe at the 'mackintosh rule'.

Source: Courtesy State Reference Library, State Library of New South Wales

disobedience. Authorities bowed to the force of public opinion with inaction, excepting for the policing of swimming costumes. In the 1930s a few people were fined or ordered off the beach for inappropriate costumes, and the Minister for Local Government in NSW, the Honourable E. S. Spooner, 'updated' the dress regulations by announcing that from 1 October 1935 bathers would have to wear costumes with legs at least three inches long, covering the body in front up to the armpits and on the back up to the waist. There was a public outcry and this regulation, like so many others before it, was honoured in the breach rather than the observance.

Yet the urge to regulate beach costumes lingered. The *Sydney Morning Herald* reported 'Melbourne's first "beach dress war"' on 3 December 1951. St Kilda Council at the weekend had cautioned hundreds of men and women who attempted to leave the beach in bathing costumes. Women in two-piece suits were told they could not leave the beach unless they wore a jumper, buttoned-up cardigan or dressing-gown. Men in trunks were not allowed off the beach unless they wore shirts over their trunks. People were warned that the next week St Kilda Council would prosecute people who walked about the promenade 'not completely covered from shoulders to hips'.

In 1956 the *Sydney Morning Herald* on 23 December a retiring Bondi beach inspector described how Waverley Council had banned the bikini costume (the bikini being a scanty two-piece bathing costume): 'I have had to order girls off the beach for wearing the Bikini . . . I came to the conclusion that the scantier a girl's costume the scantier her brains . . . girls who wear sensible one-piece costumes are full of sound sense'. In 1961 fifty women were ordered off the beach for wearing bikinis, and one young woman was fined £3 in October that year for wearing too brief a costume. But in that same month the ordinance prescribing the type of costume to be worn was repealed, to be replaced by the simple directive that swimmers should be clad in 'proper and adequate bathing costumes'. Gradually resistance to the wearing of increasingly briefer costumes crumbled. In 1978 Waverley Council decided unanimously that no action would be taken against topless bathers using the southern end of Bondi, and 'going topless' came to be generally tolerated.

In an ironic twist, however, concern about the damage caused by ultraviolet radiation has led to a greater 'covering up' by many beachgoers. As well as the application of sun-protective creams and lotions, sun-protective clothing has become popular, especially for little children, whose neck-to-knee costumes hardly differ from those of the last century, except that they are made from sleek and colourful lycra rather than regulation black or navy wool or cotton.

Reasons for restrictions on the freedom of the beach

WHY SO MUCH RESISTANCE, for so long, to untrammelled use of the beaches? The simplest answer is the effect of the triumph of bourgeois values of respectability and propriety in Victorian society, allied with the power of the churches, particularly the evangelical churches. From the mid-nineteenth century the influence of Methodism had been increasing, and the temperance and Sabbatarian movements were strong as the proportion of 'respectable' members of the colony increased. Dunstan refers to the 'extraordinary power of the Nonconformist churches in Victoria and South Australia' in seeking to explain why laws against free use of the beach were harsher and in force until later in these states. Bans on Sunday bathing were an issue in Melbourne for many years, the Melbourne *Argus* of 21 December 1911 stating that bathing was banned on Sundays, Good Friday, Christmas Day, and any day after 10 a.m.; but no such regulation was imposed in New South Wales.[19]

Anglicanism, the church of the most influential and respectable members of society, set its face against the liberalisation of bathing laws. Lowe stated that in the 1880s his parents had refused all attempts to entice them into 'the Church organizations which frowned on ocean bathing in daylight hours and which were responsible for getting the various councils to prohibit daylight surf-bathing'. He noted that 'the Allday Bathing Ban was led by the Anglicans', who exerted pressure to maintain the ban on several Manly aldermen who were otherwise sympathetic to all-day bathing. Following the English example, local government had become the appropriate authority to regulate the beach, and the beachside councils enlisted police assistance to enforce observance of their by-laws.[20] The franchise for local government favoured property holders, and it may have been the case here, as in England, that evangelical groups, with their concern for public morality, were disproportionately influential in local government.[21]

Local government and the churches acted in concert, in accordance with ideals of decency and proper behaviour. Perhaps they were also driven by a fear of disorder that had its origins in the foundation of the colony. Lurking beneath the threshold of public discourse was a not-entirely suppressed awareness of the ignominious beginnings of settlement—the 'convict stain'. As Stephen Knight observes in *Freedom Was Compulsory*, habits of law enforcement were maintained after the relationships between the gaoler and the gaoled that had made them necessary had disappeared. From the perspective of depth psychology, David Tacey sees repressive authority in colonial Australia as a defensive reaction common to newly settled societies: 'Colonial high culture is far more reactionary, oppressive and dictatorial than the conservative element in the parent culture. The stronger the upsurge of instinct in colonial consciousness, the more severe is the resistance erected to defeat it'.[22]

Certainly C. D. Paterson, President of the Surf Life Saving Association and the man who tried to introduce skirted costumes into lifesaving competitions, showed a lack of confidence in the ability of local bathers to conform to standards of behaviour prevailing on other (overseas) beaches when he addressed the Committee on Surf-bathing in 1911:

> [On the beach at Atlantic City] the bathers are permitted to promenade with a freedom never dreamed of among our surf bathers. From end to end the beach is covered with people in bathing attire, ordinary walking costumes, or by sightseers in deck chairs, and the greatest decorum appears to prevail, but it is a state of affairs which I do not think for a moment should be permitted here.[23]

Reasons for lack of opposition to these restrictions

WHY DID PEOPLE put up with these prohibitions for so long? Nowhere is Stephen Knight's observation—'a country [Australia] that prides itself on disregard for repressive law is also a culture that constantly makes rules'[24]—more persuasively illustrated than in the case of regulation of the beaches. The *NSW Government Gazette* of 27 March

1912 published Ordinance No. 52 relating to amendments of Acts relating to Public Baths and Bathing: the rules cover three foolscap pages of small print, and were published in association with the repeal of an Ordinance of the same number, dealing with the same regulations, which had been proclaimed in 1908.[25]

For many years, bathers put up with the regulations when and where they could not successfully evade them. Perhaps there was a social consensus in favour of them, and many who might otherwise have enjoyed a swim had internalised the norms and conventions that underlay the various bathing bans. Even the leader writer in the *Newcastle Chronicle*, who so often praised the cleansing and health-giving aspects of ocean bathing, was submissive in his editorials of 2 October 1869 and 26 October 1872 to the better judgement of the law:

> the law must be obeyed till it's amended. Good things may be brought [*sic*] at too dear a price. If the feelings of decency and modesty be outraged, or become so blunted as to be made indifferent to indelicate exhibitions, the practice that leads to it cannot be tolerated.

Year after year, this editorial writer denounced the overzealous prosecution of bathers, and advocated the building of baths as a solution to the problem, but never did he suggest that a campaign should be mounted to change the law.

Knight identifies what he considers to be a crucial element in Australia's postcolonial society: 'the self-restraint of the underclass in its effort to be judged respectable by the rulers. Much of the insistent love of legality by the apparently free, ordinary, neo-colonised Australian is a nervous defence against the risk of being unruly'.[26]

He traces this back to the early, basic conflict between the 'land-takers' and a coalition of colonised, disaffected groups—what could loosely be defined as antipathy between 'sterling' and 'currency'. Robert Hughes, in attempting to distinguish any lasting effects of convictry, discerns in Tasmania (where the effects of transportation were most concentrated) 'a malleable and passive working class, paternalistic institutions, a tame press and colonized Anglophile values'.[27] Whether or not one accepts these sweeping cultural and political assessments as explanatory, there is no evidence of concerted opposition to the bathing bans until shortly before they collapsed.

5

The Achievement of Freedom on the Beach

WHY DID BEACHGOING eventually become accepted? A consensus in favour of existing regulations was lost as fewer working hours meant more opportunity for enjoyment and 'respectable' members of society who had moved in the late nineteenth century to suburbs nearer the beaches began to enjoy the pleasures of surf-bathing. The leaders in movements against the bans were middle-class professionals: Gocher was an Englishman and a newspaper proprietor; Lowe's father was a successful lawyer, and the family had several servants in their household. A Bondi clergyman and doctor, the Reverend Robert McKeown, accompanied by Frank McElhone, a lawyer and the son of a former Lord Mayor of Sydney, were prosecuted for bathing at Bondi a few weeks after Gocher's famous swim. George Philip, who in *Sixty Years' Recollections of Swimming and Surfing in the Eastern Suburbs* took the credit for breaking down the law against daylight bathing at Tamarama, was an Inspector of Schools and a successful writer and publisher of school textbooks.

Philip described with relish his fight with Waverley police over three weekends. On the first Sunday a policemen appeared and read out the law to the lawbreakers on Tamarama beach.

> After it was all over he pocketed his blue book and started to return the way he came ... Next Sunday another policeman

appeared—a more popular one who said that that particular blue book was out of date, the other policeman was a silly fool who didn't know what he was talking about. Next Sunday the Superintendent of Police came. The Writer gave him his card, and asked him what he was going to do about it.[1]

'The Writer gave him his card': the surfers were clearly persons of substance in the community, not mere layabouts. Victory was won, and surfing became permissible, if not yet legal.

Perhaps ordinary people had been indulging in unobserved (or unrecorded) illicit enjoyment of the surf long before this. However, much as the idea of a proletarian uprising might appeal to those who

The law and the surfers' victory: George Philip showing his card to the hapless policeman. Both women and men surfers are shown to be challenging the edict against daylight bathing. (E. A. Holloway)

Source: G. B. Philip, *Sixty Years' Recollections of Swimming and Surfing in the Eastern Suburbs and Kindred Subjects* (1940)

believe in the power of the people, it was not the masses but men of status and authority who achieved the freedom of the surf.

Hegemonic support for surf-bathing was enlisted by appeals based on two persuasive arguments and one important development. The first and probably more influential argument related to the health-giving properties of beachgoing—an argument that had strong racial overtones. The second was the citing of evidence that money was to be made out of the popularity of the beaches. And the important development, one that greatly increased surfing's social acceptability and allayed the anxieties of those who feared that disorder might result from unrestricted freedom, was the rise of the surf lifesaving movement.

The health of the race

NOT ONLY WAS surf-bathing promoted for its health-giving properties (perhaps building on old beliefs about the therapeutic value of sea-water) but it was seen as superior to any other type of bathing:

> There is no doubt about the fact that surf-bathing is wonderfully healthy. In the first place, it is quite different to bathing in ordinary calm water. One is always moving about in the surf, diving, swimming and dashing through the waves, and consequently plenty of physical exercise is taken. Then the action of the surf breaking against the body keeps it in a healthy glow. Then again the surf contains phosphorus and other chemical qualities that serve to strengthen and invigorate the system. The sun also has a very beneficial effect on the body ... The strong salt seabreeze, too, helps blow away the cobwebs ... corpulent people get rid of their loose unnecessary flesh by regular surf bathing, while thin people put on flesh ... the muscles are hardened, and the blood corpuscles of the skin improved ... *Surf-bathing is helping to build up a race of fine young hardy Australians, and everything should be done to encourage it.*[2]

The last sentence needs to be understood in the context of the times. The late nineteenth century had seen the development of theories of race that helped to underpin the foundations for modern nation states in Europe. These nations consciously traced their roots to a great and glorious past based on racial groupings. Australia had attained nationhood with the achievement of Federation in 1901, but had anything but a 'great and glorious past' with which to nourish the idea of an Australian race. For some, there was strong adherence to the belief that Australia would perpetuate and enhance the greatness of the British race; but a forward-looking vision, of a future race of Australians who would surpass the excellence of their European forebears, was a heady one in those optimistic early days of Federation. Integral to this idea of race was a conviction of the need for racial purity, that the race should be a *white* race: one of the first acts of the new Federal Parliament was the adoption of the White Australia Policy.

Ideas of racial destiny sat comfortably with a belief in social Darwinism. If the triumph of 'the race' depended on 'the survival of the fittest', then it followed that the race needed to be *fit*, to maintain its supremacy over other lesser but potentially aggressive races. There was also a new consciousness that the health of the general population could be greatly improved by public health measures. The introduction of sewerage, improvements in garbage disposal and the appointment of health and safety inspectors to monitor public hygiene had resulted in a marked decrease in infant and child mortality in the 1880s. Fatalistic acceptance of high mortality rates gave way to an expectation that good health could be achieved and sustained by encouraging the population to engage in health-giving practices and pastimes—like surf-bathing.

Outbreaks of plague in various parts of Sydney in 1900 could only have reinforced the common belief that cities were unhealthy places—a belief supported by statistics that show substantially higher rates of illness and death in urban as compared with rural areas in the late nineteenth century.[3] Most people lived in the cities, unable to enjoy the health benefits ascribed to life in the country. The fortuitous proximity of surfing beaches to the cities was therefore all the more welcome: 'The pastime [surfing] ... is helping to build up a fine vigorous race from amongst the young people who live in the cities bordering on our shores'.[4]

Australian Beach Pattern, Charles Meere's classic 1940 painting, manifests this exaltation of the physical, literally embodying an ideal of racial perfection. The people on the beach, heroic in form and stature, loom up from the picture as in a monumental grouping, frozen in mid-movement. Where other nations erect monuments to honour

Those on the beach are here represented in a triumphalist style, true representatives of a fit and heroic Australian race.

Charles Meere, 1890–1961, *Australian Beach Pattern*, 1940. Oil on canvas, 91.5 × 122 cm

Source: Art Gallery of New South Wales, Image no. OA20.1965. Reproduced with permission

soldiers, revolutionaries or workers, this painting is an Australian equivalent, celebrating the people on the beach. (Anne Zahalka's 1989 colour photograph, 'The Bathers', is an updated version of Meere's painting. In the colouring and features of some of its modern beach-goers it celebrates the changes in the Australian population over the past half-century that have transformed Meere's 'Aryan' idealisation.)

The final seal of approval was the reaction of an 'overseas expert' to the experience of surfing. William Henry, founder of the Royal Life Saving Society in England, paid a visit to Manly, and the *Sydney Morning Herald* of 23 October 1910 reported his reaction:

> It is magnificent. There is some wonderful chemical influence in your surf that makes it a tonic bath, and the invigorating effect on the body is marvellous. I have often heard of it, but never expected anything so delightful.

In the honeymoon stage of Australians' love affair with the beach in the 1920s, articles were written with such titles as 'The Race on the Sands: Showing What Surf and Sun Are Doing for the Inhabitants of the Australian Coastline' and 'The Shores Set Free: What Surfing Is Doing Towards the Making of a New Race along the Pacific Coast of Australia'.[5] The surf-bathers were described as 'young Greek gods', and the healthful physical effects of surfing eulogised.

The perceived health-giving properties of the surf are the key to the lack of opposition to allowing women the same opportunities to enter the surf as men: '*The women, the mothers of our race*, are inclined to stay indoors, and take less exercise than the men ... The surf is Nature's remedy for the slackened constitution'.[6] The health advantages of the surf for women were perceived to be so great that they outweighed disapproval of mixed bathing, and enabled the respectable to argue that fears about its dangers were unfounded:

> The association of the sexes so far from suggesting impropriety has the very opposite effect. Amidst the tumult of the waters can be heard shrieks of feminine laughter, showing that the wives, daughters, sisters, cousins, and aunts are having a right good time. The introduction of mixed or Continental bathing is one of the best things that has happened for the ladies and children of Sydney. Many an erstwhile weary woman and pallid girl is today rejoicing in life and energy.[7]

Just as the dangers of mixed bathing were seen to be groundless, so the nuisance posed by 'the rough element' faded in the minds of the proponents of surf-bathing. The situation here seems to have paralleled that in England, where

> By the end of the nineteenth century in some of the well-established popular resorts, a common recreational culture was developing at the seaside for the pleasure-loving of all classes. Mainstream middle-class attitudes were relaxing, and working-class behaviour was widely perceived to be improving.[8]

Thus, while the leader writer of the *Newcastle Morning Herald and Miners' Advocate* (formerly the *Chronicle*) on 18 April 1884 had condemned 'Filthy larrikins' in extravagant terms—'the all-pervading larrikin has changed a resort fit for the gods into a mephitic horror'—as surfing became popular the tune changed:

On Eight-Hour Day 20 000 people visited the village [Manly] and their behaviour was exemplary ... I will admit that some years back an undesirable class of visitor was in evidence ... but times have changed for the better.[9]

One of the chief arguments against surf bathing in NSW was that it would bring an undesirable class of people to the beach ... How wrong that argument was has since been amply verified. There are no more orderly or respectable parts of the Common-wealth than our beaches ...[10]

Even where a correspondent in an article headed 'Disgraceful scenes at the beach' in the *Sydney Morning Herald* of 22 January 1908 railed, as if by force of habit, against 'a riotous condition of affairs' at Coogee, a sober look at the facts in an article the following day headed 'The Coogee Disorder' revealed that 'The misconduct complained of is chiefly connected with the practice of lying about the beach'—surely a particularly passive and innocuous form of 'riotous' behaviour. Sometimes, in fact, the behaviour of the lower orders was seen to be *more* decorous than that of their betters:

It is noteworthy that the rougher element always to be met with on the surf-bathing beaches is particularly careful in this respect [immodest behaviour in the dressing sheds], more so, in fact, than the average public schoolboy who has been brought up in disdain of prudery.[11]

John Walton wrote that 'The seaside expressed class and cultural differences; the insoluble problem is to show how it influenced them'.[12] The influence of beachgoing in Australia was probably to blur con-sciousness of class and cultural differences, partly because of the idea of racial health and fitness which was associated with the beach. If *race* was an idea that excluded people from exotic places and with dark skins, it was inclusive of members of all classes within the nation as long as they were white. Where the concept of race was salient, consciousness of class difference became less marked.

Opportunities for profit

TO THE PROPERTIED CLASSES, rises and falls in property values are of the highest importance. Before surf-bathing became popular, it was considered that the presence of people disporting themselves in the surf detracted from the amenity of the beach suburbs. A Randwick alderman complained that 'The value of property is reduced, and people are attracted to Coogee who Coogee could afford to do without'.[13]

This argument was turned on its head as proximity to beaches was promoted as a selling point in land and house sales. A. W. Relph asserted in an article headed 'Surf-Bathing' in the *Sydney Morning Herald* of 11 September 1909 that

> Wherever there is a beach land has jumped from a few shillings to as many pounds per foot. Whether it is at Maroubra, where 5 years ago land was unsaleable, or at Freshwater, Curl Curl or Narrabeen, where water or beach frontages are almost unobtainable . . . prices have gone up and up.

A report in the *Daily Telegraph* of 19 October 1907 stated that a meeting of representatives of surf clubs had said that property had tripled in value in five years, the population had increased 50 per cent and house rents had doubled, as had rates. Alderman Quirk of Manly in the *Daily Telegraph* of 23 October rejected these claims as exaggerated; but the association of the beaches with opportunities for profit in the residential market facilitated acceptance of the activities that took place there, at the same time increasing pressures for 'improvement' of the beaches themselves.

As usual, examples of how things were done overseas were invoked as municipal councils (or, should their enterprise be lacking, would-be entrepreneurs) were exhorted to make their fortunes by developing the resort potential of the beaches. The leader writer in the *Sydney Morning Herald* on 24 January 1907 urged would-be entrepreneurs to greater efforts:

> In places like Brighton, Bexhill, Eastbourne, Blackpool, Hastings, Margate [and in Europe] . . . the municipal authorities . . . make great profits, which are used to increase public conveniences and enjoyments . . . There should be bands and music, organised amusement, rational recreation, and open-air dining to draw the people to our beauty spots. Manly beach and Bondi have the chance of being to Sydney what Coney Island is to New York, and Blackpool to the Midlands.

When both local government and commerce showed no eagerness to rise to the challenge, the tone became reproachful, as in a *Sydney Morning Herald* article headed 'Beach Mismanagement' on 2 December 1911:

Anyone who has seen popular watering resorts in Europe and America will remember them as filled with evidence of pride, and care . . . The marine front, the gardens and lawns, the seawall, the terraces, the esplanade—in a thousand seaside resorts these are details of organisation which have built places not remarkably dowered with natural beauty to a splendid height of picturesqueness . . . The contrast between any of these places and our own Manly, or Coogee, or Bondi, is painful to think of.

Time would tell whether dreams of Antipodean Coney Islands and Blackpools were to be realised. Meanwhile, their promotion served to secure acceptance of beachgoing by those who were not themselves attracted by the physical delights of the beaches.

The rise of the surf lifesaving clubs

THE ENORMOUS INCREASE in the popularity of surf-bathing in the first half of the twentieth century would almost certainly not have been realised without the formation of the surf lifesaving clubs. The clubs were established in response to clear and urgent need. The *Sydney Gazette* had recorded the first reported drowning of a bather in the surf at Bondi on 18 July 1818: 'A young man by the name of Allen, clerk to Messrs Jones and Riley, was drowned on Sunday last at Bundye [Bondi] by venturing into the surf which was very high and rapid at the time, from the force of which when once involved he could not extricate himself'. And as the numbers flocking to the beach increased, so did the number of those who got into difficulties and drowned.

Histories of individual clubs show a common pattern: a drowning tragedy or a series of drownings, followed by a public meeting and the establishment of the Club. Sometimes there was already a kind of informal club in existence, where a group of regular surfers organised themselves to watch out for inexperienced swimmers getting into difficulties. Bondi and Bronte are contenders for the credit of being the first club to be established, as early as 1903 informally, more officially in 1906 or 1907. What is certain is that similar initiatives were taken on many beaches within a very short space of time, not only in New South Wales but on Queensland and Western Australian beaches as well. Clubs all over Australia affiliated to become members of the Surf Life Saving Association of Australia, adopting similar rules, procedures, and techniques of rescue and resuscitation.

The status of the clubs was uncertain during a period when questions of management and control were sorted out with local government. Councils in beachside suburbs were often ambivalent towards the growing popularity of surf-bathing, and a desire to 'pass the buck' to the state government for the provision of facilities needed on the beaches conflicted with concern that the taking on of such responsibilities by the government would undermine council control. Tension also developed as some councils, Manly for example, perceived the lifesaving clubs as rivals in a struggle for control over the beaches. Before the surf clubs began operating, collections taken up on Manly ferries had funded a lifeboat operated by the Sly brothers, fishermen from Fairy Bower who often rescued those in difficulties. There was little initial financial support or assistance with accommodation from councils for the fledgling clubs, and they kept going with donations and their own funds.

These early tensions soon disappeared, however, as the public embraced the idea, indeed the ideal, of the lifesaving movement, and its indispensable role in improving the safety of the beaches was recognised. The 1911–12 Committee on Surf-Bathing, while affirming that all powers relating to care, control and management of beaches were vested in local councils, also advanced thousands of pounds in the form of loans to the Councils, payable within ten years without interest, for the erection of clubrooms for the surf lifesaving clubs.

The lifesavers, with their patrols, their equipment, and their distinctive yellow-and-red flags and caps, soon became a symbol of safety on the beaches. It was the proud record of the clubs that no lives were lost while a lifesaving patrol was on duty until Black Sunday in February 1938. The voluntary nature of the movement was especially admired, the lack of gratitude of so many of those rescued, condemned. The lifesaver became an urban hero, praised in extravagant terms: 'The lifesavers represent the very highest class [among the social distinctions of the beach]. They are the Samurais [*sic*], the oligarchs, the elite'.[14]

Jaggard argues that there was an implicit social contract between councils and lifesaving clubs, whereby the larrikinism of many lifesavers

The idealisation—and the reality.

In *Resuscitation* by E. A. Holloway, Christ blesses the efforts of the lifesavers as they seek to revive a drowning beachgoer.

Source: G. B. Philip, *Sixty Years' Recollections of Swimming and Surfing in the Eastern Suburbs and Kindred Subjects* (1940)

While some lifesavers hold back the crowd, others work frantically to resuscitate surfers after the mass rescue on 'Black Sunday' at Bondi on 6 February 1938.

Source: Waverley Library Local Studies Collection

was rarely publicised as an image of a disciplined and reliable community service was highlighted.[15] The lifesaving movement became a universally approved social institution, the only element of order amidst the anarchy of the beach. The aspiring lifesavers had to undergo a series of difficult tests to gain their bronze medallion, without which they could not become club members. Training was rigorous, the skills of rescue and resuscitation constantly practised, and the self-discipline required of lifesavers was constantly stressed. Frequent surf carnivals pitted club against club: 'The association encouraged this competitive involvement . . . club members would train relentlessly and compete against themselves'.[16]

Qualities accorded high esteem and respect in the wider society—hard work, self-discipline, order, competition, and public service—were now embodied in the lifesavers, and the beach thereby gained legitimacy. Beachgoers were reassured by the sight of these superbly fit young athletes and their proven record of protecting the surf-bathing public. An ever-visible Presence, they seemed to guarantee safety against not only the hazards of the surf but also the dreaded menace of sharks.

Fear of sharks was undoubtedly a significant disincentive to swimming in unfenced waters. The description of the beginnings of surfing at Bondi quoted earlier reveals that the Bondi boys would not enter the surf until they noticed that Aboriginal swimmers were not taken by sharks: 'If the sharks do not touch them, what about us?' There were comments on the abundance of sharks in the waters around Sydney when the settlement was first founded, and their numbers probably increased significantly as tanneries and abbatoirs, discharging their effluent directly into harbours and rivers, increased their food supply. My uncle, Bill Butterfield, a Bondi lifesaver, wrote of the 1930s:

> I am reminded of the frequency with which sharks cruised along the channels within yards of the beach. Shark attack was no empty threat. Surfers and board riders, an elite band with their heavy redwood boards, were far more cautious in those days, with the possible exception of Bea Miles [a well-known Sydney eccentric] who, armed with a knife, used to swim unconcernedly around Ben Buckler . . .[17]

One of the tasks of lifesavers was to maintain a watch for sharks, sometimes atop a lookout tower that was erected on the beach for

GREEN / RED

S.H.A.R.K

The Lookout Man. (Attributed to E. A. Holloway)
Source: G. B. Philip, *Sixty Years' Recollections of Swimming and Surfing in the Eastern Suburbs and Kindred Subjects* (1940)

that purpose. The sighting of a shark resulted in the ringing of a bell or the wailing of a siren, a signal recognised by those in the water and followed by a rapid return to the shore. Knowing that the trusted lifesavers were watching out for them was psychologically comforting to bathers, a reassuring component of the 'mantle of safety' they seemed to cast over the beach, even though shark attacks were not eliminated by this surveillance. The Australian Shark Attack File, held at Sydney's Taronga Park Zoo Aquarium, lists 491 recorded shark attacks in Sydney over 200 years, of which 182 were fatal. The meshing of popular Sydney beaches (meshing is also practised in Queensland and was proposed for South Australia) has done more than any other measure to reduce the number of shark attacks. Bill Butterfield recalled that 800 sharks were caught in the first six months after meshing was introduced in 1937, the number dropping dramatically as time went on.

Lifesavers never had, and were never perceived to have, a policing function. The task of policing the beach remained firmly in the hands of the council, usually delegated to a beach inspector, now sometimes called a lifeguard, employed by the council, with the assistance of the police to be invoked as a last resort. But in supervising the safety of those who packed the beaches, and in rescuing the incompetent, the foolish or the unlucky, they constituted a benevolent, trusted form of authority that held at bay the beach's potential for disorder and danger.

C. Bede Maxwell's *Surf: Australians Against the Sea* and the histories of the various surf lifesaving clubs contain accounts of incredible feats of bravery and selflessness by lifesavers rescuing drowning surfers despite dangerously high seas or treacherous rocks and rips. With vacuous celebrities currently being promoted as models for the young to emulate, such stories could be resurrected and retold in ways that connect with contemporary needs and attitudes.

6

The Australianising of the Beach

THE RED-AND-YELLOW BATHING CAPS of the lifesavers, and the red-and-yellow flags indicating the areas that were patrolled and where it was therefore safe to bathe, were merely the most visually arresting signs that the beach was acquiring distinctively local, or indigenous, features. As the beach gained in popularity, so a characteristically Australian way-of-being-at-the-beach developed.

Knowledge of, and adaptation to, local conditions

AT THE ENGLISH SEASIDE and on the Continent, the models from which Australians' idea of the beach had been derived, bathing was generally abandoned when the seas became rough. On Australia's ocean beaches, a lively surf was the normal state of affairs. Hence, when it came to the achievement of maximum pleasure and minimum danger at the beach, the imported example provided no inspiration nor guidance.

With respect to beach safety, many were the helpful suggestions regarding types of lifesaving equipment by correspondents to the newspapers. Work on designing a reel for lifelines began about 1903, and soon the reel, lifeline and belt method of rescue was perfected and adopted by all the clubs, resulting in the saving of thousands of lives. Rescue and resuscitation procedures, and flags for the demarcation of safe areas for bathing, were similarly devised and uniformly adopted. Surfboats were based on the design of the Sly brothers' Manly life-boat, but were adapted for better handling and steering in the surf. They remain the highlight of surf carnivals, but have now been replaced for practical purposes by speedy inflatable rubber boats with outboard motors.

A major cause of difficulty and drowning were the parts of the surf—variously called the undertow, the drawback, the backwash, and now, rip—where swimmers and bathers were most in danger of being swept out to sea. In newspapers, magazine articles, and no doubt from one person to another, instructions were given on how to avoid being caught in a rip, and how to escape from a rip if caught, as regular surfers shared the fruits of their experience with others.

A similar passing on of knowledge occurred in the case of body-surfing, or surf-shooting, as it was first called. Tommy Tanna, a native of the then New Hebrides (now Vanuatu) who worked as a gardener in the home of one of Lowe's neighbours, is usually credited with having brought the skill to Australian surfers. But Lowe claimed that he had worked out how to shoot a wave before Tanna showed him how to do it better; and it is plausible that a strong, well co-ordinated swimmer, at ease in the surf, could discover for him- or herself how to use the momentum of the wave to assist propulsion of the body towards the shore. Of course marine creatures such as seals and dolphins are superb 'bodysurfers', and perhaps their example has inspired human imitation.

Thus the novel conditions encountered on Australian beaches precluded reliance on an imported way of doing things. Local inno-vations and solutions became a source of nationalistic pride as, for example, belt-and-reel rescue equipment and methods were copied and used on overseas beaches, and a style of swimming became known internationally as the Australian crawl. The new national-istic spirit was sometimes manifested as pride in the local rather than the imported. The *Sydney Morning Herald* (p. 7) on 28 Sep-tember 1909 expressed its satisfaction that 'Luckily for Australia, it [Manly] has never become infected with the snobbishness that would have abolished an interesting old name and set up a New

Margate, or East North Sydney, or Sandville-on-Sea instead. Manly's Manly still'.

There is a doubly delicious irony here. The heading of the article in which these words appeared was 'The Boulogne of Australia'; and the writer was evidently ignorant of the fact that in 1877 Manly was proclaimed a municipality after having unsuccessfully petitioned in 1876 to become a municipality called Brighton. If 'Manly's Manly still', it was a close thing.

Freedom of access to, and occupation of, the beaches

ARTHUR LOWE RECALLED an occasion when his father stood with him looking out over Manly beach. Lowe's father, a lawyer, waving his hand at the sand and the promenade, told his son: 'It belongs to the people, for a hundred feet above the highwater mark . . . It belongs to the people, all of the people'.

Like most statements about land ownership, the situation is more complicated than Lowe senior asserted. It is true that under English common law the Crown reserved, to a depth of 100 feet (30 metres) adjoining the highwater mark, water frontage on the sea coast. The majority of beaches in all states are Crown land.

However, there is no inalienable right to beach access and occupation in Australian law. In the nineteenth century land grants were made that encompassed beaches. If there was no land access to a beach entirely surrounded by private property, it was to all intents and purposes alienated from the public. This was the situation at Dee Why, where the Salvation Army owned all the land adjoining the beach, a wire netting barrier extended all the way along it, and any trespassers were threatened with prosecution by the Army.[1]

Nevertheless, there seems to have been a widely-held conviction that the public should have free access to the beaches, as a cultural right transcending mere law. This idea of freedom of access was expressed in two ways: first, that the beaches should be available to all irrespective of income; and second, that they should not be alienated for private use and profit.

This first meaning is clearly expressed in discussion of proposals to charge for access to dressing sheds:

The people who cannot afford to pay the few pence that would be demanded are precisely those whose interests have to be conserved. The beach offers them at present a healthy outing at the cost of a tram fare and no scheme should be entered upon which does not regard the preservation of that opportunity as its first duty. The leading principle should be that the ocean is free to all.[2]

With respect to the second meaning of 'freedom of access', this idea might have been fostered by an early victory over commercial interests. In 1906 the pleasure grounds at Wonderland City at Bondi were enclosed by an eight-foot-high fence with a strong concrete foundation, preventing free entry to Wonderland City, but also blocking off access to the beach. To the annoyance of managers of the pleasure park, children and youths kept cutting the barbed wire that was intended to secure the boundary.

Keeping the beach for the people: 'Members of the Club cutting the wires [around the boundary of Wonderland City] to the disgust of the Manager'. (E. A. Holloway)

Source: G. B. Philip, *Sixty Years' Recollections of Swimming and Surfing in the Eastern Suburbs and Kindred Subjects* (1940)

A rumour spread that Wonderland City management was planning to gain a lease for an indefinite period that would exclude the public from the beach. This galvanised George Philip, the conqueror of the police on Tamarama Beach, and his colleagues to mount a campaign to thwart any such decision. Adopting the slogan that there was a plot to 'take away beaches and parks from the people', Philip used his familiarity with the social and political system to good effect. He visited the houses of members of parliament, arranged a deputation to the Minister for Lands, and pressed the case against a lease with such success that it was never thereafter proposed. Philip himself believed that his campaign had been crucial: 'I am convinced had we not so strenuously taken up the fight the lease would have been given'.[3] Philip refers to this campaign in his book *Sixty Years' Recollections*, publishing correspondence that illustrates his familiarity with political tactics and processes.

There is other evidence of more general acceptance of the principle that private interests should not be allowed to alienate beaches:

> J. G. Mosley has pointed out that from the 1860s Australian governments made a practice of reserving the coastal foreshore and the banks of lakes and streams for public use, showing foresight in a generation not much given to the use of the beach for pleasure.[4]

When the beaches became popular and access had been difficult or impossible because private land ownership had previously been granted, government and councils resumed land to create beachfront reserves:

> During the past five years ratepayers of Warringah have paid £68,956 for purchase of foreshores and reserves . . . Probably no other council in New South Wales could show such a fine record, the Shire President said. But they couldn't be expected to go on burdening the ratepayers in that way indefinitely. Beaches were used by people who came in their thousands from all parts, and acquisition of places of access, in his opinion, should be a national work.[5]

The point at issue here was where the money for resumption should come from—not the desirability of resumption in itself.

This belief has remained strong. While in other countries an area around a beach and including the beach may be ceded to private ownership, attempts to appropriate the beach in any way are met with fierce resistance in Australia, as shown by examples eighty years apart in time:

> The proposed shutting of the public off the foreshore of Manly beach, and handing them over to showmen, is exactly what the Minister for Lands has already declined to permit other gonce-grubbing councils to do . . . What is now wanted is that the Minister for Lands promptly points out to the Manly mugwumps that the Manly parks and beach foreshores are for the public, and not for individual or collective side showmen, or speculative syndicates.[6]

> Mosman Council has decided to reject a controversial proposal to allow corporate sponsorship at Balmoral Beach because the notion of stamping a corporate logo on the harbour beach has been seen as distasteful.
> The Town Clerk . . . and the Mayor . . . had recently agreed to let a sponsorship company, *Lightning Rod*, secure a company to 'adopt' Balmoral beach in return for money for capital works.
> However, when the secret deal was revealed in the *Herald* last week, the aldermen were horrified and voted unanimously to reject the idea.[7]

Even so, the price of keeping commerce from putting its mark on the beach is eternal vigilance; and there are plenty of examples of waterfront residents in wealthy suburbs exercising a kind of informal ownership of beachfronts bordering their properties. There are always exceptions to the rule where money is concerned.

A well-publicised recent eruption of opposition to appropriation of the beach was the anti-Baywatch campaign in the northern Sydney beachside suburb of Avalon. In 1998, when a couple of episodes of the popular US television series *Baywatch* were filmed at Avalon, its producer became so enamoured of Sydney's beaches that it was decided to move the location for the series to Sydney—specifically, to Avalon.

Furious controversy raged when the local community heard of this proposal in early 1999. On one side were those who scented opportunities for profit in the business a large television production unit would bring; those who liked the idea of promoting the charms of Avalon to the world; and the local surf lifesaving club, chronically short of money, whose clubhouse had already been refurbished with *Baywatch* help (and the promise of more to come). Those opposing it had resented what they saw as an attempt by *Baywatch* to take over the beach, aggravated by the perceived high-handedness of *Baywatch* staff during the previous year's filming. One organiser of the protest was reported in the *Sydney Morning Herald* of 13 February:

> We're used to *Home and Away* [an Australian television series] but they use only three trucks and mostly use the far end of Palm Beach. Baywatch had 15 trucks and, frankly, they had a Hollywood approach, thinking they were God's gift to the beach.

Others reported *Baywatch* staff frogmarching a surfer off the beach, and patrolling the beach in black outfits and walkie-talkies.

At a meeting called by the local council the strength of feeling against the proposal was such that the producer announced *Baywatch* would not go ahead with its plans to film at Avalon. The Prime Minister of Australia rebuked Avalon residents for costing Australian jobs and investment, while residents of other suburbs condemned them as selfish silvertails. Businessmen fumed at the thought of lost opportunities for investment, and Greg Bonnan, producer of *Baywatch*, expressed the view, reported in the *Sydney Morning Herald* on 13 February 1999, that the protesters were 'very non-Australian. These are people who don't want to share things, like surfers who don't want to share the wave . . . I'd think . . . it's not my wave, it's not my beach, it's the public beach'.

If Mr Bonnan had known more about the history of the Australian beach he would have realised that resistance to occupation of beaches by commercial interests, far from being 'non-Australian', is a very Australian thing to do.

The latest clash over appropriation of the beach—this time successful for the appropriators, though temporary—has been between residents and lovers of Bondi Beach and the New South Wales government and Olympic authorities, over the building of a stadium there for staging the 2000 Olympic beach volleyball matches. There was fierce opposition to the stadium, overridden by the juggernaut of Olympic preparation.

Arguments about the justification for alienating a large part of the beach in this way can be mounted on both sides. From a televisual viewpoint, the benefit derived from situating the competition on Australia's iconic beach is dubious: televising of the matches themselves focused on the players and the area in which the contest was fought; it could have been a square of sand anywhere. Aerial shots of the venue showed the two ends of the famous beach, with a large blue lump—the stadium—in the middle.

From the point of view of spectators the stadium was a great success. An exuberant party atmosphere prevailed; the good humour and sheer enjoyment of the crowd was infectious. For the players, the impact was probably mixed: the noise may have been distracting for some, but the Australian women's team exceeded expectations and carried off the gold medal. Some might fantasise that the Spirit of Bondi was on their side, as well as the boisterous spectators (the men's team, on the other hand, seemed to enjoy no similar inspiration).

True to the promise of the authorities, dismantling of the stand began immediately after the beach volleyball competition finished. Many Bondi aficionados hope that such incursions will be resisted in the future.

The unadorned beach

THE PUBLIC COULD NOT HAVE it both ways. Either the beaches could be at least partly given over to commercial interests, or they would remain undeveloped. It was as much as councils could afford to provide basic dressing sheds and toilets and the essential surf-club houses even with government loan assistance. From the point of view of a writer in the *Sydney Morning Herald* of 15 February 1912, this was all that was needed: 'The average surf-bather has no desire to be palatially housed and so long as he can hang his oldest clothes and a towel upon a peg (with some reasonable prospect of finding them there when he comes back) he is perfectly well satisfied'.

Others retained dreams of the beaches becoming 'what Coney Island is to New York, and Blackpool to the Midlands', foreseeing 'the inevitable time to come when smart business enterprises will set about it'.[8] But their visions were based on an overestimate of the real profit-making potential of the beaches. The few amusement parks that were built were never as popular as similar ventures in the United States, and soon struggled to attract patronage. Wonderland City closed in 1911, and by 1914 other beachside amusement parks were struggling to pay their way.[9] Even in England, with its much more densely packed seaside resorts, only the most popular entertainment parks and palaces made large profits. While many entrepreneurs found the seaside an attractive investment prospect, in northern England particularly 'The few successful dividend-earners were far outweighed by the failures and abortive schemes'.[10]

If English seaside resorts, patronised by a much larger population, found it hard to sustain profitable entertainment venues, then it was almost inevitable that their Australian imitations would fail. The various aquaria, Wonderland City, attractions built with so much hope and fanfare, decayed and were demolished. Some piers built for promenading remain in more sheltered bays, mainly on the coast of the southern states whose longer winters mean less time for enjoying the beach itself—St Kilda in Melbourne being the best-known example. But most of them disappeared, either swept away in storms or demolished because of the high costs of maintenance. Coogee Pier was demolished in 1934, only six years after it had been built.

As the beaches lost most of their built accoutrements and became barer, they kept increasing in popularity. It seemed that the lure of the beach was sufficient unto itself.

The 'suburbanity' of popular beaches and its consequences

IT HAS BEEN SIGNIFICANT in the development of the meaning of the Australian beach that the primal, most popular beaches fringed the suburbs, as noted by the travel writer Jan Morris: 'I suppose there is no other great city with quite such a gift: the beaches of Los Angeles or San Francisco have none of the domestic appeal of these Sydney ocean fronts, which are like sand-and-surf extensions of the family suburbs behind them'.[11]

Years before, Jean Curlewis had written in celebration of this very ordinariness, the casual interweaving of suburban life with the enjoyment of the beach:

> Our long coast scalloped as neatly as a beach towel. Behind each beach, a village . . . In the steep gardens husbands and wives garden domestically in their bathing suits. Butcher boys dash on their rounds with towels round their necks . . . Business men come home from the office and go for a dip before dinner as inevitably as men in other cities wash their hands.[12]

For many of those who lived and worked near the beaches, or who could reach them easily by public transport, the beach was a place to be unselfconsciously enjoyed, not a setting for courting the public gaze through self-presentation or display of the body beautiful. There were plenty of those (beautiful bodies), of course. Ben Travers, the English playwright, wrote of a visit to Bondi in the 1920s:

> Nowhere in the world had I ever seen a lovelier setting for the recreation ground of thousands of magnificently proportioned young males with bronzed torsos, escorting an equal number of young females, who revealed, so far as the regulations allowed, that their forms were as attractive as their faces ... the whole experience was Paradisiac.[13]

Appreciation of the beautiful bodies to be seen on the beaches has never been lacking; but observers have also noted that being a superb physical specimen is not a prerequisite for entry to the beach:

> Contrary to the belief general among those who don't know, the feminine surf-bather is not often a roguish damsel of the type pictured on illustrated post-cards but a sedate, and frequently middle-aged, married woman, who is usually accompanied by her offspring ... she seeks the water for its own sake and cares nothing for her appearance ...[14]

> Here on the beach an elderly lady happily parks her spectacles with her towel and wades happily into the fray.[15]

> There are many men—and, curiously enough, mostly well over middle age—and women, too, who never miss their morning dip in the long Pacific swell.[16]

The beaches became favourite holiday places for those who did not live close to them. Fine holiday beach houses were built by the well-off, fibro or wooden beach shacks by the less wealthy. Others patronised guest houses or private hotels: in a story entitled 'Weather- board Swastikas', Barry Humphries recreates the tone of holidays at a 'respectable' beach Guest House on Victoria's Mornington Peninsula in his usual ironic style and with his seemingly total recall of detail:

> Dava Lodge at Mount Martha, and Ranelagh at Mount Eliza, were two favourite seaside resorts on the Mornington Peninsula ... After each successful season of maximum occupancy by the families from Malvern, Camberwell and Kew, another century-old Norfolk pine would be felled, another Victorian wisteria arbour

deracinated, to make way for yet another wing of chilly, linoleum-floored bedrooms.

Before each meal, and all in black, with white starched apron, cap and cuffs, a maid hurried down the labyrinthine corridors sounding the dinner gong or strumming an inane tunelet on a miniature marimba, and in her wake streamed the famished families. Piebald with sunburn, sand chafing in each secret crevice, they hurtled towards the dining-room.[17]

Unions and friendly societies built clusters of beachside holiday cabins for their members; families put up their tents or swarmed into caravan parks to spend the long summer holidays by the beach. But while there were always tourists and holidaymakers among the locals and those who arrived from other suburbs by tram, bus or ferry (and later, cars), the suburbanity of the popular beach added to its casual atmosphere and inclusiveness, and influenced attitudes to beachgoing generally.

Many of the beaches were still referred to as 'resorts' until well into the twentieth century; however, it was a description that faded, as for many people beachgoing was an experience not necessarily synonymous with holidays. 'Resort' became a label applied to exotic places whose special purpose was to cater for the needs and dreams of those seeking pleasure and escape—ski resorts, Barrier Reef resorts, overseas holiday destinations—not the local beach.

The label of 'the seaside' when applied to Australian beaches was even less appropriate. In England and Europe a 'majestic seaside architecture' had blossomed during the nineteenth century. Terraces were landscaped and paved or planted with gardens. Promenades, esplanades and parades, lined by hotels and lodging-houses, fascinated travellers, one of whom noted in 1824 that 'a continuous train of carriages and men and women on foot or on horseback [moved back and forth] a hundred times on the same site'; seaside architecture was characterised by its 'cumbersome magnificence'.[18] This use and arrangement of space overwhelmed the beach: the beach had become the seaside.

In Australia the beach itself remained the focus of attention, assisted by its lack of adornment. The occasional grand hotel and beach pavilion failed to dominate the tiled roofs, houses and flats of the suburbia bordering the beaches. The names given to streets along the beach of esplanade, parade and terrace only serve as a pale reminder of what might have, but probably never could have, been.

7

The Beach from the Mid-twentieth Century to the Present

THE HUGELY POPULAR lifesaving movement brought both safety and glamour to the beaches during the years between the two world wars, and surf lifesaving carnivals attracted enormous crowds of spectators. But the lifesavers largely disappeared when 70 per cent of club members enlisted in 1939; and the beaches themselves became a focus of wartime anxiety, especially when the coming of war to the Pacific in 1941 heightened Australians' awareness of their isolation. Barbed wire was laid along some of the more popular beaches, while groynes (walls of rock or concrete built out at right angles from the beach in an effort to halt erosion or sand drift) were blown up, reportedly at the direction of American military authorities. Some Sydney beaches were strewn with tank traps, small concrete pyramids apparently designed to disable (or at least discourage) advancing Japanese tanks.

Such measures considered as deterrents against invasion might seem futile, even ludicrous, today; but hindsight is always a comfortable perspective, and the vulnerability was keenly felt. Australia's sandy frontier was breached by Japanese bombs and shells: along the north-western Australian coast, repeatedly at Darwin in the Northern Territory, near Townsville in Queensland—and at Bondi and Newcastle by shells fired from a Japanese submarine several miles out to sea. My family blamed my grandmother's too-early death in

September 1942 on the shock she suffered in June that year when shells exploded nearby as she and my grandfather sheltered under a table in their Bondi home.

Not only were the beaches less inviting with their barbed wire and sandbags, but the exodus of lifesavers to the warfront threatened to leave them relatively unprotected. Women's lifesaving clubs had been formed almost as early as those of the men, and 20 000 people watched the Manly women's team compete at a surf carnival there in 1912; but the Surf Life Saving Association of Australia banned women from gaining the bronze medallion necessary for them to qualify as lifesavers, and an official ban on women lifesavers was maintained despite the depletion of the ranks of lifesavers when they enlisted.[1] But there was a degree of adaptation to the exigencies of the times: the secretary of the Victorian Surf Life Saving Association told the Melbourne *Argus* in 1940 that 'their [women's] training, identical to

Bondi beach in the 1930s and 1940s: a study in contrasts.

A crowded day on Bondi beach in the 1930s, showing concrete groynes built to prevent sand movement, cars parked along Marine Drive, and Norfolk pines recently planted in Bondi Park.

Source: Waverley Library Local Studies Collection

that undergone by the men, is sufficient to enable them to take their place in patrols', and women lifesavers, without fanfare, took over the men's duties all over Australia.[2]

'Out of Uniform and into a Jantzen!' proclaimed an advertisement for a very popular brand of swimming costume in the *Australian Women's Weekly* in 1946. The 'real' lifesavers resumed their prominence on the beaches, the Surf Life Saving Association refused to grant women lifesavers official recognition, and by 1953 the message was again that women were 'not strong enough physically to carry a heavy belt and line'.[3] Monday newspapers in the 1950s regularly reported shark alarms, bluebottle stings, rescues, and the drama of big waves and challenging surf.

After World War II patterns of beach use changed with rising affluence and the consequent increase in car ownership. 'Going to the beach' no longer meant travelling to the beach most conveniently

A very different view of the same beach. The groynes have been blown up, and barbed wire laid along the beach to repel invading Japanese troops (there were gaps where bathers could get in and out). A chilly winter's day (the photograph was taken on 7 July 1943) is the main reason the beach is deserted. Since the taking of photos was prohibited, it is rare to see pictures of the beach in this state.

Source: Waverley Library Local Studies Collection

Women lifesavers, 'not wanted' by the Surf Life Saving Association.

Freshwater beach lifesaving ladies, c. 1908, dressed in starched white long dresses: ready, willing—and able?

Source: Warringah Library Local Studies Collection

Coffs Harbour Ladies Life Saving Club, between World Wars I and II: much more suitably dressed and ready for action, but, alas, they were still not wanted. Women would not be admitted as lifesavers to the ranks of the Surf Life Saving Association of Australia for another half-century.

Source: Bicentennial Copying Project, State Library of New South Wales

reached by public transport each weekend; enjoyment of a wider range of beaches became possible. The mobility associated with car ownership was especially attractive to surfboard riders, who could strap their surfboards onto their roof racks and cruise from beach to beach looking for the best waves. Developments in surfboard design, combined with changes in lifestyle, ensured that boardriders—'boardies', surfriders, or simply 'surfers', as they are variously called—were to become an increasingly prominent category of beachgoer in the decades to come.

Surfboards and surfboard riding

THE BEGINNINGS of the modern surfboard (surfing) movement in Australia can probably be dated from the visit of Hawaiian surfboard riders to the Melbourne Olympic Games in 1956. Attempts to devise 'improved' ways of riding the waves had been around for a long time, however. Boards with which to catch the waves were improvised from the early days of surfing: Lowe reported that a bodysurfer named Frank Bell, who had read about board-shooting in Hawaii, brought a church door with a pointed top to Freshwater and tried (unsuccessfully) to shoot the surf with it. Surf skis were invented in Australia— probably adapted from the wooden canoes used for paddling around North Bondi.

Duke Kahanamoku, a champion Hawaiian swimmer, first introduced Australians to riding the solid redwood board at Harbord beach in December 1914, at one point riding in tandem with a local girl, Isobel Letham. A friend of my uncle's, a Swiss-born woman, rode a surfboard in the 1920s at Bondi.

After demonstration of the new, lighter malibu boards by the Hawaiian surfers at a number of Australian beaches in 1956, board-riding became a popular fad, promoted in the popular mind by the 'Gidget' series of movies, 'Surfin' U.S.A.', sung by Chuck Berry, and the music of the Beach Boys, with California as the centre of the new surfing movement. Shorter and lighter boards made of balsawood and fibreglass were sold in their thousands, and from the 1960s onwards in both California and Australia there was constant experimentation and innovation with respect to board shape, length and design.

A new type of Australian memorial, a new type of hero.

A memorial to Duke Kahanamoku, the Hawaiian who brought surfboard-riding to Australia, on the headland above Harbord (Freshwater) beach.

Source: The author's private collection

Moves to regulate boardriders

For the first few years of the modern surfing movement, the public image of surfers was quite favourable: a beachside council mayor was of the opinion that '99.9% of board riders are wonderful young people with a fine approach to sport'.[4] But as boardriders became more numerous, the public began to regard them with some unease; for surfing was acquiring the characteristics of a subculture at a time of great cultural change. As the 1960s went into the 1970s 'counter-cultural' values of 'doing your own thing', anti-authoritarianism, spontaneity, rejection of discipline and of the values of the older generation, all challenged the existing order. Devotees of the new surfing movement came to be seen as exemplifying those values, with their disregard of the work ethic, their individualism and apparent

Sculpture of the lifesaver, hero of the beach, erected near the pavilion on Bondi beach.

Source: The author's private collection.

irresponsibility. In 1963 there were newspaper reports of working-class young gangs, known variously as 'rockers' and 'westies' and 'mods', roaming the beaches and beating up surfers.

Influential in the shaping of the cult were the surfing magazines produced here and in the United States. While *Surfing World*, which started in 1962, expressed countercultural values, *Tracks*, first published in 1970, was regarded by many of its readers as being in the vanguard as far as surf literature went. It was seen by them as the truly independent voice of an alternative culture to mainstream Australia. In contrast to other surfing magazines, the text, with its outspoken views on many issues, was more important than the pictures of spectacular feats of surfing. The values of the young surfers in *Puberty Blues* (1979) are reflected in the 'Letters' columns of magazines like

Tracks and *Surfer*. In the crudity of their language and the aggressive and sexist attitudes they often express, surfing magazines were and still are designed to appeal to adolescent boys and to alienate parents who might venture to peruse their pages.

The boardriders now described themselves as 'surfers', appropriating the name hitherto used by bodysurfers; and for a while they seemed likely to take over the beaches as well. Sydney beachside councils responded to moves to ban the use of boards in 1958 by stating that they were 'not a problem yet'; but by 1959 they were designating special areas of the beaches for the use of boardriders and excluding them from other areas. Registration of boards was introduced in the 1960s, with a ten-shilling (one dollar) fee and a requirement that a registration sticker be affixed to the board. Reports of injuries caused by boards began to appear in newspapers, and riders who did not comply with orders to move from non-board areas were liable to have their boards confiscated by beach inspectors. In 1966 boards were banned totally on Harbord beach, and restricted at other beaches under the control of Warringah Council.

Surfers hit back against these bans. Signs on beaches defining boardriding areas were vandalised or removed. Surfers and supporters launched a 'Fight the Warringah Board Ban' campaign, with 'Share the Surf' car stickers, petitions, and letters of protest. With the growing number of surfboards and few resources to police the bans, the bans only lasted one season.

Anxiety over boards intensified with the introduction of surfboards with fins, which were seen as 'lethal weapons', although the President of the Australian Surfriders Association denied that they were dangerous. Loose boards were a bigger problem, unguided missiles liable to plough into bodysurfing areas after their riders had fallen or been washed off. The invention of leg ropes, enabling a rider to stay attached to his board after falling off, were designed to prevent this happening and to save riders a lot of paddling; but when a rider with a leg rope was killed after his board knocked him out, a committee of inquiry was set up by the Minister for Sport and Recreation to investigate the safety of leg ropes.

Reading the report of the committee reminded me of the *Report of the Surf-Bathing Committee* more than sixty years previously: there is the same mixture of commonsense and the impulse to regulate. It concluded that commercially-produced leg ropes probably reduced rather than increased the risk of accident, and that they should be sold with instructions as to their proper use; but it also recommended that boards should be inspected annually, and that a registration fee of $2 be introduced.[5]

The registration fee imposed during the 1960s had proved to be impossible to administer, and was soon dropped. Only 1600 boards had been registered at that time; now it was estimated that there were 195 000 boardriders in New South Wales alone. The *Sydney Morning Herald* reported on 5 May 1975 that the Minister had commended the committee on its work, noted that he favoured the use of regulatory or legislative powers only as a last resort, and commented that some of its recommendations were 'of a far-reaching nature and require further thought'. No more was heard of the proposal to register surfboards.

The widespread adoption of leg ropes greatly reduced the danger posed by loose boards. Newspaper reports of injuries decreased, and boardriders and bodysurfers mostly confined their activities to separate areas. The urge to regulate boardriding weakened, as the impracticability of enforcing bureaucratic restraints became evident, and time showed that the beach could accommodate a variety of ways of enjoying the surf.

The relationship between surfriders and lifesavers

Surfboards were associated with lifesaving clubs from the time they were introduced by Duke Kahanamoku. During the 1920s and 1930s boardriding was a popular recreational pastime for club members, boards appeared in club rescue competitions and were occasionally used for rescue purposes.[6] The need to store the heavy boards close to the beach restricted their use and popularity, and for some lifesavers the convenience of the club house as a place to store their boards was a major reason for their membership of the movement. The Surf Life Saving Association organised 'special' malibu surfing events at the NSW championships in 1962–63. When the Australian Surfriders Association was formed in 1963 to represent the interests of boardriders, one of its aims was 'to assist the Surf Life Saving Association in any way possible to help the public on the beaches'.[7] The numbers of young men joining the lifesaving clubs steadily increased up to 1965, so boardriding was not seen as a rival attraction competing for the allegiance of potential lifesavers.

This changed after the mid-1960s as countercultural values became more prominent, the number of boardriders not affiliated with clubs grew, and club membership started to decline (the Young Nippers training program was started at this time to counteract this trend). The president of the Freshwater Surf Life Saving Club referred to the noncommitted boardriders as 'a hoodlum element which is causing members a great deal of concern'[8]—a reminder of mutterings about 'the rough element' during the struggle for free access to the beaches at the beginning of the century.

On 7 November 1966 the *Sydney Morning Herald* reported a clash between 350 board riders and surf club members at Palm Beach, with police being called in to restore calm. Surfers' hostility towards 'clubbies' was expressed by the cartoon character in *Tracks*, Captain Goodvibes, who ridiculed lifesavers' sexism, homophobia, and predilection for beerdrinking (qualities by no means lacking among boardriders themselves!)

Craig McGregor highlighted differences between the lifesaving movement and the 'boardies', characterising lifesaving as 'hidebound, loyalist', ruled by 'puritan regulations, rigorous discipline and "authoritarianism"', while surfers were 'cool, modern, uncommitted', 'freewheeling, anti-authoritarian, hedonistic'.[9] And in a submission to the committee of inquiry into leg ropes, the editor of *Surfing World* magazine, Bruce Channon, complained that 'The Surf Life Saving Association people always join in the cry, jumping at any opportunity to turn kids away from surfing and into their depleting ranks. Kids like these ... aren't at all interested in military-like training schemes and officious administrators'.[10]

It has been argued that conservatives within the surf clubs caused unnecessary tensions as they strove to maintain their control of the beaches and that rank-and-file lifesavers were generally sympathetic to the boardriders.[11] A letter from the captain of the Palm Beach Surf Life Saving Club in the *Sydney Morning Herald* on 2 May 1975, supporting boardriders in arguing against the recommendations in the Report on leg rope safety, gives credence to this view. He wrote that 'The decision that [registration] fees should go to the clubs rather than the surfriders association discriminates against boardriders in general (they rescue as many as organised patrols do)'. Today the sting has gone out of the conflict as the decline in membership of clubs experienced during the 1960s and 1970s has stabilised (partly because women were accepted as lifesavers from 1980 onwards), and co-existence between lifesavers and boardriders in their use of the beach has prevailed.

In search of better waves and less crowded beaches, surfers travel all round the Australian coast: to Burleigh Heads and Kirra in Queensland; Byron Bay and Angourie on the New South Wales North Coast; Bell's Beach on the Victorian coast; Cactus Beach in South Australia, where surfers share the long waves rolling in from the Antarctic with the great white sharks, and camp in hollows among the dunes; the beaches of the Margaret River region and Kalbarri in Western Australia, where surfers wear crash helmets as protection against the rocks; and many others. Some have settled near favourite beaches well away from crowds, making a modest contribution to the reduction of population density in the major cities.

Ed Jaggard argues persuasively that the clubs had always contained members whose main enjoyment was perfecting their surfing skills and being in harmony with the sea—similar aims to those of the boardriders. And he is probably right when he concludes that 'the surfing mentalité [sic] did not suddenly appear on the beaches in the late 1950s and 1960s with the coming of the malibu board; it had been present among surf lifesavers since the movement's formation in 1907'.[12] But the emphasis on teamwork and training within the clubs ensures that there will always be a tension between the ethos of the two movements and that, in a more individualistic age, more of the young will be attracted to boardriding than lifesaving.

Surfriding and the world beyond

From the time the Hawaiian Duke Kahanamoku brought surfboard riding to Australia, the surfing movement has had an international focus. The Hawaiians always commanded special respect as the fathers and creators of the sport, and the waves rolling onto the beaches of the Hawaiian islands are still regarded as the biggest, most powerful and challenging. But from the 1950s California was the headquarters of the surfing cult, and its fashions, style and jargon were adopted by Australians.

The traffic was by no means one way, however. The designers and makers of boards in Australia were as innovative as the Californians, and there was an interchange of ideas and techniques across the Pacific. Australian-designed surfwear dominates the fashion scene internationally. An Australian, 'Midget' Farrelly, won an international surfing contest in 1962, and as the trend towards professional surfing contests gained momentum top Australian surfers travelled to Hawaii and California to compete. This interchange has continued, with the honours in world championships being shared between Australians, Hawaiians and Californians.

Surfers from other countries have also gained international status, and the search for the perfect, uncrowded wave has led surfers all over the globe. Australian surfers swelled the numbers of young Australians who were travelling overseas from the 1970s onwards in search of freedom and personal growth, not on the time-honoured trip to England or Europe but to more culturally diverse locations. These experiences helped to form a generation of Australians less insular and more global in their thinking.

Their pursuit of better waves also led to an increasing awareness among surfers of how many beaches had been spoilt or were endangered by human activities. An environmentalist ethic came to be characteristic of surfers, vague and passive in some but focused and activist in others. In their desire to protect the beaches and the oceans in general, surfers were developing attitudes towards preservation of the beaches that were also growing in strength among the general population as the century progressed.

The beaches and environmental activism

Pollution

Outrage over beach pollution was first expressed when a sewer outfall was built at Bondi in the 1880s, and has continually provoked condemnation and protest. In its introduction to a humorous poem entitled 'Compensation', the *Bulletin* of 17 December 1914 noted that 'For years past complaints have been made of the refuse which is cast up on Bondi Beach'. The poem concluded:

Those people with a taste for fruit who find the local price
More swollen than their pockets can afford
May get enough for nothing at Bondi to suffice
The most voracious crowd, or tribe, or horde.
And if they long for cabbages, or lettuces or peas
By paying twopence for a surf they also can have these.

So let us not condemn a spot where I may buy a swim,
And for the same expenditure acquire
A host of little articles that are of use to him
Whose luck may be described as poor or dire.
The Land of Promise flowed with oil, so Scripture writers tell;
So does the Sea of Bondi—and with other things as well.

'Other things' were likely to include raw sewage, grease balls, and other disgusting objects when the wind and tides were in the right (or wrong) direction.

Every coastal sewerage outfall elicited the strongest community protest, invariably met by the clinching argument of the exorbitant cost or the technical impracticability of alternative methods of sewage disposal. For Sydneysiders the discharging of untreated sewage near its finest beaches has long been a matter for shame. It became a catalyst for outrage when the *Sydney Morning Herald* reported in 1989 that fish caught near Sydney's sewerage outfalls contained more than 120 times the recommended safety limit of pesticides, and that these findings were being kept from the public by the 'deceit and collusion' of government authorities. It was argued that extending the outfalls further into deeper ocean, as the authorities proposed, would only move the toxic wastes and viruses a little further offshore, and would therefore not stop pollution of the beaches, even if the pollution were less visible.

Public protest intensified, resulting in the formation of People Opposed to Ocean Outfalls (POOO) and culminating in the 'Turn Back the Tide' concert on Bondi Beach. The extended outfalls were built, but measures to monitor pollution of the beaches and to facilitate public scrutiny of responsible authorities were introduced. Following a poll indicating that two-thirds of Sydneysiders would be prepared to pay more to prevent pollution of the beaches, an environmental levy was introduced to fund improvements.[13]

Today the beaches south of Sydney are sometimes polluted, but at the more popular beaches the water is usually clear and clean, to

visual inspection at least. The Beachwatch Program, which daily
reports on water quality between October and April, was set up in
1989 by the Environmental Protection Authority and reports that
sewage pollution on the beaches is greatly reduced compared to ten
years ago. At least one coastal town (Byron Bay) has adopted a policy
of restricting residential development rather than opting for an ocean
outfall. Others have been less successful. But new technologies and
techniques for the recycling and re-use of waste (biosolids) have
ameliorated the problem. Much effort is now expended by government
authorities on public relations and in keeping the public informed
about new schemes and developments. The outrage of 1989 has
receded from consciousness—at least until the next scandal comes
along.

The mining of sand minerals

In the late nineteenth century the black sands of beaches from southern
New South Wales to north Queensland were mined for small amounts
of gold, tin and platinum. There was little public awareness of this
commercial value until about 1950, but public opposition began to
increase as beaches on Queensland's Gold Coast, the islands of
Moreton Bay, and beaches around the Myall Lakes on the mid-north
coast of New South Wales were mined. A vocal campaign to 'save' the
dunes of the beaches on the Myall Lakes eventually led to a decision
by the New South Wales government in 1977 to allow no further
sand mining in national parks and reserves. In 1976 the Common-
wealth government under Malcolm Fraser announced withdrawal of
export licences for minerals mined on Fraser Island in Queensland,
effectively ending mining there.

Sand mining continues in Queensland, New South Wales and
Western Australia, but has a low profile. Although Australia is the
largest producer of minerals from sand, with exports (mostly from
Western Australia) earning $1100 million in 1999/2000, 45 per cent
of the known economic mineral sands resources of Australia's east
coast have been frozen because of environmental considerations. The
sand-mining companies point to the success of their efforts to restore
and to revegetate dunes disturbed by mining; conservationists argue
that there is a reduction in biodiversity in such 'restorations' and that
the dunes never return to their original state.[14]

Beach erosion

Severe storms in the 1960s and 1970s that washed away some houses on the New South Wales coast led to concerns that beaches were being irrevocably undermined and destroyed because of the encroachment of buildings onto the dunes. Realisation that knowledge of the dynamics of forces operating on the coast was scant has led to more intensive studies of dune and beach formation and the effects of weather patterns, winds and waves.

In ecological and political contexts the beach has been subsumed under the concept of 'the coast'; thus local councils wrestle with coastal management policies, dealing with would-be developers and conservationists who pursue their conflicting agendas. There is agitation against building too close to beaches and against factors seen as contributing to beach erosion. Boardriders are divided between those who fight to preserve the natural features of the beaches and those who are tempted to advocate the 'improvement' of beaches for surfing through the building of artificial reefs.

The beach today

IN AN ARTICLE ENTITLED 'Shifting Sands' in the *Sydney Morning Herald* of 6 December 1997 Deirdre Macken looks at the place of Sydney's beaches in the lives of the city's residents in the 1990s. She observes that Bondi has become a beach where the beautiful people go to be seen—'Bondi beach as decor'. Old weatherboard weekenders have been pushed aside to make way for beach homes for the rich. Pollution and violence are associated with the beach in a way that they never were before. While she concludes that 'The beach has always represented the Sydney way of life. It still does', she also notes that 'the estimated 200,000 pools in Sydney backyards . . . have wiped out the cultural collective that once comprised the beach culture'.

It is true that many homes around the nation have captured and tamed their own little piece of beach, the inground backyard pools that stand out like blue squares or ovals as one flies over the cities. The light-coloured paved area surrounding the pool now serves as the family's private beach. So many thousands thronged the popular beaches in the middle of the century that they almost hid the sand.

Today, except on a hot Sunday at Bondi, there is usually plenty of space.

But comparing today's beach with its past is like trying to compare the quality of love at the beginning of an affair with the deep affection of a long marriage. Children might be happy with the pool at home when they are small, but once they can travel independently they head towards the beach. In the old days people went to the beach for the whole day, soaking up the sun until sunburn set in, taking it all in greedily, almost frantically, like lovers who cannot get enough of the presence of the beloved. Today visits to the beach are often brief, a kind of 'touching base', woven in amongst other busy comings and goings. People trust the beach to be there whenever they need it for pleasure, excitement, exercise, company, solitude, contemplation, solace or peace. After an apparently disturbed Frenchman, Roni Levi, was shot by police on Bondi Beach, an observer reflecting on why Roni had been on the beach that morning was reported in the *Weekend Australian* of 7–8 March 1999 as saying 'in many respects it's . . . the Australian way—where do you go to when you're in trouble, depressed, burdened? You go to the beach'.

Despite many competing attractions, the beaches are still crowded on warm days. Those who now venture into the water at the beach are a diverse lot. Boardriders are prominent wherever the waves are favourable; but they are no longer exclusively members of the type of youth subculture that first blossomed in the 1960s and 70s. There are grey and balding heads among the figures standing and swaying on the boards: a love of riding the waves does not disappear simply because one gets older. Boards of different length and design for different kinds of waves, including 'boogie' boards and kneeboards, are now seen where once the short boards ruled. A wetsuited surfer may be either a man or a woman. There are fewer bodysurfers; the young generally prefer the excitement and power of riding the boards.

Windsurfers are a thrilling and colourful sight as they skip over the tops of the waves when a strong wind is blowing, but the expertise, strength and equipment needed mean that their numbers are relatively few. A few jetskis (PWCs, or personal watercraft) growl around the outskirts of the surf, their noise and smell provoking distaste in many beachgoers. They are prohibited from entering designated surf and swimming zones, and whether or not they will become sufficiently numerous to constitute a significant nuisance is yet to be seen. Most of those in the water on summer weekends are still the men, women and children without special skills but who simply love to play at the beach.

Paul Carter in *The Road to Botany Bay* analysed the beginnings of Australia's European spatial history in terms of appropriation and conquest, with the early explorers and squatters the agents of imperial power. The spatial history of the beach, by way of contrast, has been haphazard, unplanned, comparatively nonexploitative, and essentially democratic.

The transformation of the beach from an imported idea of the seaside to an Australianised space was accomplished by the time the first part of the twentieth century was over. There were three phases in this evolution. In the first, during the first forty or fifty years of settlement, the newcomers emulated the original inhabitants in a relaxed and informal enjoyment of bathing and swimming. In the second phase, which prevailed until the end of the nineteenth century, an imported idea of the seaside or pleasure resort held sway, with social mores, backed by legal prohibitions and policing, restricting bathing to prescribed areas. In the final phase, the spread of suburban development and public transport made ocean beaches increasingly accessible, resistance to unrestricted bathing was gradually worn down, prohibitions crumbled, and universal free access to the beaches was a fact of Australian life by the time the early part of the twentieth century was over. The rest of the twentieth century has seen a consolidation and confirmation of the beach's abiding contribution to Australian life, irrespective of passing fads and fashions.

PART 2

Representations of the Beach in the Twentieth Century

8

Early Representations and Emerging Themes

IN THE SECOND of his 1998 Boyer lectures David Malouf refers to 'the real work of culture', whereby direct experience is transformed by being represented imaginatively—through paintings, photographs, music, and especially the written word. When this 'real work' is done, a hitherto unexamined and unfamiliar landscape is drawn from the 'objective' world into the world of feeling. This transformation is essential if we are to feel grounded, at home in a particular place.[1]

As Australians moved onto the beaches and into the surf at the beginning of the twentieth century, the process of taking possession of the beach imaginatively, as well as in fact, began. Like the spatial history of the beach, the earliest representations of the 'new' beach could be characterised as haphazard: the end of the daylight bathing ban arrived with no great fanfare, no awareness of the significance the beach would accrue in the years to come. It came hard on the heels of the achievement of Federation and a buoyant mood was abroad, generated by justifiable pride in the peaceful way this union had been achieved, and optimism about the future.

Thus it was probably coincidental that instead of the melancholy tone of earlier poetry exemplified in Henry Halloran's verses on Bondi, 'poems' written about the beach now struck a different note: of playful, pleasurable, active human engagement with the beach. What had

previously been a site for meditation and reflection now evoked a
much merrier reaction:

> For the morning gleams with promise, and a gladness fills
> the land,
> As I mark where young Australia goes a-romping on the
> sand . . .
> And though every little footprint will be cleanly washed
> away,
> With a happy heart the ocean joins Australia at her play.[2]

The ideal that had prompted acceptance of surf-bathing—of the
glorious Australian race that would develop from these promising
beginnings—is reflected in verse:

> Souls big as is the sea's wild soul,
> Mysterious, undivined;
> And hearts untamed as Nature's,
> And minds free as the wind . . .
> A nation of sweet women,
> A race of noble men![3]

Roderic Quinn, who had anticipated the happier beach poetry to
come in a playful poem 'Spring-Song' in 1899, celebrated the surfer in
'The Surrender'—perhaps the first self-consciously 'literary' verse to
do so:

> Here, in the new day's golden splendour—
>   Headlands pushing their foreheads forward—
> Sweet is the surfer's sad surrender
>   To the will of the wave, as it rushes shoreward.
>
> Nought in his ears but the breaker's thunder,
>   Arrowing on through the surf he flies,
> Foam about him and clean sands under,
>   Over him arching the radiant skies.
>
> Yielding himself as a toy to the ocean,
>   Locked and mute in its fierce embraces,
> Thrilled and filled with the joy of motion,
>   Limbs outstretched, through the swirl he races.
>
> Here, in the gold day's new-born splendour,
>   Sea winds sighing in tree and cave,
> Sweet it is in a glad surrender
>   Thus to yield to the will of the wave.[4]

As well as expressing active enjoyment, poems and paintings created during this period often focused on the people on the beach, rather than the beach itself. Perhaps the most memorable pictures of the beach were the black-and-white photographs of Harold Cazneaux, a predecessor to another famous photographer of a slightly later period, Max Dupain. Some of these photographs concentrate on the effects of sun and moonlight on the wave-edge spreading over the beach or other effects of light on water, while others capture brilliantly the action of surfers in a wave, lifesavers in competition. Dupain's work was also remarkable for the clarity and evocativeness of his portraits of bathers and sunbakers, often capturing a moment of stillness in the midst of movement.

There seems to have been a kind of cultural lag in imaginative treatment of the opening up of the beach during the first third of the century. As far as novels and more substantial works of literature in that period are concerned, the beach is virtually invisible. There is one early novel of apparent relevance, *The Passage*, by Vance Palmer (1930).[5] The book is set almost entirely around Caloundra, which for many years has been a popular surfing beach. But the image of the beach in *The Passage* is unfavourable: it is the site of an ephemeral holiday resort that fails and eventually disappears. The central character, Lew, maintains a secure sense of place through his work as a fisherman and his closeness to nature in the tiny nearby fishing settlement. Lew and the other members of the fishing community are 'grounded', authentic, in a way that Lew's go-getting brother Hughie, the property developer Osborne, and the holidaymakers at the beach are not.

The holiday resort, with its beach, is meretricious and artificial. In contrasting the fishermen's affinity with nature with the developer's greed for profit, Palmer alludes to a fundamental and continuing opposition within Australian society. The major theme of the novel is the search for meaning and stability in a country with little sense of its own past or of roots, poised uncertainly on the edge of an unknown future. In many ways it has more in common with the literature of the bush than with the modern view of the beach.

Incongruous though it may seem, one of the first novels to deal with the Australian beach was written by an English visitor: D. H. Lawrence's Australian novel, *Kangaroo* (1923). Watching people on

the beach provoked Lawrence to the irritation and ambivalence that is
so characteristic of his response to the Australian people and landscape:

> To the right the sea was rolling on the shore, and spurting high on
> some brown rocks . . . And near at hand Somers saw another youth
> lying on the warm sandhill in the sun . . . he lay like an animal on
> his face in the sun . . .[6]
>
> Two men in bathing suits were running over the spit of sand to
> the surf, where two women in 'waders' were paddling along the
> fringe of the foam. Three boys, one a lad of 15 or so, came out . . .
> to roll in the sand and play. They were extraordinarily like real
> young animals, mindless as opossums, lunging about . . .
>
> Freedom! That's what they always say. 'You feel free in Aus-
> tralia.' And so you do. There is a great relief in the atmosphere, a
> relief from tension, from pressure. An absence of control or will
> or form . . . Not the old closing-in of Europe.
>
> But what then? The vacancy of this freedom is almost terrifying
> . . . The absence of any inner meaning: and at the same time the
> great sense of vacant spaces. The sense of irresponsible freedom
> . . . And all utterly uninteresting . . . nothing. No inner life, no
> high command, no interest in anything finally.[7]

The references to 'animal . . . animals' are indicative of the aversion to the physical that underlay Lawrence's fascination with sexuality, one reason for his ambivalence about Australia. He felt that the
country encouraged sensuality at the expense of the intellectual side
of life ('mindless as opossums'; 'no inner life at all'). And in sensing
an 'absence of inner meaning' Lawrence detected a truth about the
rawness of Australian society: that the accumulation of shared meanings resulting from the acculturation of a people to each other and to
the land they inhabit was at a very early stage here.

Lawrence writes as an outsider, his physical awkwardness in the
surf an analogue of the emotional and psychological dislocation he is
experiencing:

> He ran quickly over the sands, where the wind blew cold but
> velvety, and the raindrops fell loosely. He walked straight into the
> forewash, and fell into an advancing ripple. At least it looked a
> ripple, but was enough to roll him over so that he went under and
> got a little taste of the Pacific. Ah the fresh cold wetness—the
> fresh cold wetness! The water rushed in the backwash and the
> sand melted under him, leaving him stranded like a fish. He turned
> again to the water. The walls of surf were some distance off, but

near enough to look rather awful as they raced in high white walls shattering towards him.

Of course he did not go near the surf. No, the last green ripples of the broken swell were enough to catch him by the scruff of the neck and tumble him rudely up the beach, in a pell-mell.[8]

It is interesting to contrast Lawrence's descriptions of the beach with those in the earliest Australian novel to have the beach as its principal setting. *Intimate Strangers* (1937) by Katharine Susannah Prichard, opens on a Western Australian beach (given a fictitious name, but clearly one of the popular beaches just south of Perth) and does not stray from it for the first half of the novel. It contains some of the most detailed and loving descriptions of sea, sand, swimming and surf to be found in any novel before or since:

Such a sight it was on hot summer mornings, this tapestry of the human swarm on the beaches, under a bare blue sky. When the smoke of bush fires sent a haze out from the land, the sea, satiny calm, lifted long rollers, translucent green, against the sand. If a breeze sprang up, the azure and sapphire deepened, cut like a mighty jewel by waves that glittered on every face and flung a rising surf towards the shore.

Here and there groups of boys practised running dives, 'chesters', swallow diving, duck shooting. Girls held themselves taut and alert, ran and dived into a green wave as it reared. Men, women, boys and girls, splashed and swam, laughing and exclaiming with each other, to the third line of breakers, farther than which only strong swimmers cared to go. Children played in the last shallow wash along the shore, bowled over and tossed high on the sand by a heavy wave, now and then. Screaming with joy and quite fearless, they pranced back into the water again or lay, flat-stomached, waiting for another roller to send them flying.

When the breeze stiffened, in the late afternoon, every wave on the far-out sea carried a white feather and rollers along the sandbank became breakers, raising gigantic jaws, clear as glass and ripping foam. But the ardour of the sunworshippers never languished or waned . . . All day, the edge of the sea braided an eager, feckless crowd of men, women, girls and boys, diving into the combers, riding in on them: and the sand its spawn of brown and red bodies, stalwart and slender, lean and potbellied, spread in the blazing sun to dry.[9]

The behaviour and the 'tapestry' of the crowds on the beach, the way the beach changes from morning to afternoon: the vivid and authentic detail and colour in this passage is inspired by the direct experience of a writer who cherishes the scene she describes. As Elodie in *Intimate Strangers* passes among the people on the beach 'she smiled at them with shy secret rejoicing that they *too* were stealing ecstasy from the monotony of their workaday lives':[10] she is one of them. She is able to understand the feelings of the people on the beach in a way that had not been possible for Lawrence, a stranger.

Dymphna Cusack's novel *Jungfrau* (1936) broke new ground in its depiction of a trio of modern young women living and working in inner Sydney. The beach is introduced at several points, seemingly more as an aspect of the lifestyle of these independent women than for reasons of plot or character. Marc, as befits a modern girl, is an accomplished 'surf-shooter': 'For a moment she hung poised on the curling crest, taut, exhilarated; then with a sudden powerful sweep the wave broke and she went riding swiftly shorewards in a flurry of hissing foam'.[11] On another occasion Thea and Eve go to Maroubra to 'shoot the breakers': enjoying the beach is part of the way of life of a 'city girl' of the 1930s.

Both *Intimate Strangers* and *Jungfrau* tell of the drama of illicit love affairs and their unhappy endings, while in *Kangaroo* Somers feels a heightening of desire after his dip (tumble) in the surf. In this respect, and in many novels written subsequently, they follow a well-established Romantic tradition where the beach is associated with eroticism, the arousal of desire and the blossoming of love.

English and European writers in the Romantic tradition realised that the sea symbolises the dark regions of the unconscious: Shelley's work, for example, reveals a clear 'sense of the correspondence between marine depths and psychological depths'.[12] The ebb and flow of the tides mirrors the fluctuations of the menstrual cycle and other bodily rhythms, the correspondence between bodily sensibility and the rhythm of the sea. Robert Drewe, in the Introduction to his *Picador Book of the Beach*, refers to Shelley and Byron's love of the sea and swimming, to 'the erotically minded Flaubert, who longed to be littorally transformed, with the sea's "thousand liquid nipples" travelling all over his body', and Valery, for whom 'swimming was simply, a *fornication avec l'onde*'.[13]

While the beach was an erotic site for writers in the Romantic tradition, it was not yet a setting for the free display of sensual delight;

for nineteenth-century codes of decency and taboos surrounding nudity precluded the explicit sexualisation of the beach at this time. As the twentieth century went on, the treatment of love was to became more heavily sexualised, its connotations of passion and desire more explicit.

As might have been expected after so many years during which bodies were concealed beneath layers of clothing, verses written early in the twentieth century express a kind of voyeurism, the gaze being blatantly directed at the forms now revealed on the beach, especially the female. This interest—and appreciation—intensified as bathing beauty competitions became popular and models posed in swimming costumes for fashion parades and for photographers. The sensuality of the beach is captured in the soft shapes and colours of the figures in William Dobell's and Arthur Murch's beach paintings; and Brett Whiteley both satirised and exploited its erotic potential in the exaggerated curves of bodies on the beach in his paintings and line drawings. Many other painters and photographers have taken advantage of the opportunities to observe the human form the beach so plentifully provides.

But the beach is also often linked with death and loss as well as sensuality and desire. It can be a place for the melodramatic suicide, as has been noted in the case of Adam Lindsay Gordon. C. Y. O'Connor, builder of the water pipeline from Perth to the goldfields at Kalgoorlie who appears in Robert Drewe's *The Drowner* (1996), also rode a horse into the surf and shot himself, just before his project proved successful. Henry Lawson confided to a doctor that he had attempted suicide at Fairy Bower in 1902 by jumping from the path by the sea that goes from Manly to North Head.[14] It is said that newspapers stopped reporting suicides off The Gap, the cliff above the sea near the entrance to Sydney Harbour, so as not to encourage others to imitate them. And an Australian Prime Minister, Harold Holt, famously disappeared, presumed drowned, while snorkelling off a beach near Portsea in Victoria in 1967.

The more one examines Australian writing on the beach, the clearer it becomes that ideas of life, love and desire are inextricably interwoven with those of loss and death: that life is fragile and precious; that loss and death are inescapable consequences and accompaniments of life; and that life is lived most fully where the inevitability of death is recognised and accepted. These are themes that emerge early, and remain a constant feature of Australian beach writing.

Life and death, love and loss, are linked with the beach in novels as diverse as Christina Stead's *For Love Alone* (1944), Martin Boyd's *Lucinda Brayford* (1946), George Johnston's *Clean Straw for Nothing* (1969), Christopher Koch's *The Doubleman* (1985), Beverley Farmer's *The Seal Woman* (1992), and Fiona Capp's *Night Surfing* (1996); in Tim Winton's and Robert Drewe's short stories; and in beach poetry by Bruce Beaver and Andrew Taylor.

These connections are manifest in a particularly concentrated fashion in an episode in Patrick White's *Voss* (1957). Early in the novel, set in the mid-nineteenth century, Voss turns up unexpectedly as Laura and her household prepare to leave on a beach picnic, and is invited to join them. The party quickly divides into two groups: one, consisting of Laura, Bella, Willie Pringle and Voss, goes down to the beach; the other, the men of substance and property who are financing the expedition, sit away from the sand on the rocks talking about

> the English packet. And the weather. And vegetables. And sheep . . . Their seams and their muscles cracked . . . One young man . . . 'the owner of a property that many consider the most valuable in New South Wales' . . . had begun to tell of the prevalence of worms in his merino flock at Camden.

There is a cluster of associations here: worms (corruption and death), wealth, rejection of 'the life of the body'. The 'men talking upon the rocks' form a static group contrasting with the activity of the others on the beach. The separation between those on the (living) beach and the (dead) rocks reflects the differences in their values and their preoccupations. Those on the beach respond to the life of the moment:

> In the rapt afternoon all things were all-important, the inquiring mouths of blunt anemones, the twisted roots of driftwood return-ing and departing in the shallows, mauve scum of little bubbles the sand was sucking down . . .

with the behaviour of the girls becoming increasingly uninhibited:

> Bella had taken her bonnet off. Her hair fell gold. Her skin, too, was golden beneath the surface of which the blood was clearly rioting and as she breathed, it did seem almost as though she was

no longer the victim of her clothes. Ah, Bella is released, Laura Trevelyan saw and was herself closer to taking wing . . . The hem of her skirt had become quite irregular, she saw, with black scallops of heavy water.

Bella is 'no longer the victim of her clothes . . . released' and even Laura, who is normally imaginative and spiritual in nature rather than sensuous, is 'closer to taking wing'. These small signs are indices of a land that is changing those who engage with it. Meanwhile, Laura and Voss, walking along the beach together, 'listened to each other's presence, and became aware that they were possibly more alike than any other two people at the Pringle's picnic'[15]—a recognition of affinity foreshadowing their spiritual union.

Enjoyment of love and life, along with acceptance of death and its inevitability, are expressed with extraordinary and heartwrenching simplicity in Michael Gow's play *Away*. The beach is the setting for Harry's acknowledgement that his teenage son Tom is suffering from a terminal illness and will soon die. He reflects that

> In a funny kind of way we're happy. Even while we're very, very sad. We don't look back and we don't look forward . . . We have this boy and we don't have him for long. And whatever he does, that will have to be enough.[16]

If references to the beach in nineteenth-century writing (what might be termed the first-stage beach) were generally melancholy and gloomy in tone, in the twentieth century (the second stage) they are more often celebratory, vivid, bright and colourful. The popularity of Ken Done's paintings, with their sparkling patterns and vivid colours, attests to the positive way in which the beach here has been emotionally interpreted, both by Australians and by tourists who buy them as mementoes of the country.

The first-stage beach was a lonely place from which a solitary observer viewed the sea, often prompting religious and moral reflection. The second-stage beach is *occupied*: the subject of paintings and photographs in Geoffrey Dutton's *Sun, Sea, Surf and Sand* is generally people on the beach, rather than scenery or landscape. Many are more active than contemplative; their comings and goings at the beach are interwoven with their stories, with the events of their lives. Religion, at least of the pious and conventional sort, is usually far from the minds of the people on the beaches of the second stage.

Yet there is an apparent paradox here. Despite their great differ-ence in tone, the major themes from the first stage—of love, loss and death—persist and appear with striking frequency in the second. What is surprising—because of the pervasive impression of pleasure and delight as the modern beach's principal features—is the frequency of allusions to loss and death. The old dread of the beach as the place where wrecks and the victims of the sea's destructive powers are cast up; symbol of the yawning gulf between the homeland or the lover of cherished memory; the lonely strand where thoughts of storms and of vanished loves cast a gloomy pall: these connotations have largely vanished. How is it, then, that death and loss are such recurring themes?

The beach is now a place where writers depict their characters as primarily enjoying themselves but also talking about death and loss, or feeling with heightened intensity the impact of such events as they have played themselves out in their lives. And the paradox—that life and pleasure, death and loss, are 'celebrated' together in modern beach writing—is resolved in its hint of the reconciliation that Dorothy Dinnerstein calls for, of enjoyment of love and life with acceptance of death and its inevitability—an enjoyment and an acceptance summed up in Harry's words in *Away*.

This intertwining of death and life is even found in children's literature, where the special place of the beach in the lives of children has found expression in twentieth-century writing.

9

Childhood and the Beach

> Digging in it, lying in it, cheek against it, the length of one's
> shivering body warmed by it. What is it about an ocean beach
> that so marvellously pacifies a child's discontents? *Kids don't need*
> *to be told what to do on a beach. They know it already.*[1]

IF THE BEACH FOR ADULTS ideally recaptures the joy of childhood,
then the beach is a natural place for children to be. Here is the perfect
place for play; and play is the child's important business.[2] Habits
and patterns of playing at the beach lay down memories and attitudes
that colour adult experience; and in their openness to sensory stimulation and capacity to enjoy the moment, children exhibit in its purest
form that 'erotic intercourse with the surround' of which Dorothy
Dinnerstein writes.

One would expect the significance of the beach in the lives of
children to be primarily reflected in two kinds of writing: autobiographical accounts of childhood, and children's literature. The
reminiscences of adults show how vividly childhood beachgoing is
remembered. Robert Dessaix remembers:

> And there were all those childhood summers—what Australian
> child doesn't remember them?—salty, sandy summers that felt six
> months long because of all the emotional upheaval, growing up
> and expeditions out into the world they brought with them . . .[3]

Tim Winton, contrasting his two childhoods—one suburban and normal, the other apparently all summer and wholly at the beach—reflects:

> I often wonder about these two childhoods of mine, the one contained and clothed, between fences, the other rambling, wind-blown, half-naked between the flags. Is it just nostalgia? Have I idealised these summers and chased their myth all my adult life? ... No ... It's just that I lived the coastal life harder, with more passion.[4]

Richard Coe writes that 'proportionately to their numbers, Australian writers write more, and more frequently, and as likely as not better, about themselves-as-children than do those of almost any other cultural group outside France and England'.[5] The pleasure of summer holidays at the beach is vividly recalled in Donald Horne's *The Education of Young Donald* (1967); in *The Road to Gundagai* (1965) Graham McInnes remembered fondly his enjoyment of the beaches near his Melbourne home in the 1920s; and for Randolph Stow as the small child in *The Merry-Go-Round in the Sea* (1965), the times he spent swimming at the beach with his father were precious.

But the beach does not loom as large in Australian autobiographical writing as might be expected. In accounts of deprived childhoods spent in cruel or dysfunctional families, reasons for its absence are obvious: the child, Albert Facey, in *A Fortunate Life* (1981), was too busy working on farms and being beaten to have the time or opportunity to play on the beach. A more subtle reason in other cases might be the influence of what Coe discerns as a prevalent theme in 'Australian Childhoods' (his collective name for accounts of childhood that are primarily autobiographical): of a love–hate relationship with the surrounding culture.

For many of our writers, passionate love of the bush co-existed with a repulsion from, even contempt for, Australian suburban society. And since the Australian beach was first of all a suburban beach, it was besmirched by its suburban associations. Germaine Greer exemplifies this attitude when she castigates her mother as 'a woman who has lain on beaches all her life'.[6]

By way of contrast the artist Clarice Beckett, who trudged the streets of suburban Melbourne to the bay beaches in the years between the two world wars with her cart of paints and canvases, created works that celebrate the beauty in the commonplace, the extraordinary in the ordinary. In her paintings bathers seem to float in a dreamlike world, their costumes blobs of luminous colour. But Beckett was pilloried, dismissed and forgotten until recent exhibitions of her work brought her widespread public and critical acclaim.

Beckett ended her days in the family home in Melbourne. It is notable how many autobiographical writers, especially those of an earlier generation—Miles Franklin, Henry Handel Richardson, Randolph Stow, Graham McInnes, Maie Casey, Martin Boyd, George Johnston, Hal Porter, and Greer herself—either left Australia or spent long periods overseas. It seems that Australian autobiographies tell us more about Australian writers' problematic relationship to their culture than about meanings of the beach being generated by that culture.

Books written for children

DURING THE PAST DECADE or so, delightful picture books have been published that capture the joy and wonder of a day at the beach for young children.[7] They show in vivid detail the great variety of activities, people and things that are typically found on a popular Australian beach, authenticating the child's own experience—a valuable function in a culture when so many books have historically presented an imported reality. The importance of this 'authentication' struck me the first time I rode on a London train. It went *clickety-clack!* For years I had heard Australian kindergarten teachers reading stories about trains that went *clickety-clack*; but our trains made a different kind of sound because they run over rails joined by a different method. So these stories either taught children to disregard the evidence of their own senses or that the child's own experience was not worth writing stories about.

These beach stories arrived surprisingly late on the Australian literary scene, however. Up until the 1950s parents who wanted to read to their children had to rely largely on imported books. Older children who could read were not much better off. Imitating imported adventure stories, Jean Curlewis wrote two books in the 1920s, *Drowning Maze* (1922), which was of the ripping-yarns-for-boys style, with some of the action taking place on the waterways around Sydney, and *Beach Beyond* (1923), another adventure story containing a colourful description of a surf carnival. Stories that took the bush as their setting predominated in the 1950s and 1960s as more books began to be published here or were co-published here and overseas. Books like Roger Carr's *Surfie* (1966), J. M. Couper's *Looking for a Wave* (1973) and Gabrielle Carey and Kathy Lette's *Puberty Blues* (1979) later capitalised on the fashionable surfie culture.

In the 1970s the first of a number of modern fantasies set on the beach was published: Lilith Norman's *A Dream of Seas* (1978). It was followed by Gillian Rubinstein's *Beyond the Labyrinth* (1988), Nicole Pluss's 'The Lifesaver' in *Kindred: The Lifesaver and Other Stories* (1995) and Jackie French's *The Secret Beach* (1995).

It is notable that all the child protagonists in these stories are outsiders or from separated families; it is as if the fissure in their lives creates a space for fantasy. These outsider children engage with creatures of fantasy: the boy becomes a seal in *A Dream of Seas*; Brenton in *Beyond the Labyrinth* finds an alien in a cave on the beach; Jemmy is rescued by the ghost of a drowned girl transformed into a shark in 'The Lifesaver'; and Emily wants to go away with merpeople in *The Secret Beach*. The special and/or ambiguous status of marine animals has also become a feature of recent books with a strong environmental message—Victor Kelleher's *Where the Whales Sing* (1994), Tim Winton's *Blueback* (1997)—which deal with the coast rather than the beach, and portray creatures such as dolphins, whales and a giant blue groper in intimate and lifesaving encounters with humans.

For children as for adults, the beach is a place where they learn to come to terms with death. *A Dream of Seas* is about a boy dealing with the death of his father. In Gary Crew and Gregory Rogers's *Lucy's Bay* (1992) Sam comes to terms with his grief and guilt over his sister's drowning. When he finally visits Lucy's Bay, a place of horrific memories, he is able to move past his and Lucy's tragedy and go on with his life. And in David Rish's *Sophie's Island* (1990) Sophie comes to terms with her grief over her baby brother's stillbirth. When Jacob's Island becomes for her a symbol of loss, she makes a bracelet for her mother of stones collected on the island (as in the story Jacob made a bracelet as a token of his love) and puts the red jumper she knitted for the baby in a basket, pushing it out into the sea to float towards the island.

There is also an element of hostility to the beach in some works written for children. The critic Heather Scutter sums up the reason for this negativity: 'In the neo-Puritan mindscape, to continue to live by the sea is to indulge in hedonism and escapism, to dwell in neverland, to refuse to grow up'.[8] Thus in Colin Thiele's *Storm Boy* (1966) Storm Boy lives wild and free with his hermit-like father, his school the marvellous natural world of the Coorong and Ninety-Mile Beach, his tutor the old Aboriginal, Fingerbone Bill. Although the captain and crew of the tugboat rescued by the Boy and Mr Percival, the pelican, offer to pay to send him to boarding-school, the Boy refuses to leave until Mr Percival dies. Mr Percival's burial is both a ceremony of mourning for the death of the bird and a mark of the end of Storm Boy's childhood. He leaves for school in the city, taking on the responsibilities of maturity and civilisation.

The message that one must leave childish pleasures behind is implicitly conveyed in beach paintings of the late nineteenth century. These show children paddling in the water and playing on the sand, while adults are always out of the water—strolling on the sand or on pathways beside it. Children must come out of the water, leave play behind if they are to ripen, to graduate to the mature adult world.

In Eleanor Spence's *The October Child* (1976) the Mariner family live in a small coastal village, Chapel Rocks, which is the epitome of small-town dreariness: nothing much happens, nothing is accomplished. The novel depicts enjoyment of the beach only once, and it also happens to be the only time Kenneth and the middle brother, Douglas, are shown as being comfortable and at ease with each other. But suddenly a shark appears, and the moment is cut short: indulgence in aimless enjoyment is dangerous, to be rejected—'I'm not going swimming in the dark any more'.

The family moves to the city to seek education and treatment for Douglas's autistic brother, Carl. Douglas is able to go to music school, and Adrienne enjoys her new school and its multicultural population. Only Kenneth, the selfish and unregenerate surfer, resists the attractions of the city and joins a hippie-like sect with vague plans of starting a commune up the coast, leaving the family to cope with Carl. Trying to make some sense of the tragedy of Carl, Douglas reflects that 'if it

'When I was a man, I put away childish things . . .' Only the child in the painting stands in the water, looking toward the adults, fully clothed, on the sand. Two worlds are contrasted: that of childhood (the water, the fringing waves) and maturity—which lies landwards, away from the beach.

Charles Conder (United Kingdom, 1868–1909), *Sandringham*, 1890. Oil on wood panel, 12.0 × 21.5 cm

Source: National Gallery of Australia, Canberra

hadn't been for him, we'd never have left Chapel Rocks. And I wouldn't have gone to the Music College and met all my friends'.[9]

Perhaps the most striking evidence of current negative attitudes to the beach in writing for children lies in critical and/or academic responses to the Lockie Leonard series of books by Tim Winton. In the first book, *Lockie Leonard, Human Torpedo* (1990), when he is riding his surfboard Lockie often experiences the joy that Dinnerstein so sensitively described; but when Lockie tries to put this feeling into words it is, naturally enough, in the crass language of a thirteen-year-old boy. Heather Scutter finds this 'all rather grandiose', dismissing it as 'a boy's idyll which doesn't truly place the sacred within the frame of the mundane'.[10]

More criticism is directed towards thirteen-year-old Lockie's resistance to growing up too soon in his steady rebuffing of Vicki Streeton's sexual advances.[11] Winton himself admits to a strong autobiographical element in the Lockie Leonard books, and is cheerfully unrepentant about Lockie's values, noting that he 'spent most of my teenage years trying not to grow up too fast . . . it's a grossly moralistic book, it's painfully moralistic'.[12] His readers seem not to mind: the Lockie Leonard books are very popular. But a moralising children's writer is apparently to be condemned—except, perhaps, where issues of racism, sexism and the environment are concerned.

Winton seems to believe that where a child is not too anxious to 'grow up too fast', more can be learnt along the way. In his fable *Blueback* (1997), the young boy, Abel Jackson (his name taken from *Abel Tasman* and *Port Jackson*, Abel represents post-European contact Australians), grows up on a beach isolated from civilisation, as Storm Boy did. Unlike Storm Boy, however—who had to leave to obtain a 'real' education at school—Abel builds on what he learnt from the natural world when he goes to university. He combines his theoretical and practical knowledge to become an international expert on marine ecological and environmental problems. Winton's message is that both kinds of wisdom are valuable, that each nourishes the other; to pose them as mutually exclusive is to create a false dichotomy.

Geoffrey Dutton wrote in *Sun, Sea, Surf and Sand* that the beach has 'until very recently had a bad literary image in Australia'.[13] His judgement seems to be more relevant to writing for children than to any other form of literature. In the *Oxford Companion to Australian Children's Literature* the entry under 'The Beach' takes up about a quarter of a column, and the authors comment that 'the surf and surfing culture is noticeably absent from contemporary settings, and reflects the cautious approach of writers for adolescents'.[14] One would like to press the authors further on this point: cautious of what? and why?

10

The Prominence of Nature: Diverse Connections

The foregrounding of nature, including the beach

WRITING ABOUT THE BEACH manifests a 'foregrounding' of nature that is characteristic of much Australian art and literature. At the end of the twentieth century landscape painting remained the most popular and dominant genre in Australian art. Richard Coe notes the ubiquity of the landscape in Australian autobiographical writing: 'Of the "magical" quality of the Australian landscape, the evidence is overwhelming: not one single Childhood escapes from its influence'.[1]

George Johnston argues that 'nothing human has yet happened in Australia which stands out above the continent itself';[2] and Les Murray takes this idea a step further:

> It is even possible that the novel as a form we have adopted from elsewhere, may not be the best or only form which extended prose fiction here requires. Its heavy emphasis on the human, on character and the development of character, may tend to lead us into repeated misrepresentation of our world. Man and his classes and disputes may not be *important* enough, here, to sustain such a form. So many of our novels are portentous in essence, piling up sensibility and brilliance on themes which cannot quite bear them, trying to exclude space in order to attain intensity ... there is something anti-ecological about the novel: in its assigning of all

agency to humans, it may be seen as a product of the over-humanised landscapes of the old world.[3]

While these ideas are thought-provoking, human beings, their behaviour and their relationships remain the primary concern of most successful Australian novels. They often show awareness of the power of the landscape, however, as in Tegan Bennett's 'Bombora' (1996):

> this country does not forget itself, despite the deadening layers of tar, the hiding buildings, the heavy howl of traffic. It can make itself heard, and you will always remember that it is there. You can spend all day in the liquid cold air of an office and then step out into a heat so strong it will carry you home without your feet even touching the ground. You can hear the cicadas in the city, and see the twin gleam of a possum's eyes in the parks at night. And you can lie in the surf, you can be rolled and licked and loved by the water, the same water that has been cooling the sides of this hot island forever.[4]

The assertiveness of nature in Australia became evident to a worldwide audience during the Olympic Games period in Sydney in September–October 2000. There were bushfires on the fringes of Sydney; tragically, two shark attack fatalities on consecutive days in South Australia; and, comically, the invasion by bogong moths of Olympic venues. Myriads of moths arrived, diverted from their annual migration southwards to the high country of southern New South Wales and north-eastern Victoria by the bright lights of the Stadium. For a few nights they were everywhere: among athletes and spectators, around the runners on the track, filling the air like miniature illuminated flying saucers. One large moth even stole the limelight by literally taking centre stage during the closing ceremony, perching on the gown of a singing diva just below her bosom, the cameras obviously trying to avoid including views of the unwanted lodger as they filmed her performance. It was as if the spirits of Australia's Aboriginal Ancestors, incarnated in the moths, were sending a message: don't think you can have the biggest corroboree *ever* without inviting us to join in!

The writings of Robert Drewe and Tim Winton

MOTHS FIGURE IN ONE of Robert Drewe's short stories, 'Radiant Heat' (1989), where there is a skilful interweaving of the edginess of modern

family life with the unpredictability of the natural world. The beach
weekender where the narrator is spending an 'access' week with his
children and his new wife is threatened by bushfires; bogong moths
shower red pollen from bottlebrushes on his son's head, and

> The bloodwoods and peppermints and angophoras were peeling
> and shedding fast in the wind, dropping sheets of bark, changing
> their colour and shape . . . On rare days things come together:
> heat, a moth plague, fires, crowds of people.

They drive to the beach to escape the bushfire:

> Everyone seemed to have the same idea. Dead moths littered
> the high-tide line, moths and bluebottles that had been washed
> ashore . . .
>   'What's that red stuff in Peter's hair?' Jenna said.
>   'Pollen', I said. 'From the moths.'
>   'It'll wash off in the sea', Lucy said.[5]

Drewe has probably been more responsible for stimulating recent
interest in the meaning of the beach than any other writer with the
publication of *The Bodysurfers* (1983) and subsequent comments, his
suggestion that 'many, if not most, Australians have their first sexual
experience on the coast' being perhaps the best publicised. He empha-
sises the 'intuitive and sensual appreciation of the coast felt by the
world's great beachgoers, the Australians';[6] and there is a sense in
which sexuality pervades many of the stories in *The Bodysurfers*,
notably the title story, 'Body Oil', but also in 'View from the Sandhills',
'80% Humidity' and 'The Silver Medallist'.[7]

But Drewe is not limited by this association, as 'Radiant Heat'
shows. It is a characteristic of many of his beach stories that the
natural world, including the beach, is accorded a prominence that
advances it from background to or reflection of human experience to
a role almost of agent, protagonist, or counterpoint to the shifting,
unstable lives of his characters.

The Western Australian Tim Winton is linked in the public mind
with Robert Drewe as a writer whose work is closely associated with
the beach, especially since the publication of *Land's Edge* in 1995 and
following interviews where he makes clear the importance of the
Western Australian coast in his life and in his art. Yet too literal a
focus on the beach obscures what is a more fundamental characteristic

of Winton's writing: the way it constantly crosses and recrosses boundaries—between land and sea, city and bush, shallows and depths, the past and the present, life and death, the natural and the supernatural.

Boundaries

Winton asserts that 'I think if we accept boundaries then we're suckers—boundaries other people set for us'[8] and 'I feel this is true realism: the supernatural and the natural accepted as one thing, as inclusive'.[9] This awareness of boundaries and the implications of crossing or disregarding them are keys to interpretation of Winton's often difficult fiction.

Boundaries between the present and the past are fluid and shifting in Winton's fiction. Many of his characters carry a burden from the past that complicates and distorts their present lives. And Winton recognises no barriers between the material and spiritual world: 'this is the kind of world where pigs speak in tongues and angels come and go. And I'm not speaking metaphor here. The world is a weird place'.[10]

In a scene in *Cloudstreet* (1993) where Quick and Fish Lamb drift in a rowing boat beneath the stars, time and space are transcended: there is an 'erasure of distinction between sky and earth, night, space and water: "Heaven" is not divided from earth'.[11]

Boundaries are associated with the divide between realms of different emotional or spiritual significance, as in *An Open Swimmer* (1982) and *Shallows* (1984); they are ambivalences to be resolved, as in 'Gravity' in *Minimum of Two* (1987); and categories to be ignored or limitations to be transcended, as in *Cloudstreet* and *That Eye, the Sky* (1986).

Verges and edges

One reviewer has written that 'Tim Winton's fictional world is one of edges and marginality',[12] and this is particularly true of his short stories in *Minimum of Two* (1987) and *Scission* (1985). Winton himself observes that 'it's pleasurable and quite useful to tell a story that's on the verge of something, whether it be on the land or sea . . . it kind of feels full of tension for me'.[13]

Amid the 'edginess' of so many of Winton's characters, there is one place and one activity where direction, resolve and purpose are found: in swimming in the sea. This is particularly the case for his women characters, for whom swimming represents competence, strength, and a shedding of the burdens of the past.

The question why it is almost always women who are associated with swimming in this way is an interesting one. It could simply be, as a cynic of my acquaintance asserts, that women are more at home in the water because the distribution of fat in their bodies makes it easier for them to withstand the cold—as is implied in a verse in an article in the *Daily Telegraph* of 1 October 1906, headed 'Winter Waters at Manly':

> Oh woman! In our hours of ease,
> Uncertain, coy and hard to please;
> When icy winds and chill waves tease,
> Thy form is first to brave the seas.

But one senses a deeper reason than this! Research on dreams has indicated that women dream about swimming more than men do, suggesting that it carries more emotional significance for them.[14] Sometimes it seems that to swim is to find 'a room of one's own', a way of escaping an unhappy home or a difficult relationship. Then again, according to feminist theorists Nancy Chodorow (*The Reproduction of Mothering*, 1978) and Carol Gilligan (*In a Different Voice*, 1982) an important psychological difference between men and women is that autonomy is a key issue for men, that of relationship for women; so it could be argued that men are less at ease with immersion, unconsciously perceiving it as threatening the loss of their autonomy and separateness, whereas women experience while swimming a comfortable balance between awareness of the separate body and the surrounding medium, between being-at-one-with-the-environment and agency.

Whatever the reasons for this association, it is Winton's disregard for boundaries and his 'edginess' that make him the quintessential example of a writer who has been profoundly influenced by the beach experience.

Connections between the coast and the inland

THERE IS AN AMUSING SYNTHESIS of two iconic landscapes in a picture postcard reprinted in a Blue Mountains tourist newspaper under the heading 'Mist-erious Doings at Katoomba'. A beach scene is super-imposed on the mist that so often fills the vastness of the Jamieson Valley. Three beach girls in two-piece swimsuits perch atop the Three Sisters. A sunbaking girl 'floats' on the mist, while the heads and shoulders of two other 'beach girls' poke out from under it. The attractions of the mountains are presumably enhanced by their association with an even more popular tourist destination.

But it is usually the desert that comes to mind when connections between coast and inland are considered. When Charles Sturt pursued his dream of an inland sea during his desert explorations, he was a few million years too late. Reminders of the ancient seabed that once lay over the interior are constantly encountered by the traveller. Waves whipped up by the westerly winds crash onto the eastern shore of the Menindee Lakes or Lake Eyre in a wet season. The pure sand forming the dunes of the 'Walls of China' in Mungo National Park is the same as that found on coastal beaches, and once formed the shore of a vast lake. The razor-sharp ramparts of the Napier Range were once a coral reef growing towards the sunlight in a prehistoric sea. The inland view extends to a low flat horizon and light floods the infinite vault of the sky, as when one stands on the beach looking out to sea. The title of an early novel by Catherine Martin, *The Silent Sea* (1892) refers to the saltbush plains between the sea and the desert country in South Australia.

Robert Drewe wrote that 'When Australians run away, they always run to the coast';[15] but in Thomas Keneally's *Woman of the Inner Sea* (1992) Kate leaves the beach, 'her garden and her age of innocence',[16] and travels to the 'inner sea', inland, to shrive herself of the guilt of blame for the death of her two children. Her sins are washed away in the flood that inundates the floodprone western town where 'the earth had once been a seabed'.[17] Keneally wrote that 'Australia is periphery. It dreams of and yet abandons the core'.[18] Yet Keneally himself in this novel moves between core and periphery, exploiting their similarities and their connections.[19]

Beach poetry

NATURE ALSO OCCUPIES a central place in the work of many Australian poets; but the bush, rather than the beach, has been the primary source

of imagery from nature during most of our history. However, some
contemporary poets of considerable reputation mine a rich lode of
meaning from their experiences of the beach. One who readily comes
to mind is John Blight, whose more than fifty-year output of poetry is
noted for its originality and its frequent use of beach imagery,
particularly in the anthologies *A Beachcomber's Diary* (1963), *My
Beachcombing Days* (1968), and *Holiday Sea Sonnets* (1985). 'The
Mindless Ocean' provides a clue to its function in his poetry:

> the vast
> mindlessness of ocean confronts us with
> unknown destinations . . .[20]

For Blight, the sea, including the beach, serves as a source of
poetic inspiration. It has no meaning (is 'mindless') in itself, but is
richly available for the projection of human thoughts and emotions.
Blight finds inspiration for poetry in the countryside, in the city, in
Asia, in people, the intimate and the domestic, as well as in the things
and creatures of beach and ocean.

Blight's beach images are not associated with one particular locale.
In contrast, although his poems range widely in tone, topic and
substance, Bruce Beaver's poetry frequently connects with Manly, its
beach and its suburban streets. In 'The Poems' he declares that poems
must be derived from the poet's own environment, discovered and
woven out of the fabric of one's time and place. His life, and that of
his family, is inextricably bound up with Manly, and it is there that he
must find his poetry and make sense of his world:

> Old house,
> I'll shelter here within reach
> of the past and try again to learn
> how to accept a mutable world and grow
> as sane as I can in sight and sound
> of the endless, ageless ocean.[21]

To 'grow as sane as I can' is more of a challenge to Beaver than to
most, enduring as he does a mood-altering mental illness, the cause of
suffering that he chronicles in some of his poems and of which he
often finds echoes in his environment. Beaver recognises that

> I understand only the man
> who is at war within himself[22]

and the ambivalence that such a state entails is explored in one of his major poems, 'Seawall and Shoreline', a poem about the search for meaning, connections, about the journey through life, childhood, youth, and finding the self. The very sense of one's (in)significance brings in face of nature's vast indifference brings about an acceptance and a receptivity that is close to peace.

Another poet who has recently found the coastline with its beaches, sand and rocks to be 'a rich source of imagery, [provoking] me to wonder whether, when my turn comes, I will exit as I lived, sinking or swimming'[23] is Andrew Taylor, in whose recent book of poems, *Sandstone* (1995), the title poem, of thirty-seven sonnets, comprises more than half of the content. Like Beaver, Taylor finds in the shorelines of beaches a way of exploring the large questions of time, place and human existence.

David McCooey has written in a review of recently published poetry that 'these collections show us (if we still needed to be shown) that the Australian imagination has come to terms with its coastal situation. The desert ecology ... has been replaced by the similarly hardy, clinging ecology of the sea-coast'.[24] This suggests that dominance of the bush as major source of poetic imagery in Australia is under challenge. This is significant, given that poetry is the form of literature most likely to manifest early evidence of stirrings within the individual or cultural imagination—an index of cultural shift, a 'sea-change'.

11

The Beach and Popular Culture

Exploitation of the beach by causes and commerce

DURING WORLD WAR I a recruiting poster designed by D. H. Souter for the Win the War League sought to awaken guilt in men who were criticised for preferring to enjoy the surf rather than support their mates by enlisting. It showed the head of a bodysurfer with foam breaking around him, and bore the slogan: 'It is nice in the surf BUT what about the men in the trenches. GO AND HELP'.

If the newly popular beach was enlisted so early to manipulate patriotic feelings in support of the war, it proved even more useful in peacetime—but for more commercial reasons. In the 1930s a series of posters was commissioned by the Australian National Travel Association for the promotion of tourism. One showed a 'beach' girl, one a girl on a surfboard, a third two stylish women standing on the verandah of the Bondi Pavilion and overlooking the crowds on the beach below.

Captioned, respectively, 'Australia'; 'Australia for Sun and Surf'; and 'Surfing Australia', these indicate that the beach was already seen as a symbol of Australianness. Through the middle years of the century, as Bruce Stannard illustrates in *The Face on the Bar Room Wall: Australian Pub Posters 1929–1950*, the paintings that adorned the

This recruiting poster by D. H. Souter seeks to evoke feelings of guilt in those who are reluctant to leave all this behind and contribute to the Allied cause in World War I, 1914–18.

Source: Australian War Memorial negative number ARTV0041

walls of hotels featured lifesavers, march-past parades, shark patrols, beach scenes, boardriders and surfskiers: the beaches were as much part of the landscape as were the pubs, linked through advertising as ways of having a good time.

The latter part of the twentieth century has been characterised by what Meaghan Morris describes as the 'massive, obsessive inscription' of the beach, observing that 'a vast anthology could be compiled of beach scenes from literature, cinema, photography, painting, theatre, television drama and documentary, newspapers and magazines'.[1] The beach is incessantly invoked as an image of 'the Australian way of life' in the promotion of tourism and the advertising of products. In an article on the beach the cultural theorist, John Fiske, describes the various ways in which hegemony seeks to incorporate the beach: through the marketing and promotion of surfing equipment, sporting competitions, advertising of banks, soft drinks, electronic software, and so on; and he concludes, in effect, that the beach has become an agent of the existing order: 'it controls the desire for freedom and the threat of nature by transposing it into the natural [*the natural* being not nature, but culture's construction of it]'.[2]

Fiske recognises that the 'joy' described by Dorothy Dinnerstein and associated with the beach can be a subversive counter-pressure to this overwhelming consumerism. He refers to the ideas of Roland Barthes regarding *jouissance* (an aesthetics of pleasure sited in the body), and those of Michel Foucault (with his notion of society replacing the prison as agent of social control):

> Pleasure, which affords the escape from this power . . . becomes an agent of subversion because it creates a privatized domain beyond the scope of a power whose essence lies in its omnipotence, its omnipresence. Showing that life is livable outside it denies it . . . The desires and pleasures of the body . . . are where the subversive meanings of the surf are potentially located . . . The body is the Achilles heel of hegemony . . .[3]

Even while acknowledging the potential of the beach for subversion of the existing order, however, Fiske is pessimistic about its ability to resist the power of consumer capitalism: 'The beach and the surf are worked on by the culture so that their overflowing meanings are controlled and legitimized . . . What the culture is trying to do to the surf is to defuse its potential radicalism'.[4]

Attempts to 'defuse the potential radicalism' of the surf are nowhere seen more clearly than in the case of the modern surfing movement. In its early days surfing was seen as an opportunity to commune with nature, for the transcendental experience of surfing through the 'tube' formed by the curling wave. Psychedelic drugs and marijuana were believed by many to facilitate the attainment of exalted states of mind. The emphasis was on the spiritual and the personal.

As surfing contests began to be promoted with the lure of large sums of prize money, some surfers turned professional, enhancing their earnings from prizewinning through sponsorship deals. The balance in surfing magazines between articulating and illustrating a lifestyle and the marketing of surf gear changed in favour of marketing. The rivalry between Australian and Californian surfers was 'hyped' by marketers to stimulate interest in surfing contests.

The 'surfing industry' was estimated in 1997 to be worth about $7 billion dollars around the world each year, the Australian company Quiksilver alone having sales on the global market of $300 million a year. Spectacular photographs of surfers executing incredible manoeuvres on heartstoppingly huge or beautiful waves are sold to surfing magazines and newspapers, and made into posters. Surfers sponsored by commercial interests are towed out into the open ocean to catch waves as big as five-storey buildings for 'fantastic' photographs, pushing beyond their limits, sometimes with fatal results: 'There's people now dying in Hawaii, you know, and I've had four good friends die, drown in the last 12 months nearly. Because people are just going too hard, and no-one is showing it [the ocean] the respect it deserves'.[5]

The global market for surfing products can be seen as an example of capitalism's ruthless quest for profit and its apparent success in appropriating the image of the beach to its own purposes.

Yet private freedom uncorrupted by the desire for belongings is more often attained than cultural critics are prepared to recognise. This freedom is symbolised in 'Sunbaker' by Max Dupain (1937), a classic of Australian photography. The man's body lies flat against the sand, warmed by the sun, drops glistening on his tanned arms and back indicating that he has just come out of the surf.

This photograph attracted little notice when it was first exhibited, but since the 1970s it has become an iconic Australian image,

The beachgoer may choose to remain self-sufficient, resisting the blandishments of a consumerist culture that seeks assiduously to 'market' the beach's image.

Max Dupain, 1911–92, *Sunbaker*, 1937. Gelatin silver photograph, 37.0 × 42.8 cm

Source: Art Gallery of New South Wales, 115.1976

constantly reinvented. To cite just two recent examples, an article on baldness treatments is illustrated by a photo of a bald-headed man in the Sunbaker pose (1999); a magazine article entitled 'Wake Up Australians, You're Getting Fatter' (1996) shows the Sunbaker figure considerably plumper than the original; and Anne Zahalka's photograph 'The Sunbaker #2' (1989), shows a woman 'sunbaker' instead of a man, a statement about the rise of feminism in the years since the original photograph was taken.

In the 1970s the Sunbaker represented individualism, 'doing your own thing'. At the turn of the century pressures towards consumerism have intensified, and the Sunbaker, still solitary and self-sufficient, serving no social purpose, now also represents resistance to the blandishments of an acquisitive society. He illustrates what Sue Hailstone describes as the 'pleasing frugality' of the beach,[6] its capacity to give pleasure without a necessary investment in material equipment and accessories. For despite the efforts of marketers to alter this state of affairs, there are still plenty of people who 'travel light' to the beach. 'Soul surfing' developed as a reaction against growing commercialisation, and today most surfers are not involved in competition; they are attracted to surfing purely for the pleasure it affords. While the beach is relentlessly used by marketeers, it is a place that still affords some respite from pressures to consume.

The beach in film and television

IN THE FLOURISHING EARLY DAYS of Australia's film industry at the beginning of the century, adventure stories about the desert and desert military campaigns were often shot among the coastal sand dunes. The first notable appearance of the beach 'as itself' occurs in Raymond Longford's *The Sentimental Bloke* (1919) where, as befits its romantic associations and as actually happens in the poems, the beach is the place where the Bloke and Doreen first acknowledge their love, and kiss on the sand.

Australian films began to be produced with government assistance in the 1970s after virtually disappearing during the previous four decades. The first films in this 'new wave' mostly looked to the past, especially the rural past, for themes and stories. The beach had no part to play in *Picnic at Hanging Rock* (1975), *Sunday Too Far Away* (1975) or *My Brilliant Career* (1979). But when filmmakers became confident enough to engage with contemporary Australian suburban and urban life, films like *Goodbye Paradise* (1982) and *Coolangatta Gold* (1984) were made, celebrating both the exuberant life of the Gold Coast beaches and the sleaziness and casual violence of their tacky surroundings. In *Muriel's Wedding* (1994) Muriel and her friend are overcome with excitement and relief as they leave the oppressively narrow-minded Gold Coast suburb where they grew up, satirically named Porpoise Spit. In contemporary films and television programs set in Sydney, a walk along the promenade at Bondi beach by the principal characters is almost obligatory.

Surfers had become sufficiently numerous by the 1970s to have films made especially for them, generating a modest profit for their makers from screenings mostly attended by surfers. *Morning of the Earth* (1972) was a very successful Australian movie, showing surfing in Australia, Hawaii and the recently discovered waves of Bali. Numerous films have been, and are still being, made featuring high-performance surfing in exotic locations. They are not screened but are released directly onto videos, and appear to have a ready market.[7]

While the first television 'soap opera' to achieve enormous popularity overseas, *Neighbours*, was set in a supposedly ordinary, sun-filled Australian suburb, television companies soon recognised the advantage of combining the visual delights of a beach setting with the usual soap opera ingredients; hence *Home and Away*, set in the mythical suburb of Summer Bay. I was told by Norwegian schoolchildren as we stood on the deck of a steamer gliding past icecovered fjords about their regular viewing of *Home and Away* and of the pin-up photos in their bedrooms of their favourite actor in the series. Truly the lure of the beach is international.

If *Home and Away* appeals particularly to teenagers, the popularity of *SeaChange* is more widely based. This series quickly became one of the Australian Broadcasting Corporation's biggest successes. Superficially it is in the soap opera/nice neighbourly community genre like so many others; but its special appeal lies in its evocation of our 'sea-dreaming'; for as David Malouf recognised in his 1998 Boyer lectures, if the Aboriginal people are a land-dreaming people, we late-comers share a sea-dreaming. The yearning for the dreaming-place, Pearl Bay in *SeaChange*, was sharpened in the late twentieth century as the demands of the workplace became more insistent and ate into people's lives. Laura Gibson's escape from a high-powered city legal firm to a meandering magistracy in Pearl Bay, and her family's gradual accommodation to the local community, are a vicarious wish-fulfilment for those who feel overwhelmed by the demands and complexities of work and family life. The characters, apart from Laura and Diver Dan, are not stylish or unusually attractive—a motley collection of humanity, just like the viewers. Each episode ends with a scene with Kevin, the 'daggy' caravan park manager, and his awkward teenage son, Trevor, on the beach watching the sunset or the gradually darkening sky over the sea. They sit comfortably side by side, not looking at each other, uttering some thought that comes into one head or the other. This is unmistakeably a time of great peace, of reflection, a precious moment in the fretfulness of life. And this, *SeaChange* seems to say, is freely available to all of us, no matter how ordinary we might be.

12

The Serene and the Sinister: Contrasting Aspects of the Beach

Apprehensions of the numinous, and 'time out' or retreat

THE CLOSING SCENES of the ABC-TV's *SeaChange* episodes often touch on what Wordsworth would have called 'intimations of immortality', and which might be discerned here as apprehensions of the numinous or transcendent. A desire to hold onto the perfection of the moment is expressed in love scenes on the beach in Katharine Susannah Prichard's *Intimate Strangers* (1937) and George Johnston's *Clean Straw for Nothing* (1964), and in works as dissimilar as David Malouf's *Fly Away Peter* (1982), Bill Green's *Freud and the Nazis Go Surfing* (1986), and Kathleen Stewart's *Spilt Milk* (1995).

A sense of the beach as a place of retreat where one achieves a new perspective on human concerns, gains inner peace or re-establishes equilibrium after disturbance or effort is another common theme of beach writing. When Sylvia in *Spilt Milk* is in a state of 'murderous rage',

> There is only one thing for it. I head to the sea.
> At last I am there; the sea rushing itself against the rocks. I sit and watch. The sea boils; waves churn and dash and fling them-selves at rocks. Below the surface flurry, the sea is cold. I watch until I am calmer, but not calm . . . It is peace, of a kind.[1]

The turbulent adolescent in *Freud and the Nazis Go Surfing* is similarly affected:

> I walked from the dunes and into the ocean. It was wondrous; there was such strength in the waves. They hurled me about without effort, as if I hardly existed, and I was soon completely recovered [from an outburst of rage, during which he gratuitously attacked and destroyed trees growing behind the dunes]. I left the water knowing that people and the horrors they were carrying were ultimately nothing.[2]

In Tim Winton's *Shallows* (1984) the sights and sounds of the familiar town beach signify to Queenie the return to normality of the town of Angelus as the anti-whaling demonstrators leave, and conflict and disruption ends.

Retreat to the beach is not only for the solitary and the contemplative. Robert Drewe writes that 'the beach is . . . a place where people go to examine an old relationship that is going through troubles, re-examine their lives, fix things up if they are fixable, or find the courage to go in a new direction'.[3] In the title story from Helen Garner's *Postcards from Surfers* collection (1985) the narrator retreats from the disintegration of her affair with Phillip to spend time with her retired parents on the Gold Coast. Her depression and sense of nervous anticipation during the journey are subtly conveyed: 'The swells are dotted with boardriders in black wetsuits, grim as sharks'.[4] The history and the present state of her relationship with her father is revealed in random memories recalled as she writes to her (ex)lover Philip, through postcards that she covers with writing and eventually drops into a rubbish bin—a reluctant letting go of a relationship that is over.

In Michael Gow's *Away* (1986) the scene on the beach is an important stage in the spiritual quest of the play's characters. A magical storm (equivalent to that in Shakespeare's *King Lear*) in the previous scene having destroyed the material goods that were so important to Gwen, all the characters meet, stripped of possessions and pretensions, on a secluded beach (as the characters are reunited in *A Midsummer Night's Dream*; *Away* is rich in Shakespearean allusions). Here Gwen's sadness and inability to let go of the past are recognised and forgiven; Harry tells of Tom's fatal illness; and Coral is finally able to move forward from her son's death in Vietnam. At the end of the play the bonfire on the beach is a symbol of the purification wrought through

suffering, understanding and forgiveness. The final stage instruction
reads: 'Beyond them, as in a dream, the lights play on the blue horizon
and the sea': the play ends as it evokes the rich and complex associations
of the beach in the hearts and minds of the audience.

Tim Winton has written that

> Surfing, swimming laps, drifting a bait from the jetty or a boat are
> similarly [to diving] forgetful things. They are forms of desertion,
> retreat, hermitage, a stepping-aside from terrestrial problems to
> be absorbed in the long moment. The sea is immense, trackless,
> potent, but above all, neutral.[5]

Winton's neutrality, Blight's 'mindlessness of ocean', Corbin's
'energy of concentrated emptiness': embodying no suggestion of
comment or judgement on human behaviour or motive, the beach
provides a breathing-space, a place of temporary refuge and peace.
Drewe writes in his Introduction to *The Picador Book of the Beach*
that in this international collection of beach stories 'the vast majority
are to do with escape';[6] but this is not true of most Australian writing
on the beach. While the beach can provide respite from the cares of
the moment, or an opportunity for reappraisal of where one's life is
heading, re-entry to the everyday world is as accepted and taken for
granted, as is access to the beach itself.

Destruction, violence and regression to the primitive

WINTON ALSO WRITES that 'for every moment the sea is peace and
relief, there is another when it shivers and threatens to become chaos.
It's just as ready to claim as it is to offer'. Beachgoing is approached
with

> a mixture of gusto and apprehension, for our sea is something to
> be reckoned with. We are reared on stories of shark attacks, broken
> necks from dumpings in the surf, and melanoma. I suspect we go
> because of these warnings at times, and not simply despite them.[7]

Sometimes sharks are symbols of the sinister in the apparently
commonplace—as in Bruce Beaver's reference to

> the white, jagged rictus in the grey sliding anonymity,
> faint blur of red through green,
> the continually spreading stain.[8]

In Robert Drewe's 'Shark Logic', from *The Bodysurfers* collection (1983), the narrator has left his family in Perth (who believe him dead) to live temporarily in a rented flat in Manly, perhaps to go on to make a new life in New Zealand. A man in limbo, his old life destroyed, a new path not yet chosen, a sense of the potential for violence—of threat posed by the existential void in which he is suspended—is both projected onto and reflected back by the beach and its seedy surroundings.

Judith Wright discerns the menace of 'the grey-wolf sea' into which the joy-giving waves can be transformed in an instant, in her fine poem 'The Surfer'.[9] The subject of the poem is the vulnerability and fragility of human life; at any moment, destruction can suddenly intrude into delight. This is the also the theme of Robert Drewe's 'Stingray', also from *The Bodysurfers*, where the poisonous sting the narrator experiences as he is enjoying the surf brings sharp realisation of the arbitrariness of death:

> This country is world champion in the venomous creatures' department. The box jellyfish. Funnel-web spiders. Stonefish. The tiny blue-ringed octopus, carrying enough venom to paralyse ten grown men ... It suddenly occurs to him he might be about to die. The randomness and lack of moment are right.[10]

Perhaps an uneasily suppressed fear of the sea's potential for destruction underlies a strong apocalyptic consciousness in Australian society discerned by Meaghan Morris,[11] expressed in Peter Weir's film *The Last Wave* (1977), and demonstrated in a quickly acquired, widespread awareness of predictions of the greenhouse effect and consequent rises in sea levels. In *Night Surfing* (1996) by Fiona Capp there is a recurring nightmare, unconnected to the plot, where a giant wave gathers itself up from the ocean and travels towards the land:

> A wave of colossal size towers over the dunes. A black wave that dredges up the sunless depths, a wave that arcs so high it drags down the sun, stars and moon from the sky and turns the day to pitch.
> The wave is more than water. It carries a whole universe inside it. What is tossed up from the sea churns with the debris of the land as the inundation gains momentum. Shells, jellyfish, driftwood and deckchairs, bladder-wrack, corrugated iron, car tyres and starfish spiral down the deserted main street as Ruben's Cafe goes under, its neon lights still glowing beneath the water.[12]

And perhaps the best-known 'beach' novel with an Australian setting is Nevil Shute's *On the Beach* (1957), a story set in Melbourne with the final remnants of the human race 'beached' on the last habitable shores of the planet, extinguished by the 1950s version of Nemesis—radioactive fallout from nuclear war.

The beach is also a place where the overwhelming presence of the natural can stimulate the awakening and expression of primitive, violent and libidinal urges. Intuitive understanding of human potential for regression to savagery may have underlain those apparently priggish early restrictions on freedom at the beach. The subjects in Drewe's 'The View from the Sandhills' and 'The Silver Medallist'[13] are men with perverted and violent instincts that find expression amidst the apparent innocence of the beach environment.

A tragedy on a NSW beach where a fourteen-year-old girl attending a birthday party at a local surf clubhouse was raped and bashed to death by a boy or boys at the party has inspired two plays by Nick Enright: *Blackrock* (1996, also a film 1997) and *Property of the Clan* (1994). *Property of the Clan* is performed in schools by the Australian Theatre for Young People, and the actors report that they have been struck by the way students in a number of towns where the play has been staged, particularly beachside towns, believe the play is based on an incident that happened in their own town.[14] It appears that the dark forces unleashed in such events are a pattern, a motif in our history, going back to those scenes on the beach when the female convicts were unloaded from the ships of the First Fleet—scenes glossed over in the prim language of Arthur Bowes Smyth, surgeon on the *Lady Penrhyn*:

> The Men Convicts got to them [the female convicts] very soon after they landed, & it is beyond my abilities to give a just description of the Scene of Debauchery & Riot that ensued during the night . . . the Scene which presented itself at this time & during the greater part of the night, beggars every description.[15]

In his painting *The Baths* (1943) Arthur Boyd's grotesque figures represent the madness that can suddenly spill over onto the calmness of the sand; in *The Beach* (1944) a monster towers over frenzied lovers intertwined beside a turbulent sea, a coffin/boat floating nearby an image of death and destruction. Jeffrey Smart's painting *Holiday Resort* (1946) presents what seems at first glance an utterly banal

The dark side of the beach—its associations with primitive sexuality, death, destruction and violence—is captured in this painting by Arthur Boyd.

Arthur Boyd (Australia, 1920–99), *The Beach*, 1944. Oil on cotton gauze on hardboard, 62.8 × 75.4 cm

Source: National Gallery of Australia, Canberra. The Arthur Boyd gift 1975.

seaside scene, with a man reading a paper on a bench by the beach-front, Norfolk pine and shelter hut in the background; but the empty pram in the foreground strikes a sinister note, evoking an anxiety explored by Peter Pierce in *The Country of Lost Children*. One recalls the three Beaumont children who disappeared from an Adelaide beach in 1966, no trace of them ever being found, and the teenage girls murdered on Wanda beach at Cronulla.

These works draw on the dark side of the beach's ambivalence, of Dorothy Dinnerstein's 'hurtful, entrancing surround'. Its unstructured space, the absence of physical boundaries and limits, has as its counterpart the ignoring or the rejection of moral constraints. The catastrophic storms, the dark shapes that lurk below and beyond the sparkling surf, are as real as the delights we more often prefer to associate with it.

13

Reflections on Representations of the Beach and 'Immersion in Place'

IN THE TWENTIETH CENTURY the focus, in both literature and art, has been on the *peopled* beach. There has been development from associations of the beach with enjoyment, sensuality, love, death and loss, to a much broader range of meanings. The need to describe the scene for someone who has never been there, or as if seeing it for the first time, is no longer evident. While Sylvia in Kathleen Stewart's *Spilt Milk* (1995) meditates as she observes the sea on her walks to Bondi, Bronte or Coogee, she feels no need to describe the beaches themselves; it is taken for granted that we know them too—or at least know beaches that are sufficiently similar for us to recognise their common aspects. In novels about uncommitted inner-city young people such as Tegan Bennett's 'Bombora' and 'A Chiming of Light' in *Bombora* (1996), and Gaby Naher's *The Under Wharf* (1995), the same assured sense of place is evident: the characters move from the inner city to the beach and back as part of the ordinary course of life, a stitching of the beach into daily experience rather than something to be highlighted, described in detail, a subject in need of explanation and comment. The teenagers in the television series *Home and Away* are completely at home in Summer Bay; we respond to Pearl Bay in the ABC-TV's *SeaChange* as a loved and familiar place.

This profound incorporation of the beach into our ways of being
is playfully represented by Toni Robertson in her screenprint series
Canberra Beaches 1, 2 and 3 (1984). In *Canberra Beaches 1* people of
all ages and both sexes stroll around the Australian War Memorial in
Canberra in their swimsuits; perhaps the old men in terry-towelling
hats are survivors from those whose sacrifice the Memorial commemo-
rates. In *Canberra Beaches 2* small groups of families or friends, again
in their swimsuits, squat or sprawl across the lawn in front of the Old
Parliament House, as if on a beach; a beach umbrella flaunts its colours
on one side of the picture. In *Canberra Beaches 3* surfers occupy the
foreground of the High Court of Australia, some riding their boards
on waves cascading down the stepped levels at the side of this self-
important building. The beach has seeped not only into our lives but
into our very institutions. And these screenprints have anticipated real
life: it is a delightful surprise to discover, walking along the Southbank
promenade along the river in Brisbane, that the City Council has
constructed, almost tongue-in-cheek, a 'real' beach complete with fine
white sand, sparkling water, children building castles and adults
sunbathing, on the very edge of the central business district. The
temples of business and commerce loom over the beach, but fail to
dominate it.

Toni Robertson, *Canberra Beaches 1—The War Memorial*, 1984, screenprint.

Toni Robertson, *Canberra Beaches 2—Parliament House*, 1984, screenprint.

Toni Robertson, *Canberra Beaches 3—The High Court*, 1984, screenprint.

The superimposition of beach scenes on landmarks of the nation's capital by Toni Robertson suggests the degree to which beachlife has been absorbed into our social and political institutions.

Source: Reproduced by permission of the Artbank Collection.

If, as Simon Schama concludes in *Landscape and Memory*, 'The sum of our pasts, generation laid over generation, forms the compost of our culture',[1] perhaps enough time has elapsed for 'the compost of our culture' to have begun to accumulate, for a deposit of direct experiences to lie fallow, gather meaning and be imaginatively transformed in ways that are apprehended and appreciated by others who share sufficiently similar experiences. Ross Gibson finds possible cause for optimism in the way that we are gradually adjusting from an imported European system of meaning to seeing and understanding local phenomena in ways that are specifically Australian—'a long and painful process', still under way after more than two hundred years; which he refers to as 'a sense of subjective immersion in [Australian] place'. Perhaps it is not too fanciful to suggest that the 'sense of subjective immersion in place' to which Gibson alludes has been facilitated by the common experience of actual immersion at the beach.[2]

But Gibson's references to 'systems of settlement' in relation to 'immersion in place', and Schama's to 'the compost of our culture' exemplify a chronic semantic difficulty encountered when one is trying to 'foreground' the beach: all the relevant metaphors are of the land, or agricultural, not coastal. We could just as well, if not more appropriately, write of a gradual surge of meaning up from the depths of consciousness, as in our coastal environment, nutrient-rich upwellings of ice-cold currents from the deepest Antarctic oceans mingle with warmer coastal waters and bring life to marine plants and animals. Here is an Antipodean association—of coldness rather than warmth—with fertility.

For all these developments, works that draw on the beach still constitute a relatively insubstantial component of the corpus of Australian literature and art (even if the beach pervades popular culture). This is partly because of the comparatively recent incorporation of the beach in Australian life, but also for a more fundamental reason—there are no myths of the beach in Western culture comparable to the great Western myths of place: the city, the *polis*, site of our greatest achievements and deepest corruption; the virtues and attractions of 'Life on the Land'; and the 'Wilderness' of the Romantic imagination. The only contender for a specifically Australian myth of the beach has been the firmly other-focused myth of the 'Noble Savage', its exotic exemplars the sensuous Tahitians and the happy South Sea Islanders.

There are many reasons why such an image has long been unacceptable to us; but this may be a self–other distinction that is in the process of dissolving. If history is kind, aspects of this myth are likely be reworked into new Australian myths yet to evolve. And fantasies and fables now being written for children suggest that creatures of the sea, like seals, whales and dolphins, will embody special significance in legends-to-come (and not only in children's books: in Tom Gilling's *The Sooterkin* (1999) a Tasmanian woman gives birth to a seal pup).

There is one important writer with a sense of the significance of the sea for Australians so powerful that her work warrants consideration in relation to the idea of myth: Christina Stead describes Australia's place in the world in the Prologue to *For Love Alone*:

> This island continent lies in the water hemisphere . . . The other world—the old world, the land hemisphere—is far above her . . . From that world . . . the people came, all by steam; or their parents, all by sail . . . there is nothing in the interior, so people look toward the water, and above to the fixed stars and constellations . . . The skies are sub-tropical, crusted with suns and spirals, as if a reflection of the crowded Pacific Ocean, with its reefs, atolls and archipelagos. It is a fruitful island of the sea-world, a great Ithaca . . .[3]

Although Stead is on the right wavelength when she writes of Australia as 'a fruitful island of the sea-world, a great Ithaca', Ithaca is the island from which Ulysses set forth on his Odyssey, leaving Penelope behind. It evokes the image of Australians as travellers leaving their island in search of the Great World (as Stead herself did, returning, like Ulysses, after many years away)—not those for whom the beach is part of their lives. But her concern for and perception of Australia's place in the world inform her earlier novel, *Seven Poor Men of Sydney* (1934), where she presents a brilliant allegorical vision of the contribution of the sea to Australia's history and destiny.

At one level *Seven Poor Men of Sydney* portrays characters living in the city and trapped by poverty, but at another level the characters represent the various ways in which Australians have failed to fashion an authentic culture and to find a genuine homeland here.[4] Michael Baguenault rejects the church and the notion that Australia is to be 'a new Britannia', but he succumbs to mindless materialism for a while, goes to Europe to fight in World War I, and returns home 'weathered and self-centred',[5] deciding that life is a game with no meaning—a paradigm of the developing Australian nation. Life without belief becomes intolerable, and Michael commits suicide by throwing himself into the sea off The Gap. His half-sister, Catherine, suffers the double burden of being a woman in a society where negative stereotypes of woman are pervasive, and an adherent of an alien European political philosophy (socialism). Her way out is to commit herself to a lunatic asylum. The other poor men 'adjust' to life in Australia in various dysfunctional ways: one by indulging in cynicism and unbridled personal licence; another espousing Anglophile values and exploiting his workers; yet another leaving for America. One goes to prison. Only Joseph Baguenault endures, accepting his ordinariness and his banal life; but he is the one who tells the tale of the seven poor men at the end. He succeeds by surviving. It is a gloomy picture, foretold by the foreign schoolteacher early in the novel: 'You have no notion of history ... Doctrine, constitution, order, duty, religion, you have to find them out by long and droughty explorations of the spirit'.[6]

Reasons why 'long and droughty explorations of the spirit' had ended in failure for his companions are summed up in the 'In Memoriam' speech by Michael's friend, Kol Blount, near the end of the novel. In the grounds of the lunatic asylum (Australia?) where Catherine is living Blount describes, in a passage reminiscent of the Genesis account but with far more vivid, concentrated images, the birth of Australia: 'the water continent, solitarily uprising' from the sea in prehistoric times. He tells of the arrival of 'native youth', the original inhabitants, growing in intimate knowledge of the land, the sea around it, and all the flora and fauna of that land and that sea. The arrival of Europeans is disposed of in a paragraph: a summary tale of violence and plunder, until now

> After all this notable pioneer tale of starvation, sorrow, escapades, mutiny, death, labour in common, broad wheatlands, fat sheep, broad cattle-barons, raw male youth and his wedding to the land, in the over-populated metropolis the sad-eyed youth sits glumly in a hare-brained band, and speculates upon the suicide of youth, the despair of the heirs of yellow heavy-headed acres. What a history is that; what an enigma is that?[7]

'The despair of the heirs of yellow heavy-headed acres': even though we have drawn much wealth from the land, we are not happy.[8] Blount recognises that we need to fashion a way of life that is authentic, that accommodates to the country that we inhabit, and that using ideas imported from other cultures condemns us to be alien and second-rate:

> Why are we here? Nothing floats down here, this far in the south, but is worn out with wind, tempest and weather; all is flotsam and jetsam. They leave their rags and tatters here; why do we have to be dressed? The sun is hot enough; why can't we run naked in our own country, on our own land, and work out our own destiny? Eating these regurgitated ideas from the old country makes us sick and die of sickness. Are we vultures to eat the corpses come down here to bleach their bones in the antipodes?[9]

His view is bitter and pessimistic, suggesting that in our isolation, our timid conformity and our ineptitude, we will never belong here. It seems that Michael, unable to come to terms with the 'bitter heart of the land' has abandoned himself to the sea—another 'heart made of salt'—in his suicide. Blount sees no answer to the 'dilemma' of Australia, and laments that 'Our land never should have been won'. But a 'madman' suddenly breaks into Blount's peroration:

> The madman at this moment approached solemnly, with quiet dignity, and cried: 'My blood is running back to the sea. Out of the sea I rose, you have clipped my wings, I cannot rise again. I must drink the salt of the sea![10]

Throughout the ages prophets have appeared in the guise of madmen. If we take the utterance of the madman, with his 'quiet dignity', as prophetic, then we need to remember always that we came from the sea and the sea is in our blood. We must therefore engage with both the heart of the land (the dead heart, the inland sea) *and* our sea-surround (the 'heart made of salt') to know and to understand both, as the 'native youth' did, if we are truly to belong here. We also face the difficult task of reconciling the 'malign and bitter genius of this waste land . . . its heart made of salt [that] oozes from its burning pores, gold which will destroy men in greed, but not water to give them drink'[11] with the beauty of so much of the landscape, and the playground of delight that is our sea-edge, our beaches. And the coast with its beaches, the meeting place of, the interchange between, land and sea, where most of us live, is where it might be possible to achieve this accommodation.

PART 3

Influences of the Beach
in Australian Culture

14

The Concept of 'National Identity'

In margins and in longings: this is where all homelands begin.
—Janette Turner Hospital, 'Litany for the Homeland', *Collected Stories*, p. 411.

The beach and national identity

IF THE BEACH HAS BECOME a significant feature of Australian life, how has this affected the kind of society that has developed here? To ask such a question is to enter the arena of argument over concepts of national character and national identity, an area of fiercely contested, some would say obsessive, social and intellectual debate—a debate that has a long history.

Modern historians and cultural analysts examine contemporary life from a political perspective, and generally find much to criticise in older versions of Australianness—indeed, in the very concept of a national identity itself. Thus Richard White asserts in *Inventing Australia* that the very idea of national identity is an invention, part of the baggage we brought from Europe with us, and one of the ways in which we are manipulated to think, feel and behave by those who seek to pursue one political or commercial agenda or another.

Feminist scholars have also played their part in demolishing older versions of national identity, labelling the proudly egalitarian national stereotype of the bushman described by Ward as 'prescriptive, unitary, masculinist and excluding'; its omission of women and the reasons for this omission have been comprehensively demonstrated and canvassed in recent feminist analyses.[1] Postmodern intellectual theory has sought to deconstruct the meaning of, and thereby to lay bare the political realities underlying apparently innocuous or hitherto accepted ideas and social institutions. Nothing is 'really' as it seems; the questions that must be asked are: who chooses a particular version of reality— and why? Changes in official policy on migrants and Aboriginal people from assimilation (which in its simplest, most literal form involved the idea that everyone who lives in Australia will adopt the same culture) to multiculturalism in the case of migrants, and self-determination in the case of Aboriginal people, clearly signalled the breakdown of a monolithic, monocultural ideal of Australianness.

Where difference is valued, it follows that attempts to generalise, as in the case of defining national identity, are rejected. In *Mistaken Identity: Multiculturalism and the Demise of Nationalism in Australia*, Stephen Castles et al. regard appeals to an idea of national identity as one of the methods used to perpetuate and increase inequality and, in discriminating against migrants, to maintain an 'Anglocentric' ascendancy. They argue that national identity will be transcended in a modern world where human identity will be transnational because 'we are now all in the same boat—economically, ecologically and politically'.[2]

More recently, prophets of the new world of cyberspace, computers and the Internet predict that notions of identity will be radically transformed by the almost instantaneous communication with all parts of the world the Web provides:

> Cassandra Pybus, the editor of *Australian Humanities Review*, a journal on the Internet, observes that the absence of geographic borders in cyberspace is changing the sense of geographic limitations, and with it, geographically induced insecurities. 'The geekgirl site on the Internet, established by Sydney resident Rosie Cross, is a major international site', says Pybus. 'Nobody even thinks about that site as being Australian.'[3]

Thus a formidable array of forces combine to reinforce the message that national identity is not only an invention but an idea that is obsolete, harmful, and yet another way in which the powerful are able to assert dominance over the powerless.

At the same time, however, there are intriguing signs of a counter-vailing movement back to a qualified, almost reluctant acknowledge-ment that there is some value in identifying what Australians have in common, as well as what divides them. A significant reason for this reappraisal is the perceived threat posed by global capitalism. There is a widely held view that the powers of the nation state are being cut back to make way for an 'efficient' order of production and trade by those very 'transnational' or 'multinational' forces, corporate and political, that most actively exploit nationalist sentiments in order to promote their aims and products.[4] More recently, an ominous threat from the other end of the spectrum has become evident: the splintering of the nationalism of the nation-state into ethnic nationalisms, where groups sharing the same homeland demonise and slaughter each other.

Our continuing discussion of national identity suggests a need that lies deeper than fashionable intellectual debate. The sentiment of nationality 'usually becomes conscious through struggle against an Other with whom one is in economic, geopolitical or religious conflict'.[5] This is a phenomenon well known and used by national leaders to shore up support; but despite chronic low-level paranoia about such matters, Australians have no clearcut enemy, no geographical, historical, political or religious forces against whom they can define themselves: no aggressive neighbour, no war of independence, no bloody internal conflicts. Others might well envy us this good fortune; but, in lieu of circumstances being forced upon us, we have to make decisions based on a sense of ourselves; and if a sense of ourselves is lacking, what is our yardstick?

Thinking about this, I remembered watching a television docu-mentary on the Polish Solidarity movement. It showed the various meetings at which the trade unionists hammered out the plan of their struggle over the Gdansk shipyards. Several times the discussion seemed to evoke in all those present at the meeting a spontaneous response, whereby they rose as one and broke into song—some stir-ring evocation of past struggles known to all. While I wondered what it would be like to belong to a society where solidarity based on a common store of memories could be so much taken for granted, the fragmentation of Yugoslavia exemplifies the dangers of myths that invoke the glories of the past and exclude those who do not share them.

If not on the basis of shared past, shared ethnic identification or unification against a common foe, how might we define what it now means to be Australian? Debate over the republic has explored this question. Recognition—ranging from tolerance to celebration—of cultural diversity and difference; reconciliation with the original inhabitants of the land; commitment to a common language, a core set of values—democracy, egalitarianism, a fair go for all—are some of the values that have been advocated.

The overwhelming presence of the natural landscape noted in the last chapter connects with a profound and passionate attachment to the land felt by many Australians. Again we run up against a semantic difficulty: the lack of a word for land or landscape that also evokes and includes the coastal fringe. When Australians are overseas, it may be the reality or the memory of the scent of eucalyptus that evokes homesickness; but it is just as likely—even for those who rarely visit the beach at home—to be images of the beach that fill their imaginations.

If pressed to define their love of country, it is a fair bet that many Australians would place affection for their physical environment above regard for their fellow-citizens or a chauvinistic sense of national superiority. Attachment to the 'land' as defined here, and commitment to cherishing and managing it for the optimal benefit of future generations, would be a non-jingoistic 'core value' to take into the twenty-first century.

What, then, is the relevance of the beach to this ongoing debate over national identity? One thing is clear: it is frequently invoked as a vivid image of 'the Australian way of life' in the advertising of products and the promotion of tourism—so frequently, in fact, that its pervasiveness seems to support the view of the deep emotional significance of the beach presented in the Introduction. It is this appropriation of the beach for the purposes of capitalism, and the contesting of ideas about the beach that has captured the attention of critics adopting a cultural studies approach in analysing the meaning of the beach in Australian popular culture.

The link between national identity and the beach is directly explored in Anne Game's 'Nation and Identity: Bondi'. Rejecting the idea that representations of Bondi are either unitary or unifying, she examines the meanings of Bondi, an urban beach where

> nature is to be . . . engaged with rather than sanctified, visited and left . . . it is an everyday affair, an other that has been successfully incorporated . . . this self is not split or separated, but merged with elements of nature. Such identifications with Bondi are perhaps, then, in the pre-symbolic realm of the Imaginary . . . It brings to mind Freud's account of the 'oceanic feeling', the lack of boundary between ego and outside world.[6]

Game thus touches on ideas about the beach that are explored in this investigation; she also recognises that 'nature/culture' and 'work/play' oppositions are disrupted or overcome in the incorporation of the beach into the lives of those who feel 'at home' there. But she is more interested in the contradictions and tensions between competing ideas of Bondi held by residents, beachgoers, tourists, and those who seek to 'beautify' Bondi, detecting 'little agreement about what constitutes the "nature" or "culture" of Bondi or the relation between them'. She identifies 'contradictory discourses' in attitudes towards being Australian, being egalitarian: 'The sea is an equalizer; no one owns the sun, sea, surf—or everyone, all Australians own it'; ownership is a reward for work; pleasure can be achieved without work on the beach. Game's central argument is that, if Bondi is used as a symbol of the nation, there are so many competing meanings clustered around that symbol that its celebration merely reveals the contradictions within the idea of national identity itself.[7]

Game refers favourably to another analysis of Bondi, by Noel Sanders. This article contains much information about the beach and the suburb but is basically a stream-of-consciousness, loosely structured setting-down of ideas, themes and issues associated with Bondi, some of them similar to Game's, but expressed more obscurely. Sanders's point seems to be that there are so many aspects of Bondi, so politically charged, that 'The Barthian quest for an unalloyed "aesthetic" discourse' is impossible.[8]

Other writers in the cultural studies movement have turned their attention to the beach as an aspect of Australian popular culture. In 'Reading the Beach' John Fiske presents a set of ideas about the beach based on observation of the beaches south of Perth, notably Cottesloe, centring on the nature/culture dichotomy, or more precisely the continuum where culture gradually gives way to nature, ranging from the city to road to the lawn strip to beach to shallow water to deep water. He regards pressures to prohibit or regulate activities on the beach as attempts to control the threat of too much meaning caused by its signifying too much of both nature and culture simultaneously. Surfers, despite their language of freedom and sensuality, are individuals competing in the capitalist rat race like the rest of us. Ultimately the beach according to Fiske is 'a text of mundane pleasure'; its apparent invitation to freedom is illusory, for it too has been appropriated for the purposes of capitalism.[9]

An essay on 'The Beach' in *Myths of Oz: Reading Australian Popular Culture*, which Fiske co-authored with Bob Hodge and Graeme Turner, notes the apparent paradox that the beach, symbolic of nature and the outdoors, is usually a city beach, and that its increasing centrality to Australian myths coincides with increasing urbanisation. The bronzed lifesaver has taken over from the bushman as an idealised figure in harmony with nature and toughly physical. There are two apparently contradictory paradigms of the beach: one as intrinsically part of the city and therefore 'culture'; the other as 'nature', an alternative to the suburb. The most popular beaches accept both meanings simultaneously. Surf beaches, in the challenge they present and the vigour they require, are definitive, at the top of a hierarchy where, lower down the hierarchy, the safe harbourside beaches still contain echoes of the freedom the rougher beaches provide. There are highly conventionalised beach rituals, impregnated with clues to status and role distinctions.

The rivalry between surfers and lifesavers personifies the opposing meanings of the beach, the lifesavers representing culture and social control, the surfers representing the rejection of work and responsibility: 'the lifesaver is the land, the surfer the sea'.

Notions of youth versus age, sexism, the colonisation of the beach by the dominant culture, 'elements of resistance' possible in the surf, and other aspects of the nature/culture distinction are dealt with. The authors conclude:

> It is the flexibility of the beach, its wide potential for meaning, that allows different sections of society to find in it different ways of articulating, different ways of relating to, this deep biblical

opposition between land and sea, or the basic anthropological one between culture and nature.[10]

This book obviously has no quarrel with the notion that the beach has 'a wide potential for meaning'; and some of the ideas presented in 'The Beach' will be taken up again later. But the references to 'different sections of society', 'different ways of articulating', and 'different ways of relating' in their concluding statement exemplify the tendency of writers on popular culture to focus on contest and conflict, to note what divides people rather than what they have in common. Emphasising difference and conflict, they align themselves with the anti-national identity side of the current debate. And their sometimes illuminating observations are 'skin deep', for it is not their intention to examine the subjective experience of the beach.

In their preoccupation with difference these critics ignore shared qualities of the beach experience, what Stephen Knight calls 'the unnoticed structures, the concealed meanings, aspects of life all the more vital for being obscured'. Knight is not referring to the beach here; indeed, he lumps the beach with sport in stating that 'None of these have played much part in my experience of Australia, nor do they have, in my view, much significance in the deep laid realities of life in this country'.[11] But Knight came to Australia from England as a young man, and lacks the experience that might have sensitised him to the 'concealed meanings' of the beach. The noted cultural analyst Meaghan Morris disagrees with him: 'The beach for me has always been a "deep-laid" and thus ambiguous, reality of life . . . when I read Knight's dedication, "For Margaret, who kept me here", I realize that were I to make such a tribute I could say, most sincerely, "For the beach . . ."'[12]

Morris alludes to a complex and emotionally charged relationship with the beach that many Australians would share but find difficult to articulate. How can the effect of this relationship on our culture be described? I suggest that meanings of the beach can be identified that find an echo, or are reflected or expressed, in behaviours, attitudes and practices sometimes noted in generalisations about Australian society—the kinds of generalisations that are invoked when notions of national character and national identity are discussed.

15

Meanings of the Beach, and the Shaping of an Australian Culture

Marginality and ambiguity

FROM THE PERSPECTIVE of an eagle or looking down from a plane flying along Australia's coastline, the country's boundary is one, indivisible, a clearcut edge. The land ends abruptly as the sea takes over. No country could wish for its territory to be more unambiguously outlined:

> To live on an island nation is to distinguish
> frontiers from boundaries. One doesn't
> negotiate with oceans. I need
> no visa, after lunch on our friends'
> breezy veranda, to borrow their boat
> and float a hundred metres over stone.[1]

All Australians share this reality of containment. Wherever we go we eventually run up against an edge, which is mostly also a beach:

> Living on an island
> no matter how big, reminds me
> of edges. The coast is our skin
> and what goes on inside it goes on
> within. If we climb mountains
> swim across lakes, walk the Nullarbor
> we encounter a coast.[2]

Coast is also margin. Remote from centres of culture and power, Australians have readily conceived of themselves as a marginalised people, considered by themselves and others to be not quite the genuine article, irrelevant to the important concerns of the real world in the Northern Hemisphere. The concept of marginality has become a fashionable one in contemporary intellectual debate, particularly in writings on postcolonialism, and the relationship of the centre to the margin was first posed as that between the oppressor and the oppressed. But the idea has taken another twist with the margin now being regarded as the site of creativity and potential, for both individuals and nations:

> [The edge is where] everything is being rearranged and redefined. The edge is where things happen, where sudden discoveries illuminate hidden memories: where revelations and metamorphoses occur . . . [It is] also the edge of the self where inside and outside meet . . . indeed where all the intellectual and creative functions of our consciousness are performed.[3]

Australia has been characterised as a key site for the working out of the centre–margin opposition:

> Australia's ubiquity—its simultaneous marginality and centrality—has become explicit [recently]. It is both a long way from the world . . . *and* it is nowhere in particular . . . an unsettled load ballasted with a clutter of cargo—the mythologies of nationalism and colonialism, rural romanticism, hedonist modernism and wildstyle postmodernism.[4]

It is coincidental, yet fitting, that a maritime metaphor—of cargo and ballast—is used to characterise a disordered jostling of movements and ideas. A striking analogue of the promiscuous potpourri Ross Gibson depicts is the edge of the beach, the tideline where 'anything goes'. A flash of blue amidst tangled seaweed might be a stinging bluebottle or a fragment of a baby's rattle; a gleam of white, the side of an icecream container or a piece of nautilus shell. Crows step purposefully through dried seaweed, feasting on the shearwaters who have dropped dead from exhaustion, so near their destination after their flight from the Arctic Circle. Willy wagtails flick their tails this way and that, chasing insects attracted by rotting weed. Bits of ash and burnt leaves from inland bushfires or pellets of pumice stone from volcanic eruptions on the other side of the ocean trace out the highwater mark, joined by sauce bottles discarded from ships waiting to enter harbour. Creatures of sea and land, fish, bird, animal and insect, man-made objects, are strewn pell-mell, not belonging yet belonging. This is a zone of coincidence, even in a scientific sense: 'The shoreline is the only part of the globe where the four great spheres, the atmosphere, the hydrosphere or ocean, the lithosphere or earth's surface and the biosphere all coexist'.[5]

It has become common to write of hybridity as the product of the creativity of the margin; but this is merely to create another category. I choose not to employ this term, preferring to leave the processes occurring in this fertile zone fluid, without closure. This is a place where the apparently meaningless may suddenly acquire new relationships and reveal unexpected connections; where former oppositions and sharp-edged categories are reconciled, obliterated, or no longer apply:

> Softly and humbly to the Gulf of Arabs
> The convoys of dead sailors come;
> At night they sway and wander in the waters far under,
> But morning rolls them in the foam . . .
>
> Dead seamen, gone in search of the same landfall,
> Whether as enemies they fought,
> Or fought with us, or neither; the sand joins them together,
> Enlisted on the other front.[6]

The title of a 1910 article about surfers, 'Australia's Amphibians', hints at the potential for metamorphosis and transformation that is imaginatively realised in children's fantasies such as Lilith Norman's *A Dream of Seas*, Jackie French's *The Secret Beach*, Gillian Rubinstein's *Beyond the Labyrinth* and Nicole Pluss's *Kindred: The Lifesaver and Other Stories*.

Thus the beaches along the coast define Australia's margin: an apparently clearcut edge, a tangible boundary, but also an 'in between' space, a site where disparity is accommodated and where creative potential resides.

In descending from the heights of eagle and plane and contemplating the beach at ground-level, what seemed so well-defined from above now dissolves into something indeterminate. As the authors of 'The Beach' in *Myths of Oz* recognise,

> the beach is an anomalous category [a better word would be *ambiguous*—there are no anomalies in this zone of coincidence],

neither land nor sea, but has some characteristics of both . . . zones are vague, the boundaries ill-marked, if not unmarked, and consequently the categories and their meanings leak one into the other.[7]

This ambiguity affects even basic concepts, which, in the context of the beach, become confused and indefinite. In 'Bombora', when 'Annabel decided she wanted to go in', her intention was to go *into the water*; but sometimes a swimmer will say 'I'm going in', meaning that they are going *in(land)*, towards the beach. (For boardriders, in contrast, 'out' is *out the back*, towards what might be the perfect wave.) Because the beach is 'neither land nor sea', it is Janus-faced, looking towards and being both sea and land; thus Sanders perceives 'two beaches, one looking toward the sea ('closer to the body, to the drift') and the other across the beach to the suburb and the city beyond.

As well as being ambiguous, the beach is unpredictable. It changes constantly as waves and wind shape the distribution of its sand, and tides rise and fall. The size of the waves and the direction from which they roll onto the beach alter according to prevailing winds or forces generated by storms at sea. Visual evidence of flux is confirmed by rigorous scientific observation:

> The surf changes from moment to moment, day to day, and beach to beach. The waves are influenced by the bottom and the bottom is changed by the waves. And since the waves arriving at a beach are highly variable in height, period and direction, each wave creates a slightly different bottom configuration for the ones that come after it. The water level changes with the tide and the waves change as the storms at sea develop, shift position, and die out again. The result is that the sand bottom is forever being re-arranged. Even in glass-sided wave channels where an endless number of waves, each exactly the same, can be produced, equilibrium is never reached; the sand continues to change as long as the wave machine is running.
>
> Thus the waves change the sand at the same time the sand is changing the waves.[8]

The beach never *is*, is always *becoming*.

An important aspect of living on the margin, where the arbitrary throwing together of heterogeneous flotsam and jetsam precludes reliance on category and definition, is acceptance of ambiguity and difference, a preference for lack of closure and a resistance to boundaries separating one category from another. This is why Tim Winton, both in the 'edginess' of many of his characters and in his disregard of boundaries is a beach writer in a way that goes beyond the content of his fiction. Other writers have also made this preference explicit. Janette Turner Hospital celebrates the freedom this lack of definition, this ignoring of boundaries, affords:

> Something there is that doesn't love a boundary line. In the medieval *Books of Hours*, people step out of goldleaf miniatures and into the margins and sometimes right off the page . . . words put forth glowing tendrils . . . they swell and turn into gryphons, dragons, creatures of glowing crimson and lapis lazuli that are neither fish nor fowl, text nor subtext, not fully on this page and not quite on the next.
>
> . . . Listen, they murmur seductively: . . . rules are for transgressing, borders for crossing . . . Censors and critics alike overlook the margins. In the margins one is ignored, but one is free . . .
>
> Who decides what is margin and what is text? Who decides where the borders of the homelands run? Absences and silences are potent. It is the eloquent margins which frame the official history of the land . . .[9]

And David Malouf has stated that he 'just loathes the whole world of distinctions and categories . . . I don't believe in those distinctions between nature and man, men and women, body and soul; I don't believe in any of those dichotomies on which a lot of culture is based'.[10]

Accommodation of difference and preference for ambiguity

WHEN THE SIGNIFICANCE of the beach as edge or margin is considered, a number of somewhat contradictory associations come to mind. There is the idea of edge as 'edgy', of people 'on the edge', unstable, ready to topple over into madness or chaos. While aspects of their society arouse insecurity in Australians, many seem content to be on the edge or on the margin—on the beach, at least. There is a notable accommodation to other groups and interests in a relaxed

'Unexpected connections and apparent incongruities' at the beach.

The 'Surfboard riding in evening dress' competition during the Symphony on the Sand celebrations at Harbord beach.

Source: Courtesy of Warringah Council, and with the kind permission of James Rankin, JRP Photography

Santa Claus riding a surfboard on Dee Why beach.

Source: Warringah Library Local Studies Collection

A symphony orchestra plays classical music to beachgoers at the Symphony on the Sand concert on Harbord beach.

Source: Courtesy of Warringah Council, and with the kind permission of James Rankin, JRP Photography

The beach in the CBD: Southbank, Brisbane.

Source: The author's private collection

sharing of territory that is also generally found among crowds in celebratory events. Among these crowds can be observed an informality of dress and an ease of bodily movement, both of which may be a common feature of modern Western culture, but may also be augmented here by the unselfconscious freedom and sense of space experienced at the beach.

This judgement might seem to contradict the authors of 'The Beach' in *Myths of Oz* who, as is their wont, focus on 'clues to status and community role distinctions' within the beach crowd, citing the sociology of Cronulla Beach as revealed in *Puberty Blues*:

> There were three main sections of Cronulla Beach—South Cronulla, North Cronulla and Greenhills . . .
>
> That's where the top surfies hung out—the prettiest girls from school and the best surfies on the beach. The bad surfboard riders on their 'L' plates, the Italian family groups and the 'uncool' kids from Bankstown (Bankies), swarmed to South Cronulla—Dickheadland.[11]

Different beaches attract different kinds of beachgoers, often because of their proximity to particular suburbs with their differences in class composition; the 'image' of each beach in the popular imagination is different. It also goes without saying that wherever people collect, some are more conscious of others—for example, young children of other young children, adolescents of those of the opposite sex slightly older or younger, the voyeur and the exhibitionist, and so on. The real questions are whether the beaches are available to all and whether subgroups exclude others, whether subtly or blatantly; and Les Murray sums up both the appearance and the reality that underlie it:

> That strip of sand fifty to two hundred metres wide is a whole world, with tribes and subcultures. It is a capital location of the Kingdom of Flaunt . . . That kingdom has its aristocracies and its hangers on, its castes and scavengers, and everyone knows how he must behave to enter it. To oppose it is to lose, and to ignore it is to be relegated to the margins of life. Or so it is believed in the Kingdom of Flaunt. In fact, the margins are very roomy, and receive nearly everyone in the end . . .[12]

When Murray writes 'nearly everyone', he may be thinking about himself as an exception. He has written of his sensations as he, a large, bulky man, ventures back onto the beach where he endured agonies as a fat teenager:

> Back, in my fifties, fatter than I was then,
> I step on the sand, belch down slight horror to walk
> a wincing pit edge, waiting for the pistol shot
> laughter. Long greening waves cask themselves, foam
>   change
> sliding into Ocean's pocket. She turns: ridicule looks down
> strappy, with faces averted, or is glare and families.
> The great hawk of the beach is outstretched, point to point,
> quivering and hunting. Cars are the surf at its back.
> You peer, at this age, but it's still there, ridicule,
> the pistol that kills women, gets them killed, crippling men
> on the towel-spattered sand. Equality is dressed, neatly,
> with mouth still shut. Bared body is not equal ever . . .[13]

It is a measure of Murray's recovery from depression when he reports that he can appear on the beach now without feeling shame for the first time in his life: 'I reckon I could do the length of Bondi beach now, without even thinking about it', he says.[14]

Generally people take it for granted that everyone belongs on the beach provided they don't interfere with anyone else. This egalitarianism is one of the discourses discussed by Game: 'Everyone is happy here, together. Social harmony is possible. This discourse is evidently a denial of differences'.[15] One could argue that, in fact, there is not so much a denial of differences as a disregarding of them. This accommodation of difference is captured in Bob Graham's *Greetings from Sandy Beach*, a children's picture book that has gained such popularity since it was published in 1990 that it was one of four 'children's classics' featured in a set of Australian postage stamps in 1996.

Greetings from Sandy Beach begins with the family of two adults and two children preparing for a camping weekend at Sandy Beach. The story is told by the older child. At the campsite there are 'people on motorbikes':

> They were called The Disciples of Death.
>   Dad didn't like the look of them.
>   'Don't go near them', said my Dad.
>   'Stay away from them Gerald,' said my Mum.

The Disciples helped a struggling Dad to put up the family's tent: 'Dad looked nervous and smiled at them a lot.'

The weekend proves to be pleasant and memorable, all the disparate campers gaining something from each other's presence in a low-key fashion:

> They all passed us on the way home.
> First the bus, then The Disciples with their little white dog, his ears streaming in the wind.
> 'They were all right really', said my Dad.
> 'Once you got to know them', he added, a bit further down the road.[16]

Accommodation of difference and preference for open-endedness and ambiguity

Habits of accommodating or disregarding difference are consistent with the construction of a relatively harmonious lifestyle among people from a myriad of different backgrounds and lifestyles and the achievement of compromise, despite no-holds-barred rhetoric, which historically characterised industrial relations in this country. The sociologist Claudio Veliz claims that

> Australia is generally, and correctly, regarded by the rest of the world as an exceptionally law-abiding country with an unequalled history of peaceful and successful domestic arrangements ... Australian society and its polity have not only proved themselves able to withstand the imperfections and asymmetries of diversity, but have evidently thrived and prospered because of them ... an original and pragmatic arrangement whereby sovereignty, power and responsibility are efficiently shared by centre and periphery, without conflict or rupture, in a manner as successful as it is unprecedented.[17]

Reflecting on this viewpoint, it is interesting to study the cartoon by John Spooner on the next page. The postures of the onlookers are revealing. They are lounging, reading, enjoying the sun or the shade, but have modified their relaxed positions to indicate that they have noticed the Hitler figure. They do not encourage him by assuming attitudes of alert attention, however; nor do they cluster or move towards him, which would be to afford him some authority or power. They show a politeness that is very characteristic of Australians in public gatherings or performances: even where they disagree with a speaker or wish he would go away, they do not hiss him or boo him off the stage as others might—after all, if they wait a little while, the

tide will rise to wet his boots and he'll move on. Are they indifferent
to the problems of violence and evil in the world? Or is it simply that
the ranting of fanatics loses its power to persuade as it is dissipated
into the sky and the sea above and beyond? What is illustrated is a

'The problem raising a pogrom' (Hitler addressing a beach assembly) by John
Spooner.
Source: Reprinted with permission from *Quadrant*, November 1994, p. 23.

laissez-faire attitude, a courteous, if passive, refusal to engage with what is distasteful or extreme.

It can and will be readily pointed out that Australia has a xeno-phobic and racist history, a sorry record of discrimination and prejudice against Aboriginal people in particular. But, while being somewhat mystified as to the reasons why, Stephen Knight concludes that

> For many odd reasons Australians might be summed up as being one of the most racially tolerant, in an offhand way, of the peoples of the world ... When Geoffrey Blainey made statements about ... Asian immigration ... It was as if Australians were forced into a debate where they were uneasy ... [they] would have preferred a decent silence on the matter ... private views that many were willing to mutter to each other [they] were not able to countenance as a specific and voiced structure of values.[18]

This may account for some negative reactions to the concept of multiculturalism where it is perceived to encourage identification with particular ethnic categories rather than leaving such matters 'decently' unresolved.

Knight also notes the preference for the anti-heroic, for remembering military failures over military successes, and judges that 'much that is valuable in Australian society stems from the strange uncertainty. The virtue of nationalism here is its vagueness ... Consoling and destructive simplicities about the nation seem largely to be resisted in Australia'.[19] He refers to the 'contradictory and often curious patterns' of Australian culture, that 'inner contradiction of the national character, its sensitive soul behind the squinting mask, [which] has given Australian society for long a paradoxical quality'.[20]

Jan Morris writes in a similar vein of Sydney, the birthplace of twentieth-century Australian beach culture. Rejecting a glittery image of Sydney as 'far too explicit', she sees it as 'tantalisingly ambivalent ... not one of your absolute cities ... I was looking perhaps for the black-and-white, sharp-edged resolution that usually characterises showy young towns of ambition, and all I found instead, I thought, was aloofness and introspection'.[21]

To these observers, seemingly contradictory realities jostle each other, like flotsam and jetsam on the same stretch of beach.

The ambiguity at the heart of Australian life is expressed architecturally in the prominence of the verandah in Australian buildings—a degree of prominence that leads architect Phillip Drew in *The Coast Dwellers* to state that 'Australia is a verandah country inhabited by a verandah people'.[22] Just as the beach is neither land nor sea, so the verandah is neither inside the house nor outside it. The primary orientation of the verandah is to the outside, to openness rather than the enclosure of the house within.

Visiting the home of a European-Australian colleague I became sharply aware of this truth about our own culture. His living-room, the centre and heart of the house, was completely what I can only describe as 'indwelling', drawn in around its comfortable furnishings, no windows beckoning us outside, the outdoor environment an irrelevance. I have been in homes with verandahs attached, built by Australians who migrated as adults from Europe, but which they never use—their 'comfort zone', too, is inside, where their loved possessions are gathered and displayed. In contrast, many native-born Australians are restless unless their homes connect with the outside.

The verandah has evolved as society has developed here. At first it was a protective shell, shading the house from the too-fierce sun, shielding its inhabitants from the alien outside environment. Or it was added on when more space was needed—makeshift, impermanent, reflecting a sense of exile and displacement felt during the period when England was thought of as home. Today the verandah is often stripped back to become a 'deck' (note the maritime connotations), more frankly open to the outside than before. And we live by preference on the country's verandah, the coast.

Thus the sense of being at ease with ambiguity and preference for open-endedness noted above are reflected in the way we build and live in our homes. The verandah, deck or patio (as an extension to the outside is more grandly named, and slyly mocked in the phrase 'patio intellectuals') is an in-between, transitional place, a place to linger. This also corresponds to another significant property of the beach—its liminality.

Liminality

PHILLIP DREW IN *The Coast Dwellers* writes of the verandah—a threshold, neither inside nor outside—as associated with unwillingness to commit; here one is in a transitory state, therefore indefinite, impermanent. The beach is also a threshold, a liminal place. Here one is 'on the brink', between the two great worlds of land and sea, in a space where one can remain frozen and irresolute, or from which one can choose to move decisively into one realm or the other. Here one might pause while deciding to remain in a present situation, retreat to the past or step forward into the future unknown. Being on the threshold might also signify adaptability, a readiness to move from one state to another.

Metaphorically, the beach is a place of transition between one stage of life and the next—hence the number of occasions, in true life and in fiction, where people end their lives by deliberately crossing from the beach into the sea. Australians unconsciously respond to this liminality by enacting many of life's significant moments there.

Robert Drewe discovered that every Australian he knew had had his or her central physical and psychologically important events occur on or near the coast:

> Emotionally, they discover or lose themselves on the coast . . . most have their first sexual experience on or near the beach . . . For the rest of their lives, the beach, the coast, is not only a regular pleasure, a constant balm, but an idée fixe, an obsession that surfaces and resurfaces at each critical physical and emotional stage . . .[23]

Here a man might make decisions about his future, as reported in an article in the *Sydney Morning Herald* of 16 January 1998, headed 'Unemployed at last!' (the opening sentence of Joseph Furphy's *Such Is Life*):

> It was in the rough surf at Rainbow Beach just off the southern tip of Queensland's Fraser Island that Wayne Goss decided to quit politics.
>   'I just thought a man would have to be a mug to throw himself back into the discipline and the hours that professional politics require', he said.
>   'I came back from Rainbow Beach full of beans and enthusiasm, and not at all wanting to climb on a plane to go to Canberra . . . I'm free at last.'

Friends and families measure off the milestones of their lives against their annual reunions at beach houses or camping spots. To people past retirement age—like the men who gather at Bronte Beach celebrated in a poem by Les Wicks published in the Spectrum section of the *Sydney Morning Herald* of 4 April 1998, 'The Summer

Sumos'—the beach is a meeting-place, an Australian equivalent of
the town square, a place to ruminate on the world today and to watch
the passing parade:

> The tired metronome of half hearted waves   plop!
> can barely rise to the conspiracy being discussed
> by this mob on a griddle cement platform
> this six-pack of heartily beached whales.
> Man and bench merge
> to call themselves 'Doctor Bronte'.
> Allegedly gathered to swim but
> 'between swims' is a time that
> stretches over hours even
> 'discussion group' is a gentle deception,
> a form guide for the dogs or Italian politics their
> great brown guts attain a grace rare elsewhere.
> The Council would have to hire stand ins
> if they didn't come here
> like volunteer statuary . . .
> **They are the beach**
> their beer bellies institution like
> a series of tiny Ulurus
> from the gentle half of white Australia's dreaming.

It is clear that the beach is gradually becoming a major site of
significance for Australian culture. Ross Gibson has described Australia as 'meagrely historicised. Every plot of earth, every spike of
spinifex hasn't accrued a story, hasn't yet become a sign in the arbitrary system of meaning which is history'.[24] The beach in Australia is
'accruing stories', accumulating meaning in a way that is not easily
recognisable by those who would link cultural and spiritual significance with that which has been built, farmed or cultivated. Australians
are constructing a shared element of their culture through their
common experience of the beach.

In a society whose public spaces usually have the effect of excluding or ignoring them, there is a privileging of children at the beach:
the edge where the waves meet the sand is by common consent ceded
to them. Adults walking along the beach or heading into the surf
thread their way among sandworks, among small children dancing to
and fro through the advancing and retreating wave edge. Young adult
males boisterously engaged in vigorous activities like beach football

or throwing frisbees swerve away from the edge of the waves to avoid the children. Two things are happening here: the right of children to exercise their capacity for both pleasure and industry is accepted and encouraged; and a civilising process is at work, whereby children are being inducted into an aspect of their culture.

The emotional significance of the beach is often private and particular, less often a place where collective meaning is celebrated; but rituals, both public and private, are developing none the less. People visiting a beach for the first time walk from one end to the other, mapping it through the soles of their feet. Boards tucked under arms, surfers trot across the sand as if impatient to meet the waves. For travellers returning from overseas the first trip to the beach is a kind of symbolic homecoming. There is also a baptismal ritual: a young mother or father, sometimes both together, will lower their baby into the water at the edge of the surf. Gently and gradually the baby is introduced to the water, the parent watching the baby's face and body in order to monitor and enjoy the baby's response; and if it is positive, if the baby squeals with delight rather than shock or fear, the parent walks further into the water, the baby becoming accustomed to the movement and depth.

An Australian baptismal ritual: the baby experiences his first 'dip' at the beach.
Source: The author's private collection.

At the other end of life many choose to have their ashes scattered off the headland of their favourite beach. The scattering of ashes symbolises the crossing of the boundary between life and death, and possibly reflects a growing ability to accept the fact of our own death and to temper our fear of it—an ability that, according to Dorothy Dinnerstein's argument, is strengthened by our capacity to take joy from the moment and to live in the here and now. Evidence of cultural change in this direction is largely impressionistic; however, 'According to sociologist James H. Gadberry, writing in the US journal *Illness, Crisis and Loss*, Australia leads the world in enthusiasm for secular, celebratory services—"fun funerals" as they are known in the trade';[25] and an article by Paola Totaro, the daughter of Italian migrants, is also of interest in this respect. She explains that mention of death is taboo in her Italian family, and describes her apprehension as the funeral of her friend's father is arranged. Joining them after the funeral at their mother's house, 'ready to speak in whispers amid tears and horror', she is 'astounded' at how much happiness is mixed in with the tears: 'He had lived, he had loved, been loved and he had died. Simple as that'. The next day the mourners travel to the Catherine Hill Bay cemetery. 'The moment Jack's coffin was lowered into the ground, there was silence. Just the wind and the crash of the surf below.' Afterwards, another gathering. Totaro concludes:

> Not once did I witness the terror I had always associated with the concept of death itself . . . I've come to realise that it is not possible to truly understand a new culture until you immerse yourself in its most intimate moments, the profound events, those that are interlaced with the rituals of life and death . . . his loss gave me a new understanding of Australia, its people—his family—and death itself.[26]

A moving example of the spontaneous incorporation of the beach into a memorial ceremony following a tragic event occurred at the end of 1996 in Gracetown, a small surfing town on the south coast of Western Australia. Nine members of the community, five adults and four children, were killed when a sand cave beneath which they were sheltering as they watched a surfing contest collapsed and fell on them. The *West Australian* of 4 October 1996 described an official ceremony held a few days after the disaster at Huzza's, the section of Cowaramup Bay where the ill-fated surfing competition took place:

In a regal procession of black wetsuits and white boards, they [surfers] slipped into the water and paddled their boards into a circle around a group of family members.

They rose together on the gentle swell ... Then came their cheers of release, echoed by the hundreds [the crowd was put at more than 5000] lining the steep steps up to the carpark.

They held hands, threw flowers, lumps of seaweed, even a surf-board, with delight. Surfers emerged from the water exhilarated, all saying it made them feel better to have celebrated the lives of those who had loved that patch of water so much ... the rituals seemed to bring the mourning into a new phase.

These themes come together in a simple piece by Robert Dessaix, a contribution to a collection of responses for a magazine cover story entitled 'The Best Year of Their Lives'. Dessaix found it impossible to isolate a particular year, finding instead that his mind identified 'favourite moments':

I'm writing this in a house on a deserted cove on Kangaroo Island. The beach a few metres away is almost pink with dried-out kelp, and at this time in the evening there's a dribble of pink from the sky spattering the rockpools and the shallows as well. Out on the point there are cormorants hunched like dabs of ink. And looking out on all this, I realise I have had a hopelessly irregular life. It hasn't settled into years. I can't just rummage around in it for a favourite one.

So, with one eye on the cover and one on the small, white coffin-shaped box of Haigh's peppermint creams at my elbow, what comes to mind is that this very moment, as I write these words, is as good as perfect.[27]

In a characteristically graceful and oblique way, in Dessaix's description of the box of peppermint creams as 'coffin-shaped' he alludes to his awareness of his own mortality: appreciation of the joy of the moment, acceptance of inevitability of death, coming together in the beach setting.

The marking of events and moments of significance at the beach relates to the sense of the numinous and the transcendent noted previously. Such events and moments may constitute what could be described as invitations to spirituality in a society that has often and persuasively been described as 'determinedly secular ... unspiritual'.[28] Historian Patrick O'Farrell writes that 'In Australia ... what is most significant historically about religion is its weakness, its efforts to achieve some strength, its tenuous and intermittent hold on the minds and hearts of Australian people, its peripheral or subordinate relation to their main concerns'.[29] In his painting *Christmas Eve* (1948) John Perceval situates the nativity scene, complete with donkey and manger, in an Australian beachside town, showing the assimilation of the Christmas story into the Australian landscape; but the town's inhabitants are too busy killing and plucking chooks for the Christmas feast or roistering on the beach and amongst the waves to take much notice.

And yet, in what may be a search for spiritual meaning, Australians have, as Knight notes,

> a fascination for an unpeopled landscape that verges on the mystical . . . For white Australia, communion with nature in this country is a means of non-communication with the former owners of the land; the ecological movement, so strong here, is a movement that prefers no people at all . . . It's not that more magic is needed in the Australian people, but that more people are needed in the Australian magic.[30]

In novels cited in the previous chapter it is the peopled beach that provokes apprehensions of transcendence, even if the peopling is by a solitary figure: a surfer observed by Miss Harcourt in David Malouf's *Fly Away Peter*, and the gold of the narrator's girlfriend's body, and the slap of the water as she dives, in Bill Green's *Freud and the Nazis Go Surfing*. It is as if the immensity and timelessness of nature stands at one pole of meaning and the precious fragility and ephemerality of human existence at the other, each drawing significance from the other.

It may be the case that the search for spiritual nourishment in solitary wilderness is misguided. There is food for thought in a notice in the Visitors' Centre at Strahan in Tasmania, where thousands of tourists take cruises up the wild Gordon River to gaze at the silent primeval forests that loom over its banks:

> Wilderness . . . is imagined as the profound opposite of much that we find repugnant about our modern world; natural as contrasted with artificial . . . spiritualism as against materialism. But rather than addressing humanity's divorce from its soul, this idea of wilderness simply reproduces it.
>
> Perhaps this idea of wilderness is inadequate, and what we need are new ideas—of something as valuable because it means something to us . . . Such a step will only be possible when we cease to regard wilderness as something separate from ourselves.

Even traditional religion seems to be edging its way towards the beach, sensing that if it is truly to take root it will need to grow in places defined as spiritual by those who live here—not the cathedrals and inside spaces where generations of Europeans have found inspiration. (This applies to the bush as well. Recently I visited the little stone courthouse at Hartley, in the valley just westward of the Blue Mountains. We stood in the courtroom with its solid polished wooden furniture and cream walls, listening to a recording of a trial. There was a window high up in the wall above the judge's bench, through which could be seen a patterning of eucalyptus leaves with sunlight sparkling on them, a sky of shockingly vivid blue; and the heavenly liquid carolling of magpies tempting us outside. I had never felt the alienness of imported institutions and architecture so acutely.)

Ken Cafe is both a Franciscan friar and a Bronte lifesaver. Formerly a chief inspector at Bronte Surf Life Saving Club, in 1997 he became the first Sydneysider in twenty-five years to be ordained a Franciscan

The wholeness of joyful body and spirit in the 'holy waters' of Bronte beach: Franciscan friar Ken Cafe, former beach inspector and Bronte Surf Life Saving Club member for more than twenty-six years, celebrates his ordination.
Source: Photograph by Andrew Taylor/*Sydney Morning Herald*

friar at the Church of Mary Immaculate, Waverley. The *Sydney Morning Herald* of 8 February reported that Father Cafe spent the morning before his ordination watching the sun rise over Bronte Beach. 'I feel Bronte is a holy place', he said. 'I am as much at home on the beach or in the surf club as I am in a church. There's no reason why I can't use water from Bronte beach for baptisms.'

A notice in front of a church in Mosman announced that the Easter service would be held on the island on Balmoral Beach (weather permitting!). And for three years an annual beach service, with a sand pulpit constructed shortly beforehand, has been held on the beach beside Manly wharf. 'We thought, "Why not actually hold church on the beach in our familiar surroundings?" So it has become an annual event which we love', the assistant Anglican minister at Manly beach said, according to the *Manly Daily* on 19 January 1999. 'Because we are a beach culture and many of our congregation are dedicated surfers, the beach is a comfortable place to gather for church.'

Meaghan Morris wrote that 'had he [Stephen Knight] spent more time at the beach, he might have learned something about spirituality in our "secular" society (most Australians, I think, are pantheists)'.[31] While the contribution of the natural world to the development of an authentic Australian spirituality is yet to be adequately explored, a number of recent publications indicate that this task is beginning to be addressed.[32]

In Greg Dening's *Islands and Beaches* 'beach' stands as a metaphor for the boundary that people, ideas and other cultural phenomena must cross to create a new or to change an existing culture, with 'island' in its turn a metaphor for the culture that is being changed or constructed. Dening sees the beach being used to represent a boundary between here and there, us and them, good and bad, the familiar and the strange.

In Australia the 'beach' has been absorbed into the 'island', and Dening's dichotomies do not apply. The beach is less a boundary than a zone of creativity where ambiguities and possibilities flourish. It is a source of new meanings that are shaping Australian society, tempering the 'absence of inner meaning, inner life' so perceptively noted by D. H. Lawrence on his brief visit here in the early part of the twentieth century.

16

Balancing Acts

Poverty prevented me from thinking that all is well under the sun and in history; the sun taught me that history is not everything.
—Albert Camus, quoted in Drewe's introduction to *The Picador Book of the Beach*, p. 5.

Australians, the beach and history

THE PLACE WHERE I LIVE now is a home unit—not the house on a quarter-acre block that has traditionally been the childhood or family home of most Australians of my generation. Yet the space around the block on which our building stands is quintessentially Australian in at least two important respects.

This is 'beachfront land': I step through a gate in the fence onto a long curving strip of sand where the surf endlessly crashes, and from my window I can watch boardriders carving the swells in their water ballet; people walking along the beach parallel to the fringing waves; or solitary figures standing still and facing the rising sun as if in prayer or meditation.

If I turn my back on the beach and look out towards the road, there is a grassy central traffic island where, screened by wind-warped teatree so that one hardly notices it is there, stands a memorial to those who gave their lives in Australia's wars. There is the flagpole, stone steps leading to the altar-like monument of granite on which is inscribed in gold-leaf lettering:

In loving memory of those who died
And appreciation of all who served
1914–1918
1939–1945

Korea, Malaya and Vietnam are also there in brighter gold, indicating their more recent addition.

These two spaces—the beach and the war memorial—symbolise two of the drives identified by Dorothy Dinnerstein: the desire to live in the senses and for pure joy of the moment, and the desire to be part of history, to prove our worth to the denizens of the real world over the other side of the equator.

When Europeans settled in Australia, they entered a land apparently bereft of history. To many of the colonists, the Aboriginal people were prehistoric; at best, they seemed to live in an a-historical vacuum. In his apologia, 'The Beauties of Australia' (1838), William Woolls admits that 'this colony is not only devoid of any venerable remains of antiquity, but that it also is deficient in those interesting scenes which contribute so much to enliven and dignify the histories of other countries'; but he argues that Australia presents other 'objects of interest to persons of a refined taste': 'She may, indeed, be poor in works of art, but she is rich in those of nature. Instead of splendid piles and glorious triumphs, she can boast of her clear Italian sky, her woolly flocks, her vine and fig'.[1]

For many, these attractions have been insufficient compensation for a sense of being left out of history-making, an activity that was the prerogative of nations of the Old World, 'up there' in the Northern Hemisphere (up there being a kind of 'hemispherist' fallacy: the notion that the map of the world is naturally read from north to south, top to bottom, Old World on top, Southern Hemisphere below, with all the consequent connotations and evaluations). If we look at early photographs of crowds on the beach, it is notable how many people stand looking directly out to sea. On the edge of the continent they look outwards, over the horizon. One interpretation of this orientation is to suggest that, as migrants crowd the deck of the ship for the last glimpse of their homeland, so Australians, mostly descendants of Europeans exiled as far from their homeland as it is possible to be, cut off by the vast oceans, huddle on the edge and mourn their isolation.

'To go overseas' has for generations been the ambition of young Australians. The immensity of the sky over the empty horizon becomes a *tabula rasa* onto which can be projected one's hopes, expectations, the belief that things are better, brighter, more interesting 'over there' (a belief fostered for many years by the Anglocentric teaching of subjects such as history, geography and literature in schools and universities). Hence our deference to 'overseas experts', our desire for travel, our avid interrogation of travellers arriving on our shores, our enthusiastic adoption of fads and fashions from overseas, and the departure of so many of Australia's writers and intellectuals to live and work abroad. Peter Goodall writes of the period 1890–1930:

> Many of the people who might have formed the cultural avant-garde of Australia left the country, spending long periods overseas ... or in many cases not returning at all. The phenomenon of expatriation is one of the most striking in the period. Over one-third of Australian Rhodes scholars never returned to their native land.[2]

Such an observation would have been close to the truth during most of our history. Phillip Drew in *The Coast Dwellers* asks: 'Is Australia really so unlovable that we need to run away to travel, for an education, to see relatives, to fight in wars, to get ahead? It seems that almost any excuse will do'.[3] But is it just the unlovability of Australia that drives the impulse to leave—or a more fundamental attraction to something we sense that *overseas* will be able to provide? As wars break out in the northern hemisphere, young men from all over Australia eagerly join the call to arms, seizing the opportunity to participate in battles being fought in distant countries, risking death for causes of which they have little understanding.

How do we explain such a response? C. E. W. Bean, Australian war correspondent and historian, acknowledged the mixture of motives that drove young men, 'all the romantic, quixotic, adventurous flotsam that eddied on the surface of the Australian people' to enlist in World War I.[4] Dinnerstein's history-making drive, towards engagement in 'memorable event' and 'durable achievement' is none the less powerful for being unconscious and implicit in the motives discerned by Bean. It was as if Australians sought to legitimate their claim to membership of Western civilisation by joining its long procession of noble warriors; having, as Robin Gerster sardonically noted, 'somehow atavistically inherited the transcendent qualities of the legendary Trojan battlefield so tantalisingly close to Gallipoli itself'.[5] George Johnston wrote in similar vein of the soldiers as 'throwbacks to the earlier golden time when gods and men walked the earth together'.[6]

Even for those with no aspirations to the heroic, the lure of historic circumstance could prove irresistible. Jim in David Malouf's *Fly Away Peter* spends all his time birdwatching among the dunes, and is content with his life. But World War I is declared, those around him join up with alacrity, and

> It was as if the ground before him, that had only minutes ago stretched away to a clear future, tilted in the direction of Europe, in the direction of *events*, and they were all now on a dangerous slope . . . Jim felt the ground tilting, as he had felt it that first day in Brisbane, to the place where the war was, and felt the drag upon him of all those deaths. The time would come when he wouldn't be able any longer to resist. He would slide with the rest. Down into the pit . . .

Soon Jim bows to the inevitable, enlists, and waits to be sent overseas:

> If he didn't go, he had decided, he would never understand, when it was over, why his life and everything he had known were so changed, and nobody would be able to tell him. He would spend his whole life wondering what had happened to him and looking into the eyes of others to find out.[7]

Jim enters a new world of mud, blood and confusion. But even as he endures all the horror around him, Jim senses that being human involves the knowledge, if necessary through first-hand experience, that such things are possible:

> Jim saw that he had been living, till he came here, in a state of dangerous innocence. The world when you looked at it from both sides was quite other than a placid, slow-moving dream, without change of climate or colour and with time and place for all. He had been blind.[8]

This 'dangerous innocence' is shown in sharp relief in a moving scene in the film *Gallipoli* (1981). The troopships carrying Australian soldiers have arrived in Anzac Cove and, waiting for the invasion to commence, the soldiers respond to the transparent sea around them by shedding their uniforms and diving into the water. It is a scene of innocent delight as they frolic in the sparkling water, engaging in the horseplay so often enjoyed at home—they are only boys. Then suddenly, the shock, the disbelief, as bullets rain down and the clear, pure water becomes discoloured with blood.

The film does not tamper with historic reality in this scene. Bean wrote: 'the salvation of the troops [was] sea-bathing . . . From the day when first a section of the troops was withdrawn from the line to rest, bathing became the one officially approved recreation'.[9]

In his straightforward way and from a soldier's point of view, Albert Facey in *A Fortunate Life* recalled swimming at Gallipoli as the only enjoyable moments of an otherwise terrible experience:

> When we were resting we were allowed to go down to the beach and have a swim, but only near headquarters. The beach nearest to our position was within range of Turkish snipers and would have been too dangerous. The bay was continuously under shell-fire but this didn't worry us because we could hear a shrapnel shell coming and would dive under the water just before it exploded.
>
> We used to go on the swimming trips a section at a time under the command of a sergeant. We enjoyed them very much and were able to get ourselves clean.[10]

Bean describes these incongruous scenes in his more expansive style:

> Many of the Australians who were accustomed to sun-bathing in their seaside resorts at home, and those whose business was in the Cove quickly discarded their shirts, amusing themselves with an informal competition to become 'the brownest man on the beach' . . . by midsummer their skins were in many cases tanned darker than those of the occasional Turkish prisoners. When the struggle of the Landing had subsided, the Beach on summer days reminded many onlookers of an Australian coastal holiday-place . . . in the water the hundreds of bathers, and on the hillside the little tracks winding through the low scrub, irresistibly recalled the Manly of New South Wales or the Victorian Sorrento.[11]

Men at play in the midst of war: soldiers swimming in the sea after returning from the trenches, Gallipoli, 1915.

Source: Australian War Memorial number GO 9269.

Men at war in the midst of play? The march-past competition at the Bronte Surf Carnival in 1931. In the precision and order of the lifesavers' marching, the flags, the 'battle formation', the beach setting is reminiscent of a military parade ground.

Source: Waverley Library Local Studies Collection

Such relaxation became more and more valued as the campaign dragged on, despite ever-present and escalating danger from the Turkish snipers:

> In June the bathing became so popular that the beach took on some of the appearance of a health resort. On June 20, for example —a drowsy midsummer Sunday—404 men were counted at one time either in the water or sun-bathing, and many more sitting half-dressed, browning their backs or dressing or undressing. The result was that about this date those of the enemy's guns which normally shelled the Beach began to be frequently turned upon the bathers . . . Birdwood, although this fact was represented to him, refused to interfere with the bathing . . . he was convinced that the recreation was of great moral and physical value to the troops. The bathing continued, in spite of frequent bombardments and the consequent casualties, from the Landing until the Evacuation.[12]

Bean had described the enlisting men as 'flotsam'; he went on to paint these memorable word pictures of men at play in the midst of war. And it is worth noting that Bean, for all his propensity to draw on bush imagery and ideology in his descriptions of the soldiers, and his disparaging judgment that *true* Australians are nurtured in the bush, not among the sea-beaches and soft breezes of the coast, did more than any other writer to establish as the quintessential Australian war legend the story of the Anzacs at Gallipoli—a battle fought on a beach. Bean was passionate about the significance of the campaign: 'In no unreal sense, it was on 25th April, 1915 that the consciousness of Australian nationhood was born'.[13]

But his account really begs the question: what was it about this particular campaign above all others that crystallised this nascent 'consciousness'? In its theme of stubborn, brave endurance against hopeless odds, Gallipoli echoes and reinforces the bush myth of stoic resistance; but any number of other battles exemplifying these same qualities could have been the subject of legend. Undoubtedly the primacy of Gallipoli was an important factor: it came early, before enthusiasm for the war as a noble cause had been eroded by the bitter realities of casualty, suffering and stalemate. But it is also possible to suggest that the focus on the beach at Anzac Cove had something to do with the significance it soon acquired and maintained.

With its curve of sand and the tracks winding down the sandhills through low heathy shrub, this was a beach like the beaches already familiar to Australians; and so for those at home, as well as the soldiers themselves, there was a connection, something to be recognised in the otherwise unimaginable (or romanticised) 'theatre' of war. There was a kind of symmetry, too: when the Australians landed on the beach at Anzac—another 'fatal shore'—as part of an invading force, they were also asserting their right to participate in events of significance in the real (Northern Hemisphere) world—a world their ancestors had relinquished when they invaded the Great South Land by landing on the beaches there nearly 130 years earlier (though acknowledgement of settlement-as-invasion was firmly repressed into the national unconscious at this time).

When they were forced to remain 'on the edge', as attempts to advance were repelled, the Anzacs occupied a zone that was not visibly enculturated. Just as the beaches in Australia resisted appropriation and cultivation, so the beach at Anzac bore no obvious stamp of Turkish civilisation. In the months they were there the Australian soldiers impressed their identity on the beach for those back home— as the beach itself constructed their identity as Anzacs—in a way that was not possible where battles occurred in the interior, on the 'native land' of the countries they helped defend. And the beach was a war/no-war zone, acquiring the features of a 'health resort', 'a coastal holiday-place', at the same time as it remained a site of 'frequent bombardment', 'shellfire' and 'casualties'. It thereby manifested the ambiguity that I have identified as one of the key aspects of the meaning of the beach. On the beach at Gallipoli two very different modes-of-being-in-the-world coalesced and clashed.

In creating the legend of the Anzacs at Gallipoli Bean had drawn heavily on 'The most enduring myth of the Australian national character . . . the populist figure of the bushman'.[14] He wrote that

> The Australian was half a soldier before the war; indeed through-out the war . . . the Australian soldier differed very little from the Australian who at home rides the station boundaries every week-day and sits of a Sunday round the stockyard fence . . . in general country life produces a much better soldier than city life . . .[15]

But towards the end of his *Official History* Bean had to admit that the figures were against him: only 57 000 out of 350 000 who had enlisted gave 'country callings' as their occupation;[16] and among the city soldiers lifesavers were well represented.

Between World Wars I and II the lifesavers maintained the continuity of an important cultural tradition. Egalitarianism, absence of social distinctions and mateship were seen as qualities shared by soldiers and lifesavers, as well as bushmen. There was also continuity in the tradition of standing by your mates and, as Ed Jaggard points out, a similar 'larrikinism and deliberate flouting of authority'.[17]

After World War I, as the lifesaver took over from the soldier as a type of national hero—moreover, an *urban* hero appropriate for a nation whose population increasingly lived in the suburbs of its cities—the ethos of the individual bushman or soldier and his loyalty to his mates became an ideal of community service. There is a continuity in this regard for service to the community as the highest good that is interesting to note. For all Robin Gerster's contempt for the promotion of 'the Digger' as the exemplar of heroic racial characteristics by Australian war writers, I would argue that the most widely remembered heroes of the two wars, respectively, are Simpson and his donkey, from Gallipoli, and Captain Edward 'Weary' Dunlop. Neither is revered for feats of daring in the heat of combat, but in Simpson's case for rescuing the dead and wounded without regard for his own life; in Dunlop's for his care for his fellow prisoners-of-war in the camp at Changi, far from the lines of battle. A recent incarnation of the hero Australian, the bushfire-fighter, maintains the continuity of this ideal. And in respect of the lifesavers, it is summed up by Maxwell, who writes of the lifesaving clubs that they foster 'a spirit of selflessness, of chivalry, such as is found in no other sporting movement in all the world today, not counting the cost when a life is for the saving'.[18]

In *Resuscitation*, E. A. Holloway's 1940 painting showing lifesavers attending to a rescued person, in a photograph of lifesavers working to resuscitate those rescued on Black Sunday 1938, and in monuments built to honour the memory of Simpson and 'Weary' Dunlop, the similarities in the way the figures are grouped are striking. They stand or kneel in nurturant posture, tending to the distressed and the fallen.

The martial qualities of the lifesaver-hero are implicitly acknowledged in descriptions such as 'Samurais [*sic*]',[19] and the titles of books about lifesaving: *Gladiators of the Surf* by Barry Galton; *Surf: Australians Against the Sea* by C. Bede Maxwell; *A Challenge Answered* by Edwin

Jaggard; *The Guardians of Our Beaches* by P. Worthington; and *Vigilant and Victorious* by Sean Brawley. Parallels are explicitly drawn: Maxwell quotes a tribute to a lifesaver turned soldier, and recognises the link between training for lifesaving and for war:

> it is possible that the qualities of courage and endurance which enabled him [a former lifesaver who was awarded the Military Cross] and so many Australian men of his generation, to win the name of 'Anzacs' were strengthened first in the strenuous and often dangerous game of 'shooting the breakers' he played every week-end at Maroubra . . . They [lifesavers] made good soldiers, good sailors, grand airmen. They fitted easily into service life, took drilling in their stride, and the disciplinary vigour of the most case-hardened sar'-major left them unshaken, they who had qualified for their Bronze Medallions under the lash of club instructor's tongues.[20]

George Philip asked rhetorically:

> Cannot the work of Surf and Life-Saving Clubs be compared to any army: one is trained to save the life of the individual, the other to fight for his country? Is the comparing of the March Past illogical? The true test of both is on their different fields of battle . . .[21]

The 'different fields of battle' seemed to merge on a memorable day at Bondi in February 1938, which became known as 'Black Sunday'. The drama of the event is worth recounting in some detail. It was a very hot day with a vigorous surf. In the morning the high tide and rough sea kept most people from venturing in too far. Recognising potential trouble, the surf club captain had the patrol on duty bring down extra reels to the edge of the surf. As the tide fell, hundreds moved further into the water onto a sandbank. In mid-afternoon several large waves swept everyone off the sandbank into a deep channel and the surging sea. Beltmen raced into the sea and the many lifesavers on the beach that afternoon grabbed whatever they could find that might support those in trouble—more than two hundred of them. Mothers were crying for their children, and on every line as it was pulled in ten or twenty panic-stricken people were hanging on for dear life: 'The clubmen began bringing in drowning victims, one by one. In a short space of time *the beach resembled a battleground, with bodies everywhere* being given the resuscitation that would give life back to most'.[22]

About 250 bathers required help; 150 were rescued unharmed; 60 were suffering from immersion, 35 were rescued unconscious, and five people were dead. An American doctor who was on the beach that day commented at the inquest that 'This rescue business is a labour of love, the like of which the world cannot show anywhere else'.[23] I discovered years afterwards that one of my uncles had been involved in the rescue that day, but he glossed over it lightly, preferring to reminisce about the comradeship he found at the club: 'It was our life. I grew up in a beach culture, our beach community a tightly-knit group. We felt our job was important to us and to the community'.

Recently an attempt has been made to pass on the mantle of warrior-hero on to the boardriders, the surfing champions. Wayne 'Rabbit' Bartholomew and Tim Baker's *Busting Down the Door: The Wayne 'Rabbit' Bartholomew Story* tells how in 1978 the Australian surfer Wayne Bartholomew was beaten up by Hawaiian rivals stung by the success of a cocky outsider who seemed out to 'steal the last vestige of their heritage—surfing'. Baker noted:

> That whole story is a really proud but largely overlooked chapter in Australian sporting achievement in its finest tradition, the whole Anzac spirit of battling against all odds. The Australians going to Hawaii is not a million miles away from jumping out of the trenches and running into gunfire. It'd be great if the Australian mainstream could recognise that as a proud chapter in our history'.[24]

(In the eyes of some surfers, however, Bartholomew deserved a hiding for going to Hawaii and not respecting local customs.)

Today the glory days of the lifesaving clubs may be past, but they still flourish; there are over 260 surf clubs and 75 000 volunteer lifesavers performing an average of 10 000 rescues a year. Surf lifesaving competitions are still huge, the surfboat races and 'iron person' competitions fiercely fought and spectacular; but the march-past teams with their flags and the military precision of their disciplined marching, once the highlight of their carnivals, have dwindled away to a few remnant teams of older men with spreading girths, many clubs now only represented by youngsters, often girls. The lifesaving movement has indeed been 'a labour of love', with its participants in its heyday achieving a felicitous balance between, or a reconciliation of, Dinnerstein's 'joy of successful activity'—the satisfaction to be gained through 'the effortful achievement of purpose'[26]—and the taking of pleasure in the moment that the beach represents.

The beach, work and play

ATTACHMENT TO THE BEACH and its delights has often been seen as a temptation to indolence and to the evasion of challenge. Yet if Dinnerstein is right, pleasure such as the beach can provide should enhance and supplement 'the pleasure in exercising our talents for cerebration and complex effort, and in using our power to make at least some things happen'.[25] While work, or enterprise, cannot substitute for 'the direct recapture of . . . erotic intercourse with the surround', there is a 'direct primary pleasure' in intellectual work, and it is an erotic pleasure in that it involves 'the enjoyable exercise of a physiological capacity'. Dinnerstein thus accords intellectual activity an instinctual, healthy status, giving us 'pleasure as straightforward as the pleasure of lovemaking, or looking, or listening . . . this pleasure induces us to act in ways that turn out to keep us alive'.[27]

Is there a connection between the pleasure of erotic use of the higher central nervous system and the 'direct recapture of erotic intercourse with the surround' experienced at the beach? The answer to such a question is inevitably subjective; but if the beach is narrowly construed as the very edge between land and sea, the moving fringe where the waves swell and crash foaming onto the sand, then it is likely that most would answer in the negative. The body's interaction with the dynamic matrix is almost totally physical, an occasion of sensation rather than cerebration.

To the extent that one moves away from the zone of perpetual motion, however, motives more akin to work may come into play— the word 'play' being appropriate here, as 'pleasure gained from the effortful achievement of purpose' is suffused with the playfulness that characterises the beach experience—a playfulness of mind as well as of body. It is no mere coincidence that Sir Isaac Newton summed up his life of scientific inquiry and achievement in the image of a child on the beach: 'To myself I seem to have been only like a boy playing on the sea-shore, and diverting myself now and then finding a smoother pebble or prettier shell than ordinary, while the great ocean of truth lay all undiscovered before me'.[28]

Recalling this statement of Newton's, the historian Jacques Barzun argues that

> Out of man's mind in free play comes the creation Science. It renews itself, like the generations, thanks to an activity which is the best game of *homo ludens* ... Science is play because of the very meaning of free inquiry: not this or that urgent result, but *laisser faire, laisser jouer*.[29]

This quotation from Barzun in its turn recalls the words of the theologian Jacob Boehme I quoted in the Introduction—that the 'inward divine man [should] play with the outward in the revealed wonders of God in this world, and open the Divine Wisdom in all creatures'. The implication is that an element of play is integral to genuine intellectual activity. Yet the two are more often seen as opposites, reflecting a prevalent dualism in Western metaphysical thinking noted by Norman Brown in *Life Against Death: The Psycho-analytic Meaning of History*. Brown believes that 'mankind will not cease from discontent until the antinomy of economics and love, work and play, is overcome'.[30]

The dissolving of boundaries: children squeal with delight as waves crash over the pool wall at high tide.

Source: The author's private collection

For children at the beach, this antinomy is erased: purpose de-velops out of play as those infinitely plastic materials, sand and water, are encountered in a setting free of imposed demands and expecta-tions. Children build and decorate elaborate and extensive sandworks with an energy and singlemindedness of purpose worthy of an engineer, builder or architect absorbed in a favourite project. As the tide comes in and washes away constructions that may have taken hours to build, other lessons are learned: of the fragility and ephemerality of human achievement; and of how to relinquish gracefully the products of one's labours when these have been superseded or destroyed.

Some adults find that the beach is not only compatible with but even facilitates focused intellectual activity:

> In my experience, the beach is a place that allows greater contem-plation, as well as no contemplation at all. It is a very cerebral place; it allows you to focus on certain matters and think of nothing else; and its honesty encourages clarity of thinking.[31]

For many, reading on the beach—a cerebral activity, if sometimes not a particularly demanding one—is part of the enjoyment of being there. Don Anderson, noting that the cover of an issue of *The Times Literary Supplement* devoted to Australia featured Anne Zahalka's 1989 photograph 'The Bathers', asks rhetorically: 'What is missing? What is the absence that speaks louder than the wild waves in *Dombey and Son* or off Bondi? There is not a book in sight. And we the nation with the highest per capita book-buying habit in the world'.[32]

Perhaps Anderson is suggesting that there is a connection between 'the highest per capita book buying habit' and the popularity of the beach, and that in portraying one without the other a stereotype of mindless activity is perpetuated, one that distorts reality. For visitors and newcomers do often suspect that enjoyment of the beach is incompatible with sustained intellectual effort. John Douglas Pringle in *Australian Accent* complained: 'It is, as I know by experience, a hard thing to read or write after a day spent in the dazzle and thunder of the surf . . . Everything seems to discourage intellectual effort in a nation where intellectual effort has never been highly regarded'.[33]

But Stephen Knight, another Englishman (of Welsh parents), who lived here longer than Pringle had when he wrote those words, perceives things differently:

Australians have constructed a culture which is remarkably intellectual . . . Australian life offers rich evidence for the existence of a
vigorous, responsible and self-generating intellectual sphere [despite
the fact that] its actual intellectual virtues have been unexpressed and
set in the shadows of the simplistic Aussieramas of popular wisdom.[34]

These contradictory judgements suggest that first impressions can
be confusing, and that the relationship between work, intellectual
effort and the enjoyment of the beach is not a simple one.

When one is swimming 'off the beach' the obsessive focus on fitness
or performance that is encouraged by the constraints of a narrow pool
built for swimming laps is attenuated by the unpredictable swell of the
waves and the overwhelming presence of sea and sky, perhaps to be
replaced by playful reverie, a sense of one's smallness in the scheme of
things. And in the pools sculpted into rock platforms at the ends of
beaches, the manufactured component of built walls is dominated by
the natural surround of sea, beach and sky, sand and shells. While the
pool wall may seem a solid barrier to the sea, it is an illusory boundary,
for at high tide the waves wash over it and swimmers' bodies undulate
in the swelling water.

In the end, the most obvious connection between the beach and
the world of history-making and enterprise is the beach's capacity to
re-energise us in its 'fountain of play and erotic exuberance'[35] when
we are exhausted by that world:

Something miraculous happens, thinks David, when you dive into
the surf at Bondi after a bad summer's day. Today had been humid
and grim, full of sticky tension . . . He'd had professional and
private troubles, general malaise and misery pounding behind his
eyes as he drove home to his flat . . . He was still bruised from
his marriage dissolution, abraded from the ending of a love
affair, and all the way up William Street the car radio news had
elaborated on a pop star's heroin and tequila overdose. Then in
New South Head Road it warned that child prostitution was rife
and economic depression imminent. Markets tumbled and kids
sold themselves . . . He'd have a swim.
  The electric cleansing of the surf is astonishing, the cold
effervescing over the head and trunk and limbs. And the internal
results are a greater wonder. At once the spirits lift. There is a
grateful pleasure in the last hour of softer December daylight. The
brain sharpens. The body is charged with agility and grubby
lethargy swept away . . . He feels that he could swim forever.[36]

Urban beaches like Bondi facilitate the interweaving of work and play in the lives of many who go there. This interweaving is illustrated in a popular children's picture book, *The Tram to Bondi Beach* by Elizabeth Hathorn. The picture on the title page is a double spread of people at the beach; but the next page, the first page of the story, shows people in trams on their way to work. The story tells of Kieran's induction into the world of work as a paperboy on the trams. Kieran and his sister play in the surf at the beach, but the focus of the story is on Kieran trying become a better paperboy, coming into conflict with a rival, then eventually befriending his rival and selling papers in a new spot, on the beachfront. Kieran's pride in his work and his ambition have developed in the context of the beach life, which is portrayed in delicately beautiful drawings.

The beach is the place for a morning dip or jog on the beach before going to work; it is close enough for a quick swim at lunchtime or between shifts: 'Lunch break surfers surf in and out';[37] 'time out' can be taken between work and home by surfing at the end of the working day. The beach is not separate, a place for holidays remote from the workaday world, but very much part of it.

Because the beach is a place to experience directly rather than a story to tell, we are often unaware of the part it plays in people's lives. Its presence becomes manifest in unexpected contexts, as in a review by music critic John Clare in the *Sydney Morning Herald* of 18 March 1996:

> How many stupendous events can an exhausted interviewer take within 24 hours? First there was Bronte's day-long succession of pinnacle waves: a surf such as you rarely get more than once in a season. Then there was Judi Connelli's final concert before she heads off to New York . . .

Ease of access to the beach encourages the achievement of a dynamic balance between work and play, or a place where people can be observed 'stealing ecstasy from the monotony of their workaday lives'[38]—an idea that is reflected, with a sting in the closing line, in one of Bruce Beaver's poems:

> It is that hour of the early evening
> when the time-pressed clerks
> and the shop-girls drift wanly
> homeward, another day worn off

their lives by an egregious friction
of wasted hours rubbed together
in a time-clock's steely bowels.
But the day itself has been so
fair, and is now; so bright
and laced by exquisite breezes
I imagine the people running
through the effervescent shallows
or lazing on the wide, glowing
sands, or trailing fingers in
cool wavelets, the hair blown
back, the eyes filled with blue
vistas and the golden light
of the sun coins spun through
the deep air, or sitting on shaded
balconies that face the fading
east or aspiring west, both satisfying
the dreamed of well-being only the
habitually exploited can imagine.[39]

17

Present and Future Challenges

Reconciliations

THE QUESTION OF HOW FAR a balance is achieved in the lives of most Australians as far as history-making is concerned is problematic. A hunger to go overseas, to be involved in the 'real' world where history is made, is evident. Australians still go to the other side of the world to participate in other people's wars. In peacetime, we are driven by a great curiosity about the rest of the world, a sense that it provides experiences and truths that are not available here, and we travel widely. We still feel a need for achievement, fame and fortune to be validated by overseas recognition.

Stephen Knight has recognised a link between Australia's 'successful but anxious' society and 'the source of disturbing silence' that is our history.[1] Meaghan Morris also comments:

> Peter Sutton suggests one source of indifference to Aboriginal people is our own history of assimilation and amnesia, growing up post-war without a sense of ancestry or tradition, or any cultural means with which to *miss* such things. Faced with immemoriality, we are sceptical. Deep down, we suspect it's a scam.[2]

Modern Australian history began on the beach, where two vastly different cultures briefly overlapped before their withdrawal into

'A brief, fragile moment of engagement': a sailor and an Aboriginal man dance a jig together as others catch and distribute fish.

V. (Victor-Jean) Adam (1801–66), *Baie Jervis, Nouvelle Hollande, les marins de l'Astrolabe partagent leur peche avec les naturels* [Sailors and Aborigines Sharing a Catch at Jervis Bay], 1833. Hand-coloured lithograph, 19.4 × 29.4 cm

Source: Rex Nan Kivell Collection NK 3340/34, National Library of Australia U 1743

mutual incomprehension and violence. *Sailors and Aborigines Sharing a Catch at Jervis Bay* shows a fleeting, fragile moment of rapprochement, as sailor and Aboriginal dance together on the beach; but such moments of engagement have been all too rare.

As the tide washes from the beach the signs of commerce and disturbance from the day just past, so it seems that much that has happened here has been erased from our consciousness—particularly with regard to our convict past and the history of Aboriginal–settler contact. One consequence of such amnesia is insecurity about the capacity for, and even the criteria for, successful history-making. To the extent that we confront the past and grow in our understanding that history has been and can be made here, so we will become less dependent on overseas experience and overseas affirmation for a sense that we too are participants in humanity's history-making.

Rediscovery and re-examination of our past is only beginning, and is fraught with controversy; but one can hope that the wiping away of memories of the past represented by the waves on the beach might be replaced by a more constructive representation in the future: that the mistakes of the past can be remedied, and that as the tide leaves a smooth stretch of sand ready for new possibilities, and unexpected treasures are perhaps cast up by the ocean, so we can make fresh starts, new beginnings. Mudrooroo Nyoongah expresses hope, sadness, bitterness and pity as past histories interpenetrate the present and each other in his poem 'Beached Party':

> We all, all of us must have a beginning, a birth day,
> I, we died a thousand, thousand,
> When Governor Phillip carried to terror nullus
> His ill cargo: 'I suffer, suffer—
> Why exile me here?'
> Convict, warder, soldier, thieves—
> The ruin of a hundred, hundred futures
> Snuffed out—hurt: 'When we came,
> We found you!'—no platitudes, please—
> Do we march, progress to the sound of the drum
> Thrumming out a present tomorrow of yesterdays,
> Or to surf fumbling over sun-drenched bodies
> Seeking releases in different genres of progress,
> While lamenting over the Empire's thick arms
> Softening at the sacrifice he offers to this our future
> Emblems of Gallipoli and betrayals in Greece,
> When we discover that we have founded a nation
> And there are no more trips back to the old country.
> Now we belong and aren't we glad to be home
> In the Aussie way of slightly doing things—
> Clichés—don't rock the boat, consensus falters
> As we glance over our bodies and stare at Australia
> Where a tree is nurtured, not dismantled into the wood
>   chips
> Of our provincial selves exported to where we can't
>   understand
> The byways and the ironies of us as a holiday destination.
> This space for sale, better to ignore the worst
> Betrayals and accept the present thinking of
> Belonging as the celebration imprisons our injustices
> And we linger on an eternal holiday under an eternal sun
> On an eternal beach where all problems are TV-framed

Foreigners flickering in constant battles for victory and
    control,
While we naked and somewhat ashamed yell:
Advance Australia Bronze into the history of our future
Marked each day by Governor Phillip holding
the shattered body
Of a Koori in his white arms slowly turning brown
Under a hot sun saddened with the defects of the cold
Icing an ancient land saddened with the defects of the new,
As on this day, I finger the scars of my sorrows, and smile at
The droppings of my tears while holding the boat steady
As Governor Phillip proffers gifts;
Then the musket speaks to place in his imperial arms
The sacrifice necessary to found this, our new nation
In mourning each and every year on this date,
As indifferent skins blister with cancerous growths,
And my voice whispers a hopeful, happy birthday, Australia,
While daubing sunscreen cream over the worst lesions
of my past.[3]

Christina Stead realised more than sixty years ago that for Australia to become our genuine homeland, in order to savour living here, we will have to come to terms not only with the land, its fauna and flora, its unique place in the world, but also with the 'native youth' whom we dispossessed. She also saw that we would one day have to recognise and reconcile the split between the inland with its 'heart made of salt' and the sea-edge of delight where our population increasingly lives. Her vision is remarkably prescient given that she wrote *Seven Poor Men of Sydney* in 1934, before World War II, at a time when belief in an unlimited future for Australia's rural wealth was strong.

Today, the description of the men and women on the land as 'salt of the earth' has an ironic meaning, given that rising levels of salinity are rendering useless much previously productive farmland. Even the term 'the bush' seems to be going out of favour, replaced in political rhetoric by the clumsy phrase 'rural and regional Australia' (or even 'rural, regional and remote Australia'—irreverently shortened to *RaRaRA*). Stead's words, 'its heart made of salt [which] oozes from its burning pores', seem particularly apt as rural areas are depopulated and a sense of alienation from, and abandonment by, the coastal majority grows within the rural heartland.

There are a few intriguing hints as to how this rift might be bridged; in the recent development of the concept of 'aquaculture', for example. The word means to grow, manage, farm aquatic plant and animal life, and it does not distinguish between fresh- and saltwater species, coastal and inland locations. Farmers on Kangaroo Island have turned the sheep off marshy areas of their land and constructed networks of ponds to grow the freshwater crayfish called marron, and graziers from back o'Bourke contemplate harvesting the yabbies that flourish in their dams. The *Sydney Morning Herald* of 24 July 1997 reported the discovery by a farmer of an inland sea of warm saline waters trapped in granite below his Riverina property. He is using this water supply to farm what he hopes to be a 25-tonne annual harvest of barramundi. On 13 September 1998 the Sydney *Sun-Herald* quoted Dr Geoff Allan, from the Aquaculture Division of NSW Fisheries commenting on the sending of hundreds of snapper (a sea fish) to dams near Deniliquin in western NSW that hold water too salty to be used for irrigation: 'The opportunity exists to grow marine fish in many areas of NSW because there are unbelievable amounts of rising saline ground water. This might regenerate farming communities and create a more valuable crop than traditional commodities'.

Rivers are the arteries connecting the coast to the inland, and as catchment management becomes an urgent concern both to governments and local communities, there is incipient co-operation between estuarine management organisations on the coast and rivercare groups inland as realisation grows that what happens anywhere along the river course affects everything downstream.

Gabrielle Lord presents a cautionary tale of a dystopian future in her novel *Salt* (1990), where Australia is a land ruined by rising salt levels and high temperatures, a nightmare of social, moral and economic disintegration. We are only beginning to recognise the ways in which coast and inland depend on each other and there are enormous problems and difficulties ahead; but new ways of thinking about challenges are the first steps towards meeting them.

'Growing into the land': immigrant Australians

IT IS CLEAR that recently arrived migrants and their children have not been subject to the influences that have been described here, and that the beach for many of them may have an entirely different set of meanings, or very little meaning. As Paul Collins in *God's Earth* recognises:

> Their spiritual and cultural lives still dwell in the old country, and their emotional sustenance is still drawn from the culture they left behind ... Identification with the new country, with the ecological and spiritual aspects of that country, takes time—even generations.[4]

Some make this journey of identification more quickly than others; so attitudes to the beach can provide an interesting scale of assimilation. Here I use the idea of assimilation in its Piagetian sense: of a psychological process whereby new material is taken into an existing scheme or system, as the original scheme or system changes and accommodates to the new material—the two processes always and simultaneously occurring. Thus, as migrants are assimilated into the host culture, the host culture changes to assimilate them.

On 13 November 1950 the *Sydney Morning Herald* reported that two men, 'new Australians', had been ordered off crowded beaches for wearing only vees (very brief swimming costumes). A Bondi surf club official complained of the way the men kicked, pushed and struggled with lifesavers, and expressed his irritation over their ignorance of both safety rules and acceptable dress: 'They're a menace—they don't know our customs and that lifesavers are trying to help them'. This was early in the phase of large-scale non-British immigration to Australia, and the identification of beachgoers as 'new Australians' and impatience over their lack of understanding reflects early difficulties in the assimilation process on the part of native-born Australians. Today, the frequent drownings of newcomers and tourists in the surf remind us of how dangerous the Australian beach can be for those unfamiliar with it.

For the newcomers, their developing relationship with the beach parallels their coming to be more 'at home' here. Renate Yates, a daughter of Viennese refugees, writes of her parents' arrival at the beginning of World War II:

> For my parents Bondi was a tremendous disappointment. Where were the outdoor restaurants, the tables under colourful umbrellas, the waiters waiting to serve them ices; where were all the imaginative and beautiful settings of the summer resorts they had

left behind . . . They found the sand too hot and the surf far too rough for swimming.

It was an alien, uncomfortable landscape. They infinitely pre-ferred [the harbour beaches] to the ocean beaches as did many of the Reffos then, and so many of the migrants now . . .

In later years, as they became acclimatised, they did turn more to the ocean beaches. Perhaps for a change or because their surfing children demanded it.[5]

I recently observed secondary-school boys on a beach excursion. Some jumped into the water or explored the rock pools; but a knot of Asian boys knelt on a broad ledge of rock, engrossed in a game of cards. They seemed oblivious of their surroundings, the rock ledge existing for them only as a table for their cards. Months later, another group of lads of similar appearance played cricket while on a beach picnic; in their movements, their knowledge of cricketing rules and terms, and their accents, they were indistinguishable from any other cricket-playing group of youngsters. Clearly they were much further along the scale of assimilation than the first group. As Max Dunn writes:

> The country grows
> into the image of the people
> and the people grow
> into the likeness of the country
> till to the soul's geographer
> each becomes the symbol of the other.[6]

I have also observed the beginnings of the process of 'growing into the likeness of the country' in numerous gatherings of recently arrived families on picnics at the beach. Often they sit tightly huddled together on the grass and not the sand; to a degree they hold them-selves apart; but the process has begun.

The 'neutrality' of the beach, its 'no man's land' status, makes it a place where groups who perceive others as different from themselves have an equal right to be. Unobtrusively, even unconsciously, we observe others and find them (again, perhaps unconsciously) to be non-threatening—just as Dad found the Disciples of Death to be, in Bob Graham's *Greetings from Sandy Beach*. We watch children with darker or lighter skins than our own children playing on the sand in the same ways, jumping up and down and squealing at the fringe where the waves meet the sand.

The Australian writer Geraldine Brooks was interviewing the Iranian president, Akbar Hashami Rafsanjani, for a book she was writing on the position of Muslim women in Islamic countries, a chador covering her head in accordance with Iranian regulations. She recalls how there flashed into her mind at that moment 'a mental image of myself as I liked to be in summer, bare-skinned on the beach near my parents' home'. She wondered if Muslim women immigrants to Australia would gradually adopt the 'passionately tolerant secularism' of Australian society, or whether they would seek to impose their values as their numbers increased. On her next visit home

> I lay on that beach beside a Muslim family who seemed not the least bit troubled by the exposed flesh surrounding them. While the man splashed in the shallows with his toddlers, his wife sat on the sand, her long, loose dress arranged around her. It made me sad that the woman's tiny daughter . . . would be, one day soon, required to forgo that pleasure. But that would be her fight, not mine. At least in Australia, she would have a choice . . .
>
> Every now and then the little girl's mother fiddled with her headscarf as it billowed in the sea breeze. That woman had made her choice: it was different from mine. But sitting there, sharing the warm sand and the soft air, we accepted each other. When she raised her face to the sun, she was smiling.[7]

On the time scale of accommodation to a new culture, for some the choice of adopting new ways sometimes seems to be made quite quickly and easily:

> Over the Christmas break I travelled to a piece of paradise on the south coast of New South Wales. There, frolicking on the splendent white sand and ripples of the deep blue-green sea, were some 300 people. I guess about 50 to 75 of them were Asians (Indians, Chinese, Vietnamese).
>
> I didn't see any of them eating with chopsticks, they played cricket and touch footy, and some of the younger ones had deep Australian accents. Some were partnered by Anglo-Australians.
>
> For a brief moment I wondered if my letter-writing condemning Hansonism was not just an embarrassing waste of time: all there seemed oblivious to the current troubles. Maybe it was a temporary illusion . . .[8]

That open-ended conclusion, that note of uncertainty, are appropriate responses in face of a future that holds many questions and challenges. The global reach of commerce and telecommunications, the mass media, ease of travel, mass migration, all lead to an increasing deracination of individuals, a growing number of people for whom the contribution of attachment to place to their construction of personal identity is potentially diluted. For some, the consequent anticipated decline of nationalism and the rise of a consciousness of world citizenship is welcome: Salman Rushdie, for example, celebrates 'Melange, hotch-potch, a bit of this and that, [this] is how newness enters the world. It is the great possibility that mass migration gives the world . . . for change-by-fusion, change-by-co-joining'.[9]

Others will argue that love of the planet and of mankind is but a pale abstraction unless it is built on a foundation of an early and strong commitment to local neighbourhood and community. Certainly we are engaged in history-making now, willy-nilly; just as children inevitably grow up, so changes in our own society as well as international developments present us with challenges requiring our engagement. This will make it impossible for us to yield to the impulse to live only for the pleasure of the moment, a temptation recognised by D. H. Lawrence: 'Would the people awaken this ancient land, or would the land put them to sleep, drift them back into the torpid semi-consciousness of the world of twilight?'[10]

Some of the qualities in Australian life that I have suggested are developing in association with the beach have been identified by Ross Gibson as those that will serve us best in the uncertain future, and which can most usefully be highlighted as we adopt new views of ourselves:

> From the 1820s onward . . . agricultural wealth burgeoned as the colony turned its attention inland. But underneath this groundplan, bubbling through like a history from below, something fluid and shifting had already installed itself. Something fundamental and oceanic, a mercuric capability . . . let's just wonder if it was something that can still be summoned, like a legend of experimentation, to guide us now into the ways of invention and improvisation required by the great social and philosophical changes of today.[11]

18

In Conclusion

THE BUSH GAINED significance early in our history. Writers and artists were of crucial importance in constructing the bush and rural life as the quintessence of Australian identity—our earliest and most influential myth of place. The people took unto themselves the writers' and artists' version of Australianness.

The beach became part of Australian life in the early part of the twentieth century—a much more recent contributor to the people's image of themselves. Here the people have led the way: the writers in particular have gradually come to the party instead of inviting the people to the party, as in the case of the bush.

Reference to 'the party' seems appropriate when one contrasts the image of the Australian as dourly resilient—the image of the bushman—with more recent characterisations of Australians as feckless pleasure-seekers. David Williamson wrote of Australia in 1985 that 'The intellectuals have always hated Australia and wished they were living in Europe. The folk have always loved it because it provided them with a lifestyle that was pleasant'.[1] The beach is a major component of this 'pleasant lifestyle', and thereby tainted by its association with the aspects of Australian society so deplored by Williamson's putative intellectuals.

Certainly intellectuals have failed to apply to the beach the attention they have lavished on the bush and, more recently, the desert. Because ideas about cultural formation are based on European models, the ways in which the beach experience has been utilised in the creation of a distinctive new culture have not been recognised. While the superficial semiotics of the beach-as-exploited-by-consumerism has been noted, the deeper reality of the beach as a place conducive to apprehension of the transcendent and the spiritual has been largely ignored.

Brian Matthews recognises that our sustaining myths—of the bush, of Gallipoli—are insufficient, that 'we have no legend based on the way we do live and have always lived, as an urban coastal people.' He asks: 'Why not a coastal myth for Australia?', but concludes that 'the trouble with a beach as against a bush legend is that the beach is about leisure, hedonism, pleasure, indolence. It does not provide those Protestant/Puritan values of endurance and back-breaking work towards achievement and prosperity'.[2]

But hedonism, a philosophical commitment to pleasure as the highest good, cannot be inferred from the behaviour of people on the beach; there is no way of knowing whether or not they accord other values as high or higher priority. I have argued that the quality of commitment to other goals can be enhanced where the beach enables a balance to be struck in people's lives. Nevertheless, the influence of the unfavourable stereotype associated with the beach—of vacuous minds in sunburnt bodies—is still evident: a photograph of people in the surf at Bondi in the *Sydney Morning Herald* of 9 January 1999 is captioned: 'Rampant hedonism ... cooling off at Bondi yesterday'. Rampant hedonism? Or a sensible thing to do on a hot day? Even a writer like Peter Blazey (whose own lifestyle suggested no personal aversion to pleasure) asserts:

> Forget Gallipoli, the outback, and the Aussie battler and other tedious wowser myths from our Anglo-Irish puritan past; the essence of being Australian is, regrettably, something much more sensual. It is to lie on warm sand under a carcinogenic sun watching other bodies walking or lying and then to ritually clean yourself in the ocean.[3]

Why 'regrettably'? The thinking that underlies Blazey's choice of that word derives from the construction of a set of antagonistic opposites—enjoyment of the moment versus commitment to work, to history-making, or to engagement with others. Capacity for enjoyment of the beach is compatible with—indeed, may often be conducive to—the 'effortful achievement of purpose'. It is clear from the example of the beach that the drives identified by Dorothy Dinnerstein need not operate separately from or in conflict with each other. The nuances of their meeting, merging and interplay, the ways in which they are balanced and reconciled, enrich and add complexity to the lives both of individuals and of the society in which they have their being.

The beach has become popular in an era that has come to emphasise cultural diversity rather than unity; where appeals to unifying discourses, or unifying symbols, are criticised as glossing over differences or as disguises for political or ideological agenda. But a society whose members share no common experiences or values is a society—a commonwealth—no longer. A situation where a single continent is occupied by a single nation-state has advantages over fragmentation. Influences that strengthen social cohesion in non-oppressive ways should therefore be welcomed. 'Being Australian' is only one of the multiple and fluid identities of our complex selves; but to the extent that the beach remains a common resource and a common site for the meanings I have explored, it contributes to the fragile network of bonds that holds a people together despite their diverse and sometimes competing interests and allegiances.

The experience of the beach resonates with other patterns in our culture. Attitudes to the body and to sensuality, to life and death, to work and to enjoyment, to time and to history, all are affected by the experience of the beach. And in its contradictory and ambiguous connotations, the beach serves as a metaphor for the paradoxical quality of human existence.

I have suggested that some of our deepest psychological needs are assuaged by contact with natural phenomena, and that a culture reverberates to aspects of the natural environment in which it is set. Such arguments may seem to be on shaky ground in an age when talk of cyberspace and virtual reality supports the view that geography is increasingly irrelevant to human society. Yet that very phrase—on shaky ground—is a reminder that we are physical beings in a physical universe. A need for contact with the natural world may even be inbuilt. Some scientists have suggested that desire for sight of the colour green, the colour of the vegetation that clothes the land masses of the planet (where they have not been blasted by manmade or climate-induced desertification) is wired into our nervous systems. Robert Drewe writes in *The Drowner* of a happening based on historical fact, in the goldmining town of Kalgoorlie during a 'water famine'. 'Suddenly the hotel's billiard rooms were thronged with players day and night, men queuing in the street who had previously never held a cue, men attracted to billiards because the baize was the only greensward they would see'.[4]

In the same novel we encounter a child with Angelman syndrome, an actual medical condition named after its discoverer. Those who suffer from it have an overpowering desire to throw themselves into water—indeed, into any liquid they see, whether real or represented: 'In her obsession, a bowl of brown Windsor soup equals the Indian Ocean for excitement. She tries to climb into seaside picture books, into illustrations of streams and ponds'.[5]

Perhaps many of us carry within ourselves a trace of the Angelman syndrome. Perhaps the idea that we can plan for a future where

'The great ocean of truth lies undiscovered' before the child on the beach.
Source: The author's private collection

humans redesign the natural world to suit themselves has been a late twentieth-century manifestation of hubris, and we would sicken and die in an environment of our own making.

Matthews writes that 'we have no legend based on the way we do live and have always lived, as an urban coastal people (though this may be evolving)'.[6] The beach manifests cyclical aspects of existence: the waves that advance and retreat; the tides that rise and fall twice daily; the variations associated with annual changes from mid-summer to mid-winter; and the destruction of beaches by storms and their gradual restoration. In this respect it reflects what Mircea Eliade has described as 'sacred time',[7] which flows in a closed circle, with eternal return to the sacred and the real—a feature of the world view of Australia's original inhabitants, but one of which modern Western culture has little understanding, and with which we feel uncomfortable. We prefer the drama of linear narrative, legends of adventure and achievement. But the recurring rhythms of life, the repeating patterns and rituals of human existence, enrich and bring significance to our work and history-making, and need to be recognised and honoured.

The beach, as ocean beach, hardly existed as a meaningful space for the first one hundred years of European settlement in Australia. During the twentieth century it became an index of our accommodation to life on this continent and a spiritual site, entering deeply into our hearts and minds. Custodianship of the beach will be a challenging, vital and rewarding responsibility to carry with us into the century just beginning.

Notes

Introduction

1 R. Drewe, 'Tidal Pull', p. 41.
2 A. Game, 'Nation and Identity: Bondi', p. 120.
3 J. K. Walton, *English Seaside Resort*, pp. 1, 226.
4 L. Wells, *Sunny Memories*, p. 22.
5 J. R. Winders, *Surf Life Saving in Queensland*, pp. vii, 18.
6 E. Jaggard, *The Premier Club*, pp. 24–6.
7 Facts about the physical features of beaches are taken from A. Short, *The Beaches of the New South Wales Coast* and from M. Safe, 'The Sands of Time'.
8 Pat Dale, *Managing Australian Coastlands*, p. 1.
9 T. Keneally, *Woman of the Inner Sea*, p. 30.
10 D. Dinnerstein, *The Mermaid and the Minotaur*, p. 244.
11 Dinnerstein, *Mermaid and Minotaur*, p. 144.
12 W. Bascom, 'Waves and Beaches', p. 470.
13 W. Blake, *The Marriage of Heaven and Hell*, p. 104.
14 Freud, referring to the conclusion to Schiller's 'Letters on the Aesthetic Education of Man', quoted in N. O. Brown, *Life Against Death*, p. 33. (These works were all written at a time before sexist language became an issue.)
15 Quoted by Brown in *Life Against Death*, p. 33.
16 J. Kingsmill, 'Growing Up in Bondi', *Bondi*, p. 76.
17 M. Blakemore, 'The Straight Poofter', pp. 37–8.
18 T. Winton, *Land's Edge*, p. 8.
19 Dinnerstein, *Mermaid and Minotaur*, pp. 121, 208, 60.

1 First Impressions

1 G. Dening, *Islands and Beaches*, 1980.
2 P. Brunton (ed.), *The Endeavour Journal of Sir Joseph Banks*, p. 19.
3 J. C. Beaglehole et al. (eds), *The Journal of Captain James Cook*, p. 399.
4 A phrase first used in a convict ballad written c. 1825–30 and used by Robert Hughes as the title, *The Fatal Shore*, of his major work on Australia's convict origins.
5 The entry in the *Oxford Dictionary of Australian Colloquialisms* reads: '**Bogie**: To bathe, swim (Ab) 1788: Daniel Southwell papers—I have bathed, or have been bathing—Colby's words on coming out of the water: Bogie d'oway'.
6 M. Cannon, *Life in the Cities*, p. 163.

[7] W. Tench, *Sydney's First Four Years*, p. 273.

[8] A. Scott, Sydney Harbour Public Baths, BArch thesis 1985, University of Sydney, quoted in EJE Landscapes, *Survey of Harbourside and Ocean Pools of the Sydney Metropolitan Region*, Historical Section. A more detailed account of the early history of baths and swimming around Sydney Harbour is contained in this historical section.

[9] P. Cunningham, *Two Years in New South Wales*, p. 50.

[10] M. L. J. Sweatnam, *Journal of a Voyage on HMS Bramble*, quoted in R. Waterhouse, *Private Pleasures*, p. 41.

[11] 'Sketches Taken from Scenes About Sydney', no. 11: The Domain, *Heads of People*, vol. 2, no. 1, 16 October 1847, p. 6.

[12] W. R. Govett in 1837, quoted in J. W. C. Cumes, *Their Chastity Was Not Too Rigid*, p. 156.

[13] Quoted in A. Birch & D. S. MacMillan, *The Sydney Scene 1788–1960*, p. 74.

[14] R. Gibson, 'Ocean Settlement', p. 670.

[15] A. Frost, 'The Conditions of Early Settlement', p. 75.

[16] For first-hand accounts of voyages to Australia, see, for example: B. Moore, H. Garwood & N. Lutton, *The Voyage Out*; A. Hassam, *No Privacy for Writing*; and L. Frost (comp.) *No Place for a Nervous Lady*.

[17] A. Mitchell, 'Fiction', in *The Oxford History of Australian Literature*, pp. 28–9.

[18] E. Webby, *Early Australian Poetry*, Introduction, p. ix.

[19] A. Corbin, *The Lure of the Sea*, p. 234.

[20] H. Halloran, *Sydney Gazette*, 16 June 1831, p. 4.

[21] *Duncan's Weekly Register of Politics, Facts and General Literature*, 19 April 1845, p. 185.

[22] H. M. Green, *A History of Australian Literature Pure and Applied*, p. 83.

[23] In *The Lycett Album*, 1990.

[24] H. L. Roth, *The Aborigines of Tasmania*, p. 102.

[25] G. Dutton, *Sun, Sea, Surf and Sand*, p. 9.

[26] Tench, *Sydney's First Four Years*, p. 281.

[27] R. Hughes, *The Fatal Shore*, pp. 503–5.

[28] W. M. Whitney, 'Vagabond of Beaches', *Bulletin*, 12 December 1907, p. 25.

2   The Triumph of Respectability

[1] The relevant regulations were published in the *N.S.W. Government Gazette*, no. 50, 13 February 1833, p. 59, and no. 352, 22 August 1838, p. 659 (relating to the Towns Police Act specifying police powers 'for removing Nuisances and Obstructions . . .').

[2] Quoted in M. Barnard, *Sydney: The Story of a City*, p. 8.

[3] W. Vamplew (ed.), *Australians: Historical Statistics*, 'Immigration to the Australian Colonies 1788–1860', p. 4.

[4] This account is summarised from J. K. Walton, *The English Seaside Resort*; R. Manning-Sanders, *Seaside England*; J. Anderson & E. Swinglehurst, *The Victorian and Edwardian Seaside*; and A. Corbin, *The Lure of the Sea*. Corbin's book is a fascinating, scholarly cultural history that examines 'emotionally charged systems', tracing the origins of desires and the ways in which suffering and pleasure were experienced, leading to 'the desire for the shore that swelled and spread [in Western Europe] between 1750 and 1840'.

[5] Manning-Sanders, *Seaside England*, p. 10.

[6] Corbin, *The Lure of the Sea*, p. 70.

[7] Corbin, *The Lure of the Sea*, p. 77.

[8] Cannon, *Life in the Cities*, p. 21.

[9] EJE Landscapes, 'The Architecture of Bathing in Sydney', *Survey of Harbourside and Ocean Pools of the Sydney Metropolitan Region*, historical overview.

[10] *Harbourside and Ocean Pools*, historical overview.

[11] M. K. Stell, *Half the Race*, p. 4.

[12] Stell, *Half the Race*, p. 5.

[13] *Sydney Morning Herald*, March 1856, quoted in J. Fishbein et al., *Beside the Sea: Sydney Beaches and Resorts*, p. 7.

[14] See A. Inglis, *Beside the Seaside: Victorian Resorts in the Nineteenth Century*, Melbourne University Press, Carlton, Vic., 1999, for an account of the Victorian seaside holiday during this period.

[15] A. Vialoux, 'Manly and Warringah Shire', p. 11, quoted in P. Triglone, *The History of Manly Ocean Beach Landscape from the First Settlement to the Present*, p. 33.

[16] R. Garran (ed.), *The Picturesque Atlas of Australasia*, illus. under the supervision of Frederick B. Schell, Picturesque Atlas Publishing Co., Sydney, 1886, vol. 1, p. 71.

[17] Fishbein et al., 'Scouring the Sea Shore', in *Pleasures and Pastimes Beside the Sea*.

[18] 'Loss of a Jetty', *Historic Glenelg*, article supplied by the Manager, City of Glenelg, SA.

[19] *Cottesloe Society Newsletter*, July 1996, vol. 5, no. 2, pp. 12–14; M. & J. Laurie, *Ten Decades*, p. 15.

[20] *Beside the Sea*.

[21] This account is summarised from S. & G. Champion, *The Clontarf Case*.

[22] A. Lowe, *Surfing, Surf-shooting and Surf Lifesaving Pioneering*, n.p. Lowe's rambling reminiscences are a researcher's nightmare, bearing no publisher, no date, and no page numbers. The cover photograph suggests they were published some time in the late 1950s, when Lowe would have been almost 80.

3   Writers and Artists, the Bush and the Beach

[1] B. Mitchell's diary, 13 February 1858, quoted in G. Dutton, *Myth of the Beach*, p. 30.

[2] E. Chomley, 'My Memoirs', and Mrs Cole's diary, quoted in P. Russell, *A Wish of Distinction*, p. 97.

[3] A. Montgomery, 'Clinched', *Bulletin*, 12 December 1896, p. 17.

[4] C. Brennan, from 'Towards the Source', [1894], from *Poems 1913*, p. 2.

[5] A. L. Gordon, 'The Swimmer', pp. 115–16.

[6] A. B. Paterson, 'Song of the Future', p. 166.

[7] A. Frost, 'Perceptions before 1855', in L. Hergenhan (ed.), *The Penguin New Literary History of Australia*, p. 103.

[8] See especially W. K. Hancock, *Australia*; A. A. Phillips, *The Australian Tradition: Studies in a Colonial Culture*; R. Ward, *The Australian Legend*; G. Serle, *From Deserts the Prophets Come: The Creative Spirit in Australia 1788–1972*; R. White, *Inventing Australia: Images and Identity 1688–1980*; J. Carroll (ed.), *Intruders in the Bush: The Australian Quest for Identity*; and S. Lawson, *The Archibald Paradox: A Strange Case of Authorship*.

[9] Ward, *The Australian Legend*, pp. 1–2.

10 Some writers see the creation of the idea of the bushman as embodying national virtues as an entirely intellectual fabrication, a projection onto the outback of values idealised by an alienated urban intelligentsia (see especially G. Davison's article, *Intruders in the Bush*, pp. 109–30, and 'Bohemians and the Bush' in R. White's *Inventing Australia*, pp. 85–109).

11 H. Lawson, 'How the Land Was Won', *Collected Verse*, pp. 361–3.

12 L. A. Murray, 'Noonday Axeman', *The Vernacular Republic*, pp. 7–9.

13 M. Gilmore, 'Old Botany Bay', *Australian Poets: Mary Gilmore*, p. 10.

14 N. Krauth, 'Continental Drift: Clancy of the Undertow', p. 29.

15 D. Thomas (ed.), *Creating Australia*, p. 11.

16 Paterson, 'Song of the Future', p. 165, emphasis added. See also K. Healey, 'Ocean Outlook—A Blueprint for the Oceans;' in *Ocean Ecology*, p. 1.

4   Beginnings: A New Century, a New Nation and the Struggle for the Beach

1 A. Short, *Beaches of the New South Wales Coast*, p. 53.

2 *Tegg's New South Wales Pocket Almanac*, pp. 283–4.

3 Quoted in M. Cannon, *Life in the Cities*, p. 157. Melbourne was no better, being known as 'Smellboom' (Cannon, p. 175).

4 A. Lowe, *Surfing, Surf-shooting and Surf-Lifesaving Pioneering*.

5 Quoted in B. Jobling, 'An Early Pioneer of Liberated Surfing in Sydney', p. 7.

6 G. B. Philip, *Sixty Years' Recollections*, pp. 39–40.

7 F. A. Larcombe, 'The Stabilization of Local Government in New South Wales, 1858–1906', p. 216. See also the *NSW Government Gazette* no. 1068, 20 December 1901.

8 The diary is held in the Wellings local history collection, Manly Municipal Library.

9 Lowe, *Surfing, Surf-shooting and Surf-Lifesaving Pioneering*.

10 'Surf-Bathing. Dangers and Decencies. Separating the Sexes', *Daily Telegraph*, 20 January 1917.

11 L. Wells, *Sunny Memories*, p. 25.

12 'Surf-bathing', *Daily Telegraph*, 20 January 1917.

13 E. T. Russell, 'Australia's Amphibians', p. 254.

14 By-Law issued by the Manly Town Clerk on 22 January 1918, approved by the Minister for Local Government, Mr Fitzgerald, on 14 December 1917 [Wellings collection, Manly Municipal Library].

15 Wells, *Sunny Memories*, p. 22.

16 See 'Decency and the Surf', *Sydney Morning Herald*, 23 January 1907, p. 8; Letter, 24 January 1907, p. 10; Letter, 25 January 1907, p. 8; Letter, 26 January 1907, p. 1; Letter, 28 January 1907, p. 5; 'G. Norton Russell', 'Australian Girl', 'A Mother of Girls', Letters, all 14 February 1907, p. 8. There were some dissenters, e.g. two correspondents on 28 January; but most were in favour of 'decency'.

17 C. B. Maxwell, *Surf: Australians Against the Sea*, pp. 31–2.

18 *Sydney Morning Herald*, 1 July 1927, p. 6; 6 July 1927, p. 15.

19 K. Dunstan, *Wowsers*, p. 150.

20 F. A. Larcombe, 'The Stabilization of Local Government', pp. 215–16.

21 J. Walton, *The English Seaside Resort*, p. 189.

22 D. Tacey, *Edge of the Sacred*, p. 37.

23 C. D. Paterson, evidence to the Surf-bathing Committee, *Report*, 1 September 1911, p. 270.
24 S. Knight, *Freedom Was Compulsory*, p. 2.
25 *NSW Government Gazette*, no. 40, 27 March 1912, pp. 1933–6 (ordinances on bathing).
26 S. Knight, *Freedom Was Compulsory*, p. 8.
27 R. Hughes, *The Fatal Shore*, p. 594.

5   The Achievement of Freedom on the Beach

1 G. B. Philip, *Sixty Years' Recollections*, pp. 40–1.
2 W. Tonge & A. W. Relph, 'Surf Bathing at Manly', *Sydney Morning Herald*, 7 September 1907, p. 6 (emphasis added).
3 S. Fitzgerald, *Rising Damp*, p. 97.
4 A. W. Relph, 'Surf-Bathing', *Sydney Morning Herald*, 11 September 1909, p. 5.
5 J. Curlewis, *The Home*, March 1929, pp. 25–32, 72; and Anon., *The Home*, January 1927, pp. 26–32.
6 *Sydney Morning Herald*, 12 October 1910, p. 7 (emphasis added)
7 *Newsletter*, 18 March 1905, in Wellings Cuttings (Manly Library), Book no. 1, pp. 2–3.
8 J. K. Walton, *The English Seaside Resort*, pp. 210, 223.
9 *Daily Telegraph*, 27 October 1905, p. 6.
10 E. J. Hill, 'Freedom of the Seas', p. 415.
11 'Surf-Bathing: Report of Select Committee', *Sydney Morning Herald*, 15 February 1912, p. 8.
12 Walton, *The English Seaside Resort*, p. 225.
13 C. B. Maxwell, *Surf: Australians Against the Sea*, p. 16.
14 E. T. Russell, 'Australia's Amphibians', p. 252.
15 E. Jaggard, 'The Australian Surf Lifesaver as a National Symbol 1920–1990', 1996, p. 9.
16 N. Young & C. McGregor, *The History of Surfing*, p. 68.
17 W. Butterfield, Bondi Revisited, 1923–1981.

6   The Australianising of the Beach

1 C. Swancott, *Dee Why Lake to Barrenjoey and Pittwater*, p. 52.
2 'Surf-Bathing. Report of Select Committee', *Sydney Morning Herald*, 14 February 1912, p. 8.
3 G. B. Philip, *Sixty Years' Recollections*, p. 45.
4 J. G. Mosley, 'History of Conservation', quoted in G. Bolton, *Spoils and Spoilers*, p. 104.
5 *Sydney Morning Herald*, 9 August 1929, p. 12.
6 *Truth*, Editorial, 30 March 1913.
7 *Sydney Morning Herald*, 19 May 1993.
8 'Beach Mismanagement', *Sydney Morning Herald*, 2 December 1911, p. 16.
9 R. Waterhouse, *Private Pleasures, Public Leisure*, p. 187.
10 Walton, *The English Seaside Resort*, pp. 177–8.

11 J. Morris, *Sydney*, p. 154.
12 J. Curlewis, 'The Race on the Sands', p. 25.
13 B. Travers, 'Vale of Laughter', quoted in J. D. Pringle, *Australian Accent*, p. 40.
14 E. T. Russell, 'Australia's Amphibians', pp. 261–2.
15 J. Curlewis, 'The Race on the Sands', p. 26.
16 E. J. Hill, 'Freedom of the Seas', p. 414.
17 In S. Kurosawa (ed.), *Hot Sand: An Anthology*, pp. 12–13.
18 A. Corbin, *The Lure of the Sea*, pp. 263–9.

7 The Beach from the Mid-twentieth Century to the Present

1   M. K. Stell, *Half the Race*, pp. 97–8.
2   Stell, *Half the Race*, p. 98.
3   Stell, *Half the Race*, p. 176.
4   D. Booth, 'Surfing 60s', p. 268.
5   From the Report of the Committee of Inquiry, 1975.
6   S. Brawley, *Vigilant and Victorious*, p. 247.
7   Booth, 'Surfing 60s', p. 269.
8   Booth, 'Surfing 60s', p. 266.
9   C. McGregor, 'The Surf Life Saving Movement: Executives Out of Step with an Unsquare Age', *Sydney Morning Herald*, 11 February 1965, p. 2; and C. McGregor, *Profile of Australia*, p. 296.
10 B. Channon, submission to the Committee of Inquiry, 17 February 1975, Appendix B.
11 J. Carter, *Surf Beaches of Australia's East Coast*, p. 97.
12 E. Jaggard, 'The Australian Surf Lifesaver as a National Symbol', pp. 17–18.
13 This account of the fight against beach pollution in the 1980s is largely taken from S. Beder, *Toxic Fish and Sewer Surfing*.
14 This account of sand-mining is summarised from *The Injured Coastline* and I. W. Morley, *Black Sands*. The figures for export earnings from mineral sand-mining are from the Australian Bureau of Statistics, Canberra, ABARE.

8 Early Representations and Emerging Themes

1   D. Malouf, 'A Spirit of Play'.
2   D. McK. Wright, 'Young Australia by the Sea', *Bulletin*, 20 October 1910, p. 43.
3   W. M. Whitney, 'Beach Brownies', *Bulletin*, 29 December 1910, p. 3.
4   R. Quinn, 'The Surrender', *Poems*, pp. 97–8.
5   Dates in parenthesis indicate when the work was first published.
6   This image recalls Max Dupain's photograph, 'Sunbaker'.
7   D. H. Lawrence, *Kangaroo*, p. 22.
8   Lawrence, *Kangaroo*, p. 167.
9   K. S. Prichard, *Intimate Strangers*, pp. 44–5.
10 Prichard, *Intimate Strangers*, p. 45; my emphasis.
11 D. Cusack, *Jungfrau*, p. 102.
12 Perrin, 'Les Structures', p. 205, quoted in A. Corbin, *The Lure of the Sea*, p. 168.

13   R. Drewe (ed.), *The Picador Book of the Beach*, 'Introduction', pp. 2, 3.
14   J. Morcombe, 'Manly Inspired Very Unhappy Poet', p. 8.
15   P. White, *Voss*, pp. 65–74.
16   M. Gow, *Away*, p. 47.

9   Childhood and the Beach

1   M. Blakemore, 'The Straight Poofter', pp. 37–8.
2   See 'Puer Ludens: An Excursion into Theory', in R. N. Coe's *When the Grass Was Taller*, pp. 240–73 for a crosscultural study of autobiographical 'Childhoods'.
3   R. Dessaix, 'The Best Year of Their Lives', p. 17.
4   T. Winton, *Land's Edge*, p. 8.
5   R. N. Coe, 'Portrait of the Artist as a Young Australian', p. 127.
6   L. White, 'Greer's Rites of Passage: From Female Eunuch to Whole Woman', *Australian*, 20 February 1999, Review, p. 5.
7   See, for example, M. Balderson, *Blue and Gold Day*; J. Bedson, *Don't Get Burnt!*; A. Lester, *Magic Beach*; G. Rubinstein, *The Giant's Tooth*; H. Edwards, *My Hippopotamus Is on Our Caravan Roof Getting Sunburnt*; M. Wild, *There's a Sea in My Bedroom*; and H. M. Saxby, *Russell and the Star Shell*.
8   H. Scutter, 'Escaping the Landscape', p. 37.
9   E. Spence, *October Child*, p. 150.
10   Scutter, 'Escaping the Landscape', p. 40.
11   Scutter, 'Escaping the Landscape', pp. 39–40.
12   J. Kroll, 'Interview with Tim Winton', p. 224.
13   G. Dutton, *Sun, Sea, Surf and Sand*, p. 20.
14   S. Lees & P. Macintyre, *Oxford Companion to Australian Children's Literature*, p. 46.

10   The Prominence of Nature: Diverse Connections

1   R. N. Coe, 'Portrait of the Artist', p. 134.
2   G. Johnston, quoted in D. Tacey, *Edge of the Sacred*, p. 7.
3   Les A. Murray, 'Eric Rolls and the Golden Disobedience', pp. 166–7.
4   T. Bennett, 'Bombora', pp. 6–7.
5   R. Drewe, 'Radiant Heat', in *The Bay of Contented Men*, pp. 24, 25.
6   R. Drewe (ed.), *The Picador Book of the Beach*, 'Introduction', p. 7.
7   All in R. Drewe, *The Bodysurfers*.
8   B. Watzke, in R. Rossiter & L. Jacobs (eds), *Reading Tim Winton*, p. 22.
9   R. Rossiter, 'In His Own Words', in Rossiter & Jacobs, *Reading Tim Winton*, p. 10.
10   B. Watzke, 'Where Pigs Speak in Tongues and Angels Come and Go', in Rossiter & Jacobs, *Reading Tim Winton*, pp. 1–14.
11   A. Taylor, 'What Can Be Read, and What Can Only Be Seen in Tim Winton's Fiction', pp. 328–9.
12   Review of *Minimum of Two*, *Times on Sunday*, 1 March 1987, p. 30.
13   T. Winton, interview, in B. Watzke, 'On the Verge', in Rossiter & Jacobs, *Reading Tim Winton*, p. 15.

14 J. Hall, *Clinical Uses of Dreams*, p. 204, n. 36.
15 R. Drewe, 'Looking for Malibu', in *The Bodysurfers*, p. 55.
16 T. Keneally, *Woman of the Inner Sea*, p. 30.
17 Keneally, *Woman of the Inner Sea*, p. 205.
18 Keneally, *Woman of the Inner Sea*, p. 189.
19 For a discussion of connections between the desert and the sea, see R. D. Haynes, *Seeking the Centre: The Australian Desert in Literature, Art and Film*, pp. 38–41 *passim*.
20 J. Blight, 'The Mindless Ocean', *Selected Poems 1935–1990*, p. 225.
21 B. Beaver, 'Letters to Live Poets XXIII', in *New and Selected Poems, 1960–1990*, pp. 73–5.
22 Beaver, 'Letters to Live Poets XV', p. 65.
23 A. Taylor, 'Littoral Erosion', p. 286.
24 D. McCooey, 'By the Sea', p. 255.

11 The Beach and Popular Culture

1 M. Morris, 'On the Beach', p. 101.
2 J. Fiske, 'Reading the Beach', in *Reading the Popular*, pp. 76, 46.
3 Fiske, 'Reading the Beach', pp. 64, 73, 76. Fiske refers to two works by Roland Barthes, *S/Z*, Cape, London, 1975, and *The Pleasure of the Text*, Hill & Wang, New York, 1975; and to Michel Foucault's *Power/Knowledge*, Harvester, Brighton, UK, 1980.
4 Fiske, 'Reading the Beach', pp. 75, 74.
5 B. Lynch, Australian surfer, interviewed in 'Billion Dollar Breakers', Background Briefing, ABC Radio National, 13 April 1997, transcript.
6 S. Hailstone, 'The Special Place', Encounter, ABC Radio National, 3 July 1996, transcript.
7 A history of Australian surf movies has recently been published; see A. Thoms, *Surfmovies*.

12 The Serene and the Sinister: Contrasting Aspects of the Beach

1 K. Stewart, *Spilt Milk*, pp. 28–9.
2 B. Green, *Freud and the Nazis Go Surfing*, p. 10.
3 R. Drewe, 'Tidal Pull', p. 41.
4 H. Garner, 'Postcards from Surfers', p. 3.
5 T. Winton, *Land's Edge*, p. 31.
6 R. Drewe (ed.), *The Picador Book of the Beach*, p. 4.
7 Winton, *Land's Edge*, pp. 39, 40.
8 B. Beaver, 'Letters to Live Poets I', in *New and Selected Poems, 1960–1990*, pp. 49–50.
9 J. Wright, 'The Surfer', in *A Human Pattern: Collected Poems*, p. 12.
10 R. Drewe, 'Stingray', *The Bodysurfers*, p. 160.
11 M. Morris, 'Fate and the Family Sedan', pp. 113–34.

12 F. Capp, *Night Surfing*, p. 4.
13 Both stories are from *The Bodysurfers* collection.
14 'Sticks and Stones: The Killing of Leigh Leigh', Background Briefing, ABC Radio National, 29 September 1996, transcript..
15 P. G. Fidlon (ed.), *The Journal of Arthur Bowes Smith*, entry for 6 February 1788, p. 67.

13 Reflections on Representations of the Beach and 'Immersion in Place'

1 S. Schama, *Landscape and Memory*, p. 574.
2 R. Gibson, *South of the West*, p. 18.
3 C. Stead, *For Love Alone*, pp. 1–2.
4 G. McGregor, '*Seven Poor Men of Sydney*: The Historical Dimension', pp. 380–404.
5 Stead, *Seven Poor Men of Sydney*, p. 56.
6 Stead, *Seven Poor Men of Sydney*, p. 17.
7 Stead, *Seven Poor Men of Sydney*, p. 308.
8 Echoing the words of Henry Handel Richardson: 'It was like a form of revenge taken on them, for their loveless schemes of robbing and fleeing; a revenge contrived by the ancient, barbaric country they had so lightly invaded' (from the 'Proem', *The Fortunes of Richard Mahony*, p. 13).
9 Stead, *Seven Poor Men of Sydney*, p. 308.
10 Stead, *Seven Poor Men of Sydney*, p. 308.
11 Stead, *Seven Poor Men of Sydney*, p. 309.

14 The Concept of 'National Identity'

1 G. Turner, *Making It National*, p. 5; for feminist analyses see especially K. Schaffer, *Women and the Bush*, and S. Magarey, S. Rowley & S. Sheridan (eds), *Debutante Nation*.
2 S. Castles, B. Cope, M. Kalantzis & M. Morrissey, *Mistaken Identity*, p. 13.
3 E. Wynhausen & J. Scott, 'Eye of the Storm', p. 27.
4 P. Cochrane & D. Goodman, 'The Great Australian Journey', p. 175.
5 Quoted in K. Inglis, 'Multiculturalism and National Identity', p. 19.
6 A. Game, 'Nation and Identity', pp. 109–10. She refers here to Freud's definition of the 'oceanic feeling'—a feeling of oneself as something limitless. Freud states that this occurs because the boundaries between the ego and the world are ill-defined in very early life, and also threaten to melt away when one is in love.
7 Game, 'Nation and Identity', pp. 112–20.
8 N. Sanders, 'Bondi the Beautiful', p. 23.
9 J. Fiske, 'Reading the Beach', in *Reading the Popular*, p. 76.
10 J. Fiske, B. Hodge & G. Turner, 'The Beach', in *Myths of Oz*, pp. 53–72.
11 S. Knight, *The Selling of the Australian Mind*, pp. 7–8.
12 M. Morris, 'On the Beach', pp. 101–2.

15 Meanings of the Beach, and the Shaping of an Australian Culture

1 A. Taylor, 'Sandstone 30', in *Sandstone*, p. 79.
2 Taylor, 'Sandstone 36', in *Sandstone*, p. 84.
3 M. Leer, 'On the Edge', p. 11. Notions of 'centre' and 'margin' now appear to be so interchangeable that their meanings run the risk of petering out in confusion—for example, in 'Playing Centre Field: Representation and Cultural Difference' in P. Fuery (ed.), *Representation, Discourse and Desire*, Sneja Gunew writes: 'The traditional Australian nationalist subject requires the imprimatur of the international "centre" to authenticate its reality—and paradoxically, its marginality ... My thesis here is that there are always centres though they are not always the same one (eg metropolitan, institutional, geographic, textual) and consequently there are always margins ... those who are situated in these margins are constantly bruised by running up against supposedly non-existent centres' (pp. 78, 87).
4 R. Gibson, *South of the West*, p. xi.
5 A. Short, *Beaches of the NSW Coast*, p. 7.
6 K. Slessor, 'Beach Burial (El Alamein, 1942)', in *Kenneth Slessor: Selected Poems*, p. 127.
7 J. Fiske, B. Hodge & G. Turner, *Myths of Oz*, pp. 59, 60.
8 W. Bascom, 'Waves and Beaches', p. 470.
9 J. T. Hospital, 'Litany for the Homeland', pp. 414–15, 418.
10 J. Hawley, 'An Imaginative Life', p. 13.
11 G. Carey & K. Lette, *Puberty Blues*, quoted in Fiske, Hodge & Turner, *Myths of Oz*, p. 56.
12 L. Murray, 'Summer', in *The Australian Year*, p. 76.
13 L. Murray, 'On Home Beaches', in *Subhuman Redneck Poems*, p. 36.
14 C. Armitage, 'Les Back from Dead, Lighter in Body and Soul', *Weekend Australian*, 21–22 September 1996, p. 3.
15 A. Game, 'Nation and Identity', p. 116.
16 B. Graham, *Greetings from Sandy Beach*.
17 C. Veliz, 'The Gothic Mode of Australian Culture', pp. 8–20.
18 S. Knight, *The Selling of the Australian Mind*, pp. 123, 115.
19 Knight, *Selling of the Australian Mind*, pp. 121, 122.
20 Knight, *Selling of the Australian Mind*, p. 6.
21 J. Morris, *Sydney*, pp. 235–6.
22 P. Drew, *The Coast Dwellers*, p. 21.
23 R. Drewe, 'Tidal Pull', p. 41.
24 R. Gibson, 'Camera Natura', in J. Frow & M. Morris, *Australian Cultural Studies*, p. 229.
25 J. Cadzow, 'Go Your Own Way', *Good Weekend*, *Sydney Morning Herald*, 3 June 2000, p. 24.
26 P. Totaro, 'Through Death, a New Understanding Is Born', *Sydney Morning Herald*, 23 October 1993, p. 17.
27 R. Dessaix, 'The Best Year of Their Lives', p. 17.
28 Knight, *Selling of the Australian Mind*, pp. 13, 16.
29 P. O'Farrell, 'Writing the General History of Australian Religion', p. 217. See also D. Millikan, *The Sunburnt Soul*.

[30] Knight, *Selling of the Australian Mind*, pp. 19, 20.
[31] M. Morris, 'On the Beach', p. 101.
[32] See, for example, C. Birch, *Regaining Compassion for Humanity and Nature*; D. Tacey, *Edge of the Sacred: Transformation in Australia* and *Re-enchantment: The New Australian Spirituality*; and P. Collins, *God's Earth*.

16 Balancing Acts

[1] W. Woolls, 'The Beauties of Australia', pp. 16–17.
[2] P. Goodall, *High Culture, Popular Culture*, p. 100.
[3] P. Drew, *The Coast Dwellers*, pp. 1–2.
[4] C. E. W. Bean, *Official History of Australia in the War of 1914–18*, vol. I, p. 43.
[5] R. Gerster, *Big-noting: The Heroic Theme in Australian War Writing*, p. 2.
[6] G. Johnston, 'ANZAC—A Myth for All Mankind', pp. 15–16.
[7] D. Malouf, *Fly Away Peter*, pp. 36, 55.
[8] Malouf, *Fly Away Peter*, p. 103.
[9] C. E. W. Bean, *Official History of Australia in the War of 1914–18*, vol. II, pp. 382–3.
[10] A. B. Facey, *A Fortunate Life*, p. 268.
[11] Bean, *Official History*, vol. II, p. 346.
[12] Bean, *Official History*, vol. II, pp. 382–3.
[13] Bean, *Official History*, vol. II, p. 902.
[14] Goodall, *High Culture, Popular Culture*, p. 88.
[15] Bean, *Official History*, vol. I, p. 47; vol. VI, p. 1079.
[16] Bean, *Official History*, vol. VI, p. 874.
[17] E. Jaggard, 'The Australian Surf Lifesaver as a National Symbol', p. 21.
[18] C. B. Maxwell, *Surf*, p. 302.
[19] E. T. Russell, 'Australia's Amphibians', p. 263.
[20] Maxwell, *Surf*, p. 40.
[21] G. B. Philip, *Sixty Years' Recollections of Swimming and Surfing*, p. 96.
[22] This account is taken from Waverley Heritage Leaflet number 30, available from Waverley Municipal Library; my emphasis.
[23] N. Young with G. McGregor, *The History of Surfing*, p. 71.
[24] F. Pawle, 'Rabbit's Roughest Break', *Weekend Australian*, 12–13 October 1996, Features section, p. 6.
[25] D. Dinnerstein, *The Mermaid and the Minotaur*, p. 145.
[26] Dinnerstein, *The Mermaid and the Minotaur*, p. 140.
[27] Dinnerstein, *The Mermaid and the Minotaur*, pp. 145, 146, 140, 141.
[28] D. Brewster, *Memories of the Life, Writings, and Discoveries of Sir Isaac Newton*, p. 407.
[29] J. Barzun, *Science: The Glorious Entertainment*, p. 112.
[30] N. O. Brown, *Life Against Death*, p. 53.
[31] R. Drewe, 'Tidal Pull', p. 41.
[32] D. Anderson, 'Strange Results When Foreigners Pick Our Teams', p. 9A.
[33] J. D. Pringle, *Australian Accent*, p. 116.
[34] S. Knight, *Selling of the Australian Mind*, pp. 23–4.
[35] Brown, *Life Against Death*, p. 50.

[36] R. Drewe, 'Stingray', in *The Bodysurfers*, p. 158. The next moment David feels 'an explosion of pain in his right hand: he has been stung by a venomous marine creature'. That's life!

[37] M. Stewart, 'Beachstruck on Bondi', in R. Drewe et al., *Bondi*, p. 42.

[38] K. S. Prichard, *Intimate Strangers*, p. 45.

[39] B. Beaver, 'Day 46', in *New and Selected Poems, 1960–1990*, p. 157.

17 Present and Future Challenges

[1] S. Knight, *Selling of the Australian Mind*, pp. 6, 8.

[2] M. Morris, 'Afterthoughts on Australianisms', p. 470.

[3] Spectrum, *Sydney Morning Herald*, 19 January 1991. This poem was commissioned for Australia Day as part of the Sydney Writers' Festival and is donated to the Mitchell Library archive.

[4] P. Collins, *God's Earth*, p. 180.

[5] R. Yates, original manuscript, quoted in G. Dutton, *Sun, Sea, Surf and Sand*, p. 116.

[6] 'Portrait of a Country', quoted in R. Gibson, 'Camera Natura', p. 221.

[7] G. Brooks, *Nine Parts of Desire*, p. 289.

[8] R. Agostini, 'Letters', *Weekend Australian*, 4–5 January 1997.

[9] S. Rushdie, 'Imaginary Homelands', quoted in S. Hall, 'Culture, Community, Nation', p. 363.

[10] D. H. Lawrence, quoted in D. Tacey, *Edge of the Sacred*, p. 201.

[11] R. Gibson, 'Ocean Settlement', p. 677.

18 In Conclusion

[1] Quoted by K. Betts, in 'The Rise of Savoir Faire', p. 25.

[2] B. Matthews, 'The Nation Needs New Urban Myths', *Australian*, 8 October 1997, p. 15.

[3] P. Blazey, *Australian*, 31 December 1983, quoted in G. Dutton, *Sun, Sea, Surf and Sand*, p. 50.

[4] R. Drewe, *The Drowner*, p. 126.

[5] Drewe, *The Drowner*, p. 298.

[6] Matthews, 'The Nation Needs New Urban Myths', p. 15.

[7] M. Eliade, *The Sacred and the Profane*, pp. 68–113.

Bibliography

Anderson, Don, 'Strange Results When Foreigners Pick Our Teams', *Sydney Morning Herald*, 6 November 1993, p. 9A.

Anderson, Janice & Swinglehurst, Edmond, *The Victorian and Edwardian Seaside*, Hamlyn, London, 1978.

Anon., 'The Humorous Wavelets', *Australian Town and Country Journal*, vol. 76, no. 1980, 15 January 1908, p. 41.

Anon., 'Lines Written by the Sea-Side', *Monitor*, 1 November 1827, p. 732.

Anon., 'The Shores Set Free: What Surfing Is Doing Towards the Making of a New Race along the Pacific Coast of Australia', *The Home*, January 1927, pp. 26–32.

Balderson, Margaret, *Blue and Gold Day*, illus. Roger Haldane, n.p., n.d. [1979].

Barnard, Marjorie, *Sydney: The Story of a City*, Melbourne University Press, Carlton, Vic., 1956.

Bartholomew, Wayne 'Rabbit', with Tim Baker, *Bustin' Down the Door: The Wayne 'Rabbit' Bartholomew Story*, HarperCollins, Sydney, 1996.

Barzun, Jacques, *Science: The Glorious Entertainment*, Secker & Warburg, London, 1964.

Bascom, Willard, in 'Waves and Beaches: The Dynamics of the Ocean Surface', used by permission of Doubleday, a division of Bantam Doubleday Dell, from *The Crest of the Waves: Adventures in Ocean-ography*, HarperCollins, New York, 1988, in Jonathan Raban, *The Oxford Book of the Sea*, Oxford University Press, Oxford, 1992.

Beaglehole, J. C., et al. (eds), *The Journal of Captain James Cook on his Voyages of Discovery*, vol. 1, Hakluyt Society, Cambridge, 1955–68.

Bean, C. E. W., *Official History of Australia in the War of 1914–18*, vol. I: *The Story of Anzac*, 3rd edn, Angus & Robertson, Sydney, 1934.

——, *Official History of Australia in the War of 1914–18*, vol. II: *The Story of Anzac: From 4 May 1915 to the Evacuation*, 2nd edn, Angus & Robertson, Sydney, 1934.

——, *Official History of Australia in the War of 1914–18*, vol. VI: *The AIF in France: May 1918 to the Armistice*, Angus & Robertson, Sydney, 1942.

Beaver, Bruce, *New and Selected Poems, 1960–1990*, University of Queensland Press, St Lucia, Qld, 1991.

Beder, Sharon, *Toxic Fish and Sewer Surfing: How Deceit and Collusion Are Destroying Our Great Beaches*, Allen & Unwin, North Sydney, 1989.

Bedson, Jack, *Don't Get Burnt! Or the Great Australian Day at the Beach*, Collins, Sydney, 1985.

Bennett, Tegan, 'Bombora', *Bombora,* Allen & Unwin, St Leonards, NSW, 1996.

——, 'The Chiming of Light', *Bombora*, Allen & Unwin, St Leonards, NSW, 1996.

Betts, Katharine, 'The Rise of Savoir Faire', *Weekend Australian*, 29–30 May 1999, p. 25.

'Billion Dollar Breakers', Background Briefing, ABC Radio National, 13 April 1997, transcript.

Birch, A. & MacMillan, D. S., *The Sydney Scene 1788–1960*, Hale & Iremonger, Sydney, 1982.

Birch, Charles, *Regaining Compassion for Humanity and Nature*, New South Wales University Press, Kensington, NSW, 1993.

Blake, William, 'The Marriage of Heaven and Hell', in W. H. Stevenson (ed.), *Blake: The Complete Poems*, 2nd edn, Longman, London, 1989, pp. 101–24.

Blakemore, Michael, 'The Straight Poofter', in Russell Braddon (ed.), *Australia Fair? Recollections, Observations and Irreverence*, Methuen, London, 1994.

Blight, John, *Selected Poems 1935–1990*, University of Queensland Press, St Lucia, Qld, 1992.

Bolton, Geoffrey, *Spoils and Spoilers: A History of Australians Shaping their Environment*, 2nd edn, Allen & Unwin, North Sydney, 1992.

Booth, Douglas, 'Surfing 60s: A Case Study in the History of Pleasure and Discipline', *Australian Historical Studies*, no. 103, October 1994, pp. 262–76.

Boyd, Martin, *Lucinda Brayford*, first published 1946; Lansdowne, Melbourne, 1969.

Brawley, Sean, *Vigilant and Victorious: A Community History of the Collaroy Surf Life Saving Club 1911–1995*, Collaroy Surf Life Saving Club Inc., Collaroy, NSW, 1996.

Brennan, Christopher, 'Towards the Source' [1894], in *Poems 1913*, first published 1914; facsimile edition, with an introduction by G. A. Wilkes, Sydney University Press, Sydney, 1972.

Brewster, David, *Memories of the Life, Writings, and Discoveries of Sir Isaac Newton*, vol. II, Constable, Edinburgh, 1855.

Brooks, Geraldine, *Nine Parts of Desire: The Hidden World of Islamic Women*, Anchor Books/Anchor, New York, 1995.

Brown, Norman O., *Life Against Death: The Psychoanalytic Meaning of History*, Wesleyan University Press, Middletown, Conn., 1950.

Brunton, Paul (ed.), *The Endeavour Journal of Sir Joseph Banks: The Australian Journey*, HarperCollins, in association with the State Library of New South Wales, Sydney, 1998.

Butterfield, William, Bondi Revisited, 1917–1933, unpublished.

Cannon, Michael, *Life in the Cities*, Australia in the Victorian Age, Series 3, Thomas Nelson, Sydney, 1975.

Capp, Fiona, *Night Surfing*, Allen & Unwin, St Leonards, New South Wales, 1996.

Carey, Gabrielle & Lette, Kathy, *Puberty Blues*, McPhee Gribble, Carlton, Vic., 1979.

Carr, Roger, *Surfie*, Horwitz, Sydney, 1966.

Carroll, John (ed.), *Intruders in the Bush: The Australian Quest for Identity*, 2nd edn, Oxford University Press, Melbourne, 1992.

Carter, Jeff, *Surf Beaches of Australia's East Coast*, Angus & Robertson, Sydney, 1968.

Carter, Paul, *The Road to Botany Bay: An Essay in Spatial History*, Faber & Faber, London, 1987.

Castles, Stephen, Cope, Bill, Kalantzis, Mary & Morrissey, Michael, *Mistaken Identity: Multiculturalism and the Demise of Nationalism in Australia*, 2nd edn, Pluto Press, Sydney, 1990.

Champion, Shelagh & Champion, George, *Bathing, Drowning and Life Saving in Manly, Warringah and Pittwater to 1915*, Shelagh & George Champion, Killarney Heights, NSW, 2000.

——, *The Clontarf Case*, Shelagh & George Champion, Killarney Heights, NSW, 1992.

Chodorow, Nancy, *The Reproduction of Mothering*, University of California Press, Berkeley, Calif., 1978.

Cochrane, Peter & Goodman, David, 'The Great Australian Journey: Cultural Logic and Nationalism in the Postmodern Era', in Tony Bennett, Pat Buckridge, David Carter & Colin Mercer (eds), *Celebrating the Nation: A Critical Study of Australia's Bicentenary*, Allen & Unwin, St Leonards, NSW, 1992.

Coe, Richard N., 'Portrait of the Artist as a Young Australian: Childhood, Literature and Myths', *Southerly*, vol. 41, 1981, pp. 126–62.

——, *When the Grass Was Taller: Autobiography and the Experience of Childhood*, Yale University Press, New Haven, Conn., 1984.

Collins, Paul, *God's Earth: Religion as if Matter Really Mattered*, Dove, North Blackburn, Vic., 1995.

Corbin, Alain, *The Lure of the Sea: The Discovery of the Seaside in the Western World 1750–1840*, trans. Jocelyn Phelps, Polity Press, Cambridge, 1994.

Couper, J. M., *Looking for a Wave*, Bodley Head, London, 1973.

Crew, Gary & Rogers, Gregory, *Lucy's Bay*, Jam Roll Press, Nundah, Qld, 1992.

Cumes, J. W. C., *Their Chastity Was Not Too Rigid: Leisure Times in Early Australia*, Longman Cheshire, Melbourne, 1979.

Cunningham, Peter, *Two Years in New South Wales: Comprising Sketches of the Actual State of Society in that Colony: of its peculiar Advantages to Emigrants; of its Topography, Natural History, &c. &c.*, vol. 2, 3rd edn, Henry Colburn, London, 1828.

Curlewis, Jean, *Beach Beyond*, Ward, Lock & Co., London, 1923.

——, *The Drowning Maze*, Ward, Lock & Co., London, 1922.

——, 'The Race on the Sands: Showing What Surf and Sun Are Doing for the Inhabitants of the Australian Coastline', *The Home*, March 1929, pp. 25–32, 72.

Cusack, Dymphna, *Jungfrau*, first published 1936; introduced by Florence James, Penguin, Ringwood, Vic., 1989.

Dale, Pat, *Managing Australian Coastlands*, Longman Cheshire, Melbourne, 1991.

Davison, Graeme, 'Sydney and the Bush: An Urban Context for the Australian Legend', in John Carroll (ed.), *Intruders in the Bush: The Australian Quest for Identity*, 2nd edn, Oxford University Press, Melbourne, 1992.

Dening, Greg, *Islands and Beaches: Discourse on a Silent Land, Marquesas 1774–1880*, Melbourne University Press, Carlton, Vic., 1980.

Dessaix, Robert, 'The Best Year of Their Lives', *Good Weekend*, *Sydney Morning Herald*, 4 January 1997.

Dinnerstein, Dorothy, *The Mermaid and the Minotaur: Sexual Arrangements and Human Malaise*, Harper & Row, New York, 1976.

Drew, Phillip, *The Coast Dwellers: Australians Living on the Edge*, Penguin, Ringwood, Vic., 1994.

Drewe, Robert, *The Bay of Contented Men*, Picador, Sydney, 1989.

——, *The Bodysurfers*, Faber & Faber, London, 1983.

——, *The Drowner*, Macmillan, Sydney, 1996.

—— (ed.), *Picador Book of the Beach*, Pan Macmillan, Sydney, 1993.

——, 'Tidal Pull', *Good Weekend*, *Sydney Morning Herald*, 23 October 1993, pp. 39, 41.

Drewe, Robert et al., *Bondi*, new edn, Allen & Unwin, St Leonards, NSW, 1993.

Dunn, Max, 'Portrait of a Nation', set up and handprinted by the author on a handpress dated 1730 for the Lyre-Bird Editions, Anvil Press, Melbourne [n.d.].

Dunstan, Keith, *Wowsers: Being an Account of the Prudery Exhibited by Certain Outstanding Men and Women in Such Matters as Drinking, Smoking, Prostitution, Censorship and Gambling*, Cassell, Sydney, 1968.

Dutton, Geoffrey, *Sun, Sea, Surf and Sand: The Myth of the Beach*, Oxford University Press, Melbourne, 1985.

Edwards, Hazel, *My Hippopotamus Is on Our Caravan Roof Getting Sunburnt*, illus. Deborah Niland, Hodder & Stoughton, Sydney, 1989.

EJE Landscapes, *Survey of Harbourside and Ocean Pools of the Sydney Metropolitan Region*, prepared for the National Trust of Australia (NSW), Sydney, 1994.

Eliade, Mircea, *The Sacred and the Profane: The Nature of Religion*, trans. from French by W. R. Trask, Harcourt Brace Jovanovich, New York, 1959.

Enright, Nick, *Blackrock*, Currency Press, Sydney, 1996.

——, *Property of the Clan*, Currency Press, Sydney, 1996.

Facey, Albert B., *A Fortunate Life*, Penguin, Ringwood, Vic., 1981.

Farmer, Beverley, *The Seal Woman*, University of Queensland Press, St Lucia, Qld, 1992.

Fidlon, Paul G. (ed.), *The Journal of Arthur Bowes Smith, Surgeon, Lady Penrhyn, 1787–1789*, Australian Documents Library, Sydney, 1979.

Fishbein, Johanna, Stackhouse, Jennifer, Stapleton, Maisy & Workman, Sarah, *Beside the Sea: Sydney Beaches and Resorts*, Historic Houses Trust of New South Wales, published in conjunction with the exhibition 'Beside the Sea' at Elizabeth Bay House, Sydney, December 1981.

——, *Pleasures and Pastimes Beside the Sea*, Historic Houses Trust of New South Wales, published in conjunction with the exhibition 'Beside the Sea' at Elizabeth Bay House, Sydney, December 1981.

Fiske, John, *Reading the Popular*, Unwin Hyman, Boston, 1989.

Fiske, John, Hodge, Bob & Turner, Graeme, *Myths of Oz: Reading Australian Popular Culture*, Allen & Unwin, Sydney, 1987.

Fitzgerald, Shirley, *Rising Damp: Sydney 1870–90*, Oxford University Press, Melbourne, 1987.

French, Jackie, *The Secret Beach*, Angus & Robertson/HarperCollins, Sydney, 1995.

Frost, Alan, 'The Conditions of Early Settlement: NSW 1788–1840', in John Carroll (ed.), *Intruders in the Bush: The Australian Quest for Identity*, 2nd edn, Oxford University Press, Melbourne, 1992, pp. 69–81.

——, 'Perceptions before 1855', in Laurie Hergenhan (ed.), *The Penguin New Literary History of Australia*, Penguin, Ringwood, Vic., 1988.

Frost, Lucy (comp.), *No Place for a Nervous Lady: Voices from the Australian Bush*, McPhee Gribble, Melbourne, 1984.

Fuery, Patrick (ed.), *Representation, Discourse and Desire: Contemporary Australian Culture and Critical Theory*, Longman Cheshire, Melbourne, 1994.

Furphy, Joseph, *Such Is Life*, first published 1903; Angus & Robertson, North Ryde, NSW, 1956.

Galton, Barry, *Gladiators of the Surf: The Australian Surf Life Saving Championships—A History*, A. H. & A. W. Reed, Frenchs Forest, NSW, 1984.

Game, Anne, 'Nation and Identity: Bondi', *New Formations*, no. 11, Summer 1990, pp. 105–20.

Garner, Helen, 'Postcards from Surfers', *Postcards from Surfers*, McPhee Gribble, Fitzroy, Vic., 1985, pp. 3–16.

Gerster, Robin, *Big-noting: The Heroic Theme in Australian War Writing*, Melbourne University Press, Carlton, Vic., 1987.

Gibson, Ross, 'Camera Natura: Landscape in Australian Feature Films', in J. Frow & M. Morris (eds), *Australian Cultural Studies: A Reader*, Allen & Unwin, St Leonards, NSW, 1993.

——, 'Ocean Settlement', *Meanjin*, vol. 53, 1994, pp. 665–78.

——, *South of the West: Postcolonialism and the Narrative Construction of Australia*, Indiana University Press, Bloomington, Ind., 1992.

Gillespie, Owen, 'Bondi Beach-Gold', *Bulletin*, 8 July 1920, p. 3.

Gilligan, Carol, *In a Different Voice: Psychological Theory and Women's Development*, Harvard University Press, Cambridge, Mass., 1982.

Gilling, Tom, *The Sooterkin*, Text Publishing, Melbourne, 1999.

Gilmore, Dame Mary, 'Old Botany Bay', in *Australian Poets: Mary Gilmore*, selection and introduction by Robert D. Fitzgerald, Angus & Robertson, Sydney, 1963, pp. 9–10.

Goodall, Peter, *High Culture, Popular Culture: The Long Debate*, Allen & Unwin, St Leonards, NSW, 1995.

Gordon, Adam Lindsay, 'The Swimmer', *Bush Ballads and Galloping Rhymes*, Massina, Melbourne, 1870, pp. 113–16.

Gow, Michael, *Away*, introduced by May-Brit Akerholt & Richard Wherrett, Currency Press, Paddington, NSW, 1986.

Graham, Bob, *Greetings from Sandy Beach*, Lothian, Port Melbourne, Vic., 1990.

Green, Bill, *Freud and the Nazis Go Surfing*, Pan, Sydney, 1986.

Green, H. M., *A History of Australian Literature Pure and Applied: A Critical Review of all Forms of Literature Produced in Australia from the First Books Published after the Arrival of the First Fleet until 1950, with Short Accounts of Later Publications up to 1960*, vol. I, Angus & Robertson, Sydney, 1962.

Hailstone, Sue, 'The Special Place', Encounter, ABC Radio National, 3 July 1996, transcript.

Hall, James, *Clinical Uses of Dreams: Jungian Interpretations and Enactments*, Grune & Stratton, New York, 1997.

Hall, Stuart, 'Culture, Community, Nation', *Cultural Studies*, vol. 7, 1993, pp. 349–63.

Halloran, Henry, 'Australian Scenery, Bondi Bay', *Sydney Gazette*, 16 June 1831, p. 4.

——, 'Pages from My Scrapbook of 10 Years Ago: Coogee, On the Sea-Coast', *Duncan's Weekly Register of Politics, Facts and General Literature*, 19 April 1845, p. 185.

Hancock, W. K., *Australia*, Ernest Benn, London, 1930.

Hassam, Andrew, *No Privacy for Writing: Shipboard Diaries 1852–1879*, Melbourne University Press, Carlton, Vic. 1995.

Hathorn, Elizabeth, *The Tram to Bondi Beach*, illus. Julie Vivas, Methuen, Sydney, 1981.

Hawley, Janet, 'An Imaginative Life', *Good Weekend, Sydney Morning Herald*, 20 March 1993, pp. 10–17.

Haynes, Roslynn D., *Seeking the Centre: The Australian Desert in Literature, Art and Film*, Cambridge University Press, Cambridge, 1998.

Heads of the People: An Illustrated Journal of Literature, Whims and Oddities, vols 1 and 2, W. Baker, Sydney, 1847–8.

Healey, Kaye (ed.), *Ocean Ecology: Issues for the Nineties*, Spinney Press, Balmain, NSW, 1996.

Hill, E. J., 'Freedom of the Seas: The Story of Surfing and Mixed Bathing—Some Historical Facts', *Sea, Land and Air*, vol. 4, 1 September 1921, pp. 412–15.

Horne, Donald, *The Education of Young Donald*, Angus & Robertson, Sydney, 1967.

Hospital, Janette Turner, 'Litany for the Homeland', in *Collected Stories*, University of Queensland Press, St Lucia, Qld, 1995.

Hughes, Robert, *The Fatal Shore: A History of the Transportation of Convicts to Australia 1788–1868*, Pan, London, 1987.

Humphries, Barry, 'Weatherboard Swastikas', in *Hot Sand: An Anthology*, introduced by Susan Kurosawa, Viking, Ringwood, Vic., 1997, pp. 8–20.

Illustrated Sydney News, vol. XIII, no. 3, 3 March 1876.

Inglis, Ken, 'Multiculturalism and National Identity', in Charles A. Price (ed.), *Australian National Identity*, Academy of Social Sciences in Australia, Canberra, 1991.

The Injured Coastline: Protection of the Coastal Environment, Report of the House of Representatives Standing Committee on the Environment, Recreation and the Arts, Australian Government Publishing Service, Canberra, 1991.

Jaggard, Edwin, 'The Australian Surf Lifesaver as a National Symbol 1920–1960', a paper presented at the Australian Identities Conference, History, Culture and the Environment, University College, Dublin, 3 July 1996 [my copy courtesy of the author].

——, *A Challenge Answered: A History of Surf Lifesaving in Western Australia*, Surf Life Saving Association of Australia, W.A. State Centre, Perth, 1979.

——, *The Premier Club: Cottesloe Surf Life Saving Club's First Seventy-five Years*, Cottesloe Surf Life Saving Club, Cottesloe, WA, 1984.

Jobling, Bill, 'An Early Pioneer of Liberated Surfing in Sydney', *Sydney Review*, June 1995, pp. 7–8.

Johnston, George, 'ANZAC—A Myth for All Mankind', *Walkabout*, vol. 31, 1965, pp. 15–16.

——, *Clean Straw for Nothing*, Collins, London, 1969.

Kelleher, Victor, *Where the Whales Sing*, illus. Vivienne Goodman, Viking, Ringwood, Vic., 1994.

Keneally, Thomas, *Woman of the Inner Sea*, Hodder & Stoughton, London, 1992.

Kingsmill, John, 'Growing Up in Bondi', in Robert Drewe et al., *Bondi*, Allen & Unwin, St Leonards, NSW, 1993, pp. 72–81.

Knight, Stephen, *Freedom Was Compulsory*, Reed, Port Melbourne, Vic., 1994.

——, *The Selling of the Australian Mind: From First Fleet to Third Mercedes*, Heinemann, Port Melbourne, 1990.

Koch, Christopher, *The Doubleman*, Chatto & Windus, London, 1985.

Krauth, Nigel, 'Continental Drift: Clancy of the Undertow', *Imago*, vol. 2, 1990, pp. 28–35.

Kroll, Jeri, 'Interview with Tim Winton', *Southerly*, vol. 51, 1991, pp. 222–4.

Larcombe, F. A. 'The Stabilization of Local Government in New South Wales 1858–1906', *A History of Local Government in New South Wales*, vol. 2, Sydney University Press, Sydney, 1976.

Laurie, Maxine & Laurie, Jacqueline, *Ten Decades: A Photographic History of the Town of Cottesloe*, Town of Cottesloe, WA, 1995.

Lawrence, D. H., *Kangaroo*, first published 1923; corrected edn, Harper-Collins, Pymble, NSW, 1995.

Lawson, Henry, 'How the Land Was Won', in Colin Roderick (ed.), *Collected Verse*, vol. I: *1885–1900*, Angus & Robertson, Sydney, 1967, pp. 361–3.

Lawson, Sylvia, *The Archibald Paradox: A Strange Case of Authorship*, Penguin, Ringwood, Vic., 1983.

Leer, Martin, 'On the Edge: Geography and the Imagination in the World of David Malouf', *Australian Literary Studies*, vol. 12, 1985, pp. 3–21.

Lees, Stella & Macintyre, Pam, *Oxford Companion to Australian Children's Literature*, Oxford University Press, Melbourne, 1993.

Lester, Alison, *Magic Beach*, Little Ark Book, Allen & Unwin, Sydney, 1990.

Lord, Gabrielle, *Salt*, McPhee Gribble, Ringwood, Vic., 1990.

Lowe, Arthur, *Surfing, Surf-Shooting and Surf-Lifesaving Pioneering*, [n.p., n.d.].

The Lycett Album: Drawings of Aborigines and Australian Scenery, with commentary by Jeanette Hoorn, National Library of Australia, Canberra, 1990.

McCooey, David, 'By the Sea: Some Recent Australian Poetry', *Southerly*, vol. 56, 1996/97, pp. 253–61.

McGregor, Craig, *Profile of Australia*, Penguin, Ringwood, Vic., 1966.

McGregor, Grant, '*Seven Poor Men of Sydney*: The Historical Dimension', *Southerly*, vol. 38, 1978, pp. 380–404.

McInnes, Graham, *The Road to Gundagai*, Hamish Hamilton, London, 1965.

Malouf, David, *Fly Away Peter*, Chatto & Windus, London, 1982.

——, 'A Spirit of Play: The Making of Australian Consciousness', 1998 Boyer Lectures, ABC Radio National, transcript.

Manning-Sanders, Ruth, *Seaside England*, B. T. Batsford, London, 1951.

Magarey, Susan, Rowley, Sue & Sheridan, Susan (eds), *Debutante Nation: Feminism Contests the 1890s*, Allen & Unwin, St Leonards, NSW, 1993.

Martin, Catherine, *The Silent Sea*, first published 1892; Rosemary Foxton (ed.), University of New South Wales Press, Sydney, 1995.

Matthews, Brian, 'The Nation Needs New Urban Myths', *Australian*, 8 October 1997, p. 15.

Maxwell, C. Bede, *Surf: Australians Against the Sea*, Angus & Robertson, Sydney, [1949].

Millikan, David, *The Sunburnt Soul: Christianity in Search of an Australian Identity*, based on the ABC-TV series, Anzea, Homebush West, NSW, 1981.

Mitchell, Adrian, 'Fiction', in Leonie Kramer (ed.), *Oxford History of Australian Literature*, Oxford University Press, Melbourne, 1981.

Montgomery, Alex, 'Clinched', *Bulletin*, 12 December 1896, p. 17.

Moore, Bryce, Garwood, Helen & Lutton, Nancy, *The Voyage Out: A Hundred Years of Sea Travel to Australia*, Fremantle Arts Press, Fremantle, WA, 1991.

Morcombe, John, 'Manly Inspired Very Unhappy Poet', *Manly Daily*, 20 November 1996, p. 8.

Morley, I. W., *Black Sands: A History of the Mineral Sand Mining Industry in Eastern Australia*, University of Queensland Press, St Lucia, Qld, 1981.

Morris, Jan, *Sydney*, Viking, London, 1992.

Morris, Meaghan, 'Afterthoughts on Australianisms', *Cultural Studies*, vol. 6, 1992, pp. 468–75.

——'Fate and the Family Sedan', *East-West Film Journal*, vol. 4, 1989, pp. 113–34.

——, 'On the Beach', in *Ecstasy and Economics: American Essays for John Forbes*, Empress Publishing, Rose Bay, NSW, 1992, pp. 85–130.

Murray, Les A., 'Eric Rolls and the Golden Disobedience', in *Persistence in Folly: Selected Prose Writings*, Sirius, London, 1984, pp. 149–67.

——, 'Noonday Axeman', in *The Vernacular Republic: Poems 1961–1981*, rev. and enlarged edn, Angus & Robertson, Sydney, 1982, pp. 7–9.

——, 'On Home Beaches', in *Subhuman Redneck Poems*, Duffy & Snellgrove, Potts Point, NSW, 1996, p. 36.

——, 'Summer', in *The Australian Year: The Chronicle of Our Seasons and Celebrations*, Angus & Robertson, London, 1985, pp. 69–153.

Naher, Gaby, *The Under Wharf,* Penguin, Ringwood, Vic., 1995.

New South Wales Legislative Assembly, *Report of the Surf-Bathing Committee to the New South Wales Government*, Government Printer, Sydney, 1912.

New South Wales Sports and Recreation Service, *Surfboard and Leg Rope Report to the Minister for Culture, Sport and Recreation*, Sydney, 1975.

Norman, Lilith, *A Dream of Seas*, illus. Edwina Bell, Collins, Sydney, 1978.

Nyoongah, Mudrooroo, 'Beached Party', 'Spectrum', *Sydney Morning Herald*, 19 January 1991.

O'Farrell, Patrick, 'Writing the General History of Australian Religion', quoted in Michael Hogan, *The Sectarian Strand: Religion in Australian History*, Penguin, Ringwood, Vic., 1987.

Palmer, Vance, *The Passage,* first published 1930; Cheshire, Melbourne, 1957.

Paterson, A. B., 'Song of the Future', *The Collected Verse of A. B. Paterson,* Angus & Robertson, Sydney, 1934, pp. 176–82.

Philip, George B., *Sixty Years' Recollections of Swimming and Surfing in the Eastern Suburbs and Kindred Subjects*, Geo. B. Philip & Son, Sydney, 1940.

Phillips, A. A., *The Australian Tradition: Studies in a Colonial Culture*, 2nd edn, Cheshire, Melbourne, 1966.

Pierce, Peter, *The Country of Lost Children: An Australian Anxiety*, Cambridge University Press, Melbourne, 1999.

Pluss, Nicole, *Kindred: The Lifesaver and Other Stories*, HarperCollins, Pymble, NSW, 1995.

Prichard, Katharine Susannah, *Intimate Strangers*, first published 1937; Imprint Classics, Angus & Robertson, North Ryde, NSW, 1990.

Pringle, John Douglas, *Australian Accent*, first published 1958; Rigby, Adelaide, 1978.

Quinn, Roderic, 'Spring-Song', *The Hidden Tide*, Bulletin, Sydney, 1899.

——, 'The Surrender', *Poems,* Angus & Robertson, Sydney, 1920.

Richardson, Henry Handel, *The Fortunes of Richard Mahony*, first published 1930; Australian Classics, Angus & Robertson, London, 1983.

Rish, David, *Sophie's Island*, illus. Wendy Corbett, Angus & Robertson, North Ryde, NSW, 1990.

Roth, H. Ling, *The Aborigines of Tasmania, assisted by Marion E. Butler and Jas. Backhouse Walker ... with a chapter on the osteology by J. G. Garson and a preface by Edward B. Taylor,* 2nd edn, rev. and enlarged, with map, F. King & Sons, Halifax, England, 1899; facsimile of this 2nd edn, Fullers Bookshop, Hobart, n.d.

Rubinstein, Gillian, *Beyond the Labyrinth*, first published 1988; Puffin, Ringwood, Vic., 1990.

——, *The Giant's Tooth*, illus. Craig Smith, Viking, Ringwood, Vic., 1993.

Russell, E. T., 'Australia's Amphibians', *Lone Hand*, 1 January 1910, pp. 252–63.

Russell, Penny, *A Wish of Distinction: Colonial Gentility and Femininity*, Melbourne University Press, Carlton, Vic., 1994.

Ryan, Simon, *The Cartographic Eye: How Explorers Saw Australia*, Cambridge University Press, Melbourne, 1996.

Safe, Mike, 'The Sands of Time', *Weekend Australian*, 5–6 December 1998, pp. 17–25.

Sanders, Noel, '"Bondi the Beautiful": The Impossibility of an Aesthetic', *Media Papers*, 16, Faculty of Humanities and Social Sciences, NSW Institute of Technology, Sydney, 1982.

Saxby, H. M., *Russell and the Star Shell*, illus. Astra Lacis, Margaret Hamilton Books, Hunters Hill, NSW, 1990.

Schaffer, Kay, *Women and the Bush: Forces of Desire in the Australian Cultural Tradition*, Cambridge University Press, Cambridge, 1988.

Schama, Simon, *Landscape and Memory*, HarperCollins, London, 1995.

Scutter, Heather, 'Escaping the Landscape: "It's Always Ourselves We Find in the Sea"', in *Landscape and Identity: Perspectives from Australia*, Proceedings of the 1994 Conference of the Centre for Children's Literature, University of South Australia, Wendy Parsons & Robert Goodwin (eds), Auslib Press, Adelaide, 1994.

Serle, Geoffrey, *From Deserts the Prophets Come: The Creative Spirit in Australia 1788–1972*, Heinemann, Melbourne, 1973.

Sharpe, Alan, *Shark Down Under: Shark Attacks in Australian Waters*, Book Company International, Brookvale, NSW, 1993.

Short, Andrew, *The Beaches of the New South Wales Coast: A Guide to their Nature, Characteristics, Surf and Safety*, Australian Beach Safety & Management Program, Beaconsfield, NSW, 1993.

Shute, Nevil, *On the Beach*, Heinemann, Melbourne, 1957.

Slessor, Kenneth, 'Beach Burial (El Alamein, 1942)', in *Kenneth Slessor: Selected Poems*, Angus & Robertson, North Ryde, NSW, 1988.

Spence, Eleanor, *The October Child*, Oxford University Press, London, 1976.

Stannard, Bruce, *The Face on the Bar Room Wall: Australian Pub Posters 1929–1950*, Angus & Robertson, Sydney, 1982.

Stead, Christina, *For Love Alone*, first published 1944; Arkon, Angus & Robertson, London, 1982.

——, *Seven Poor Men of Sydney*, first published 1934; HarperCollins, North Ryde, NSW, 1990.

Stell, Marion K., *Half the Race: A History of Australian Women in Sport*, Collins/Angus & Robertson, North Ryde, NSW, 1991.

Stewart, Kathleen, *Spilt Milk*, Minerva, Melbourne, 1995.

Stewart, Meg, 'Beachstruck on Bondi', in Robert Drewe et al., *Bondi*, Allen & Unwin, St Leonards, NSW, pp. 28–53.

'Sticks and Stones: The Killing of Leigh Leigh', Background Briefing, ABC Radio National, 29 September 1996, transcript.

Stow, Randolph, *The Merry-Go-Round in the Sea*, Macdonald, London, 1965.

Swancott, Charles, *Dee Why Lake to Barrenjoey and Pittwater*, D. S. Ford, Sydney, [n.d.].

Tacey, David, *Edge of the Sacred: Transformation in Australia*, Harper-Collins, Blackburn North, Vic., 1995.

——, *Re-enchantment: The New Australian Spirituality*, HarperCollins, Pymble, NSW, 2000.

Taylor, Andrew, 'Littoral Erosion: The Changing Shoreline of Australian Culture', *Australian Literary Studies*, vol. 17, no. 3, 1996, pp. 284–9.

——, *Sandstone*, University of Queensland Press, St Lucia, Qld, 1995.

——, 'What Can Be Read, and What Can Only Be Seen in Tim Winton's Fiction', *Australian Literary Studies*, vol. 17, 1996, pp. 323–31.

Tegg's New South Wales Pocket Almanac and Remembrancer for MDCCCXLII [1842] being the second after Bissextile, or Leap year, calculated from the meridian of Sydney, 7th year of publication, James Tegg at the Atlas Office & Book Repository, Sydney; microfiche held at the Mitchell Library, Sydney.

Tench, Watkin, *Sydney's First Four Years: Being a Reprint of A Narrative of the Expedition to Botany Bay and, A complete Account of the Settlement at Port Jackson*, introduction and annotations by L. F. Fitzhardinge, Library of Australian History in association with the Royal Australian Historical Society, Sydney, 1979.

Thiele, Colin, 'Storm Boy', *Storm Boy and Other Stories*, first published 1966; Lansdowne, Sydney, 1995.

Thom, B. G., *Coastal Geomorphology in Australia*, Academic Press, Sydney, 1984, in Pat Dale, *Managing Australian Coastlands*, Longman Cheshire, Melbourne, 1991.

Thomas, Daniel (ed.) & Radford, Ron (co-ord.), *Creating Australia: 200 Years of Art 1788–1988*, International Cultural Corporation Ltd, in association with the Art Gallery Board of South Australia, 1988.

Thoms, Albie, *Surfmovies: The History of the Surf Film in Australia*, Shoreline, Sydney, 2000.

Triglone, Peter, The History of Manly Ocean Beach Landscape from the First Settlement to the Present, thesis, School of Landscape Architecture, University of New South Wales, 1985.

Turner, Graeme, *Making It National: Nationalism and Australian Popular Culture*, Allen & Unwin, St Leonards, NSW, 1994.

Vamplew, Wray (ed.), *Australians: Historical Statistics*, Fairfax, Syme & Weldon Associates, Broadway, NSW, 1987.

Veliz, Claudio, 'The Gothic Mode of Australian Culture: The 1986 Latham Memorial Lecture', *Quadrant*, vol. 31, 1987, pp. 8–20.

Walton, John K., *The English Seaside Resort: A Social History 1750–1914*, Leicester University Press & St Martin's Press, New York, 1983.

Ward, Russel, *The Australian Legend*, 2nd edn, Oxford University Press, Melbourne, 1965.

Waterhouse, Richard, *Private Pleasures, Public Leisure: A History of Australian Popular Culture since 1788*, Longman, Melbourne, 1995.

Webby, Elizabeth, *Early Australian Poetry: An Annotated Bibliography of Original Poems Published in Australian Newspapers, Magazines and Almanacks before 1850*, Hale & Iremonger, Sydney, 1982.

Wells, Lana, *Sunny Memories: Australians at the Seaside*, Greenhouse, Richmond, Vic., 1982.

White, Patrick, *Voss*, Eyre & Spottiswoode, London, 1957.

White, Richard, *Inventing Australia: Images and Identity 1688–1980*, Geo. Allen & Unwin, Sydney, 1981.

Whitney, W. M., 'Beach Brownies', *Bulletin*, 29 December 1910, p. 3.

——, 'Vagabond of Beaches', *Bulletin*, 12 December 1907, p. 25.

Wicks, Les, 'The Summer Sumos', Spectrum, *Sydney Morning Herald*, 4 April 1998, p. 9.

Wild, Margaret, *There's a Sea in My Bedroom*, illus. Jane Tanner, first published 1984; Penguin, Ringwood, Vic., 1989.

Wilkes, G. A., *Oxford Dictionary of Colloquialisms*, 4th edn, Oxford University Press, South Melbourne, Vic., 1996.

Winders, J. R., *Surf Life Saving in Queensland*, Queensland Centre of the Surf Life Saving Association, South Brisbane, 1969.

Winton, Tim, *Blueback: A Fable for All Ages*, Macmillan, Sydney, 1997.

——, *Cloudstreet*, McPhee Gribble, Melbourne, 1993.

——, *Land's Edge,* Pan Macmillan, Sydney, 1993.

——, *Lockie Leonard, Human Torpedo*, McPhee Gribble, South Yarra, Vic., 1990.

——, *Lockie Leonard, Legend,* Pan, Chippendale, NSW, 1997.

——, *Minimum of Two*, McPhee Gribble, Fitzroy, Vic., 1987.

——, *An Open Swimmer,* Geo. Allen & Unwin, Sydney, 1982.

——, *Scission*, Penguin, Ringwood, Vic., 1985.

——, *Shallows*, McPhee Gribble, Ringwood, Vic., 1984.

——, *That Eye, the Sky*, McPhee Gribble, Ringwood, Vic., 1986.

Woolls, William, 'The Beauties of Australia', in Michael Ackland (ed.), *Penguin Book of 19th Century Australian Literature*, Penguin, Ringwood, Vic., 1993.

Worthington, P., 'The Guardians of Our Beaches', *Port of Sydney*, vol. 5, October–December 1956, pp. 170–3.

Wright, David McKee, 'Young Australia by the Sea', *Bulletin*, 20 October 1910, p. 43.

Wright, Judith, 'The Surfer', originally published in *The Moving Image*, 1946; in *Judith Wright: A Human Pattern—Collected Poems*, Angus & Robertson, Sydney, 1990.

Wynhausen, Elizabeth & Scott, Jody, 'Eye of the Storm', *Weekend Australian*, 16–17 November 1996, p. 27.

Young, Nat, with Craig McGregor, *The History of Surfing*, Palm Beach Press, Palm Beach, NSW, 1983.

Index